MW00334217

Special Education:
A Biblical
Approach

The lighted torch in the broken vessel represents the light of the gospel which shines forth through a life broken and yielded to the will of God.

Special Education: A Biblical Approach

*A Special Education Resource
for Christian Schools*

Edited by
Joe P. Sutton, Ph.D.

HIDDEN TREASURE MINISTRIES • GREENVILLE, SOUTH CAROLINA
John C. Vaughn, Founder/Director   John J. McCormick, Administrator

Copyright © 1993 by Hidden Treasure Ministries.
All rights reserved.
No part of this publication may be reproduced, transmitted, transcribed, stored in a
retrieval system, or translated into any language in any form by any means, without the
written permission of Hidden Treasure Ministries.

Hidden Treasure Ministries
18 Hammett Street
Greenville, South Carolina 29609

Library of Congress Catalog Card Number: 92-74588

ISBN # 0-963-4315-0-1

Suggested Dewey decimal classification: 371.9

Printing history:
20 19 18 17 16 15 14 13 12 11 10 9 8 7 6

Cover design: Perimeter Designs

Printed in the United States of America

Dedication

*This book is dedicated to all the parents
who, through the past ten years, have allowed us
the opportunity to be involved in the spiritual and academic
lives of their disabled children.
We are extremely grateful to all of you
for letting us help you to
"train up a child in the way he should go…"*

Table of Contents

4 Man's Mandates for Public Special Education
John J. McCormick

5 Recognition, Identification, and Placement in Special Education
John J. McCormick and Joe P. Sutton

6 Physical Disabilities
John C. Vaughn

7 Emotional Disorders
John C. Vaughn

8 Learning Disabilities
Ross Fichter

9 Educable Mentally Retarded and Slow Learning Students
John J. McCormick and Katherine S. Young

10 Trainable and Severely/Profoundly Mentally
Retarded Students
Mary E. Behymer

Preface

*A*lthough secular special education has realized tremendous growth in this century, very little has been done in the area of Christian special education. Christian schools across our country have failed to respond to the needs of disabled students. Likewise, fundamental churches have been slow to start Sunday school programs for disabled persons. And perhaps more important, professional Christian researchers and writers have provided very few materials and resources to assist parents and educators in understanding and helping students with disabilities.

The purpose of this present work, then, is both obvious and simple. We desire to provide an accurate, well-documented resource that will allow fundamental Christians to learn more about special education and disabled students. This book represents the collective efforts of the administrators and teachers of Hidden Treasure Christian School, Greenville, South Carolina. It presents a Christian philosophy of special education, provides instruction in basic concepts of special education, discusses legal requirements, and describes the basic characteristics and educational needs of students with various disabilities. This book is not an exhaustive presentation of special education and all of its related issues and concerns. It is an introduction, a place of beginning for pastors, parents, administrators, and teachers.

We have organized this book into ten chapters. In the first chapter, Dr. Vaughn provides a preview, with a brief history of the field of special education as well as a discussion of the people and ministry of special education. Dr. Vaughn continues in Chapter 2 with an exposition of a Biblical philosophy of Christian special education. In Chapter 3, he provides an orientation for parents and teachers and discusses three critical needs for all Christians in the area of special education.

Chapter 4 focuses on the legal mandates for public special education. Through a question-and-answer format, Mr. McCormick describes major special education provisions mandated in federal law and explains how these can be helpful in a Christian school setting. In Chapter 5, Mr. McCormick and Dr. Sutton lay the groundwork for how students with disabilities are identified and labeled. They discuss the purpose of testing and evaluation, the function of the multidisciplinary team, and the various types of special education programs.

The remaining chapters in this book focus on selected disabilities. Dr. Vaughn describes physical disabilities in Chapter 6 and emotional disorders in Chapter 7. In Chapter 8, Mr. Fichter discusses learning disabilities among elementary and adolescent students. Chapter 9, by Mr. McCormick and Mrs. Young, is devoted to educable mentally retarded and slow learning students. Finally, in Chapter 10 Mrs. Behymer provides information about trainable and severely/profoundly mentally retarded students.

While many Christian schools continue to drag their feet in developing programs for disabled students, Hidden Treasure Christian School has provided special education on a separate, self-contained campus for over a decade now. On behalf of these faithful Christian special educators, may this book bless and encourage interested readers and stir up fundamental Christians to the cause of Christian special education. May Christian parents and educators come to realize their God-given responsibility to provide for the spiritual and educational needs of disabled students. May we all move beyond mere *acknowledgment* of these students and demonstrate sincere, dedicated *action* in developing Christian school programs for them. As I Corinthians 10:31 demands, may we give God the glory for what is accomplished.

Joe P. Sutton, Ph.D.
Editor

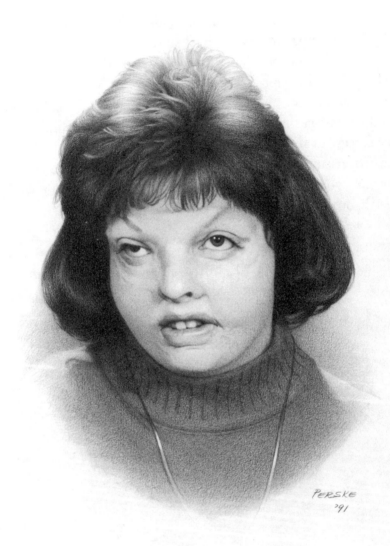

PERSKE
'91

A Personal Word from Becky Vaughn

*O*n May 20, 1978, we had a serious house fire. My mother and I were both burned. I was very young, and I don't remember the fire or being in the hospital then. But altogether, I've been in the hospital for over 37 months, many of those times since I have been in school. I have had surgery 55 times. I am a junior at Hidden Treasure Christian School, which I have attended since kindergarten. When I graduate, I want to attend a Christian college and be a writer. I want to write children's books.

I am thankful my parents started Hidden Treasure and I enjoy going there because I have wonderful friends and all of us there get the help we need. Some of us cannot work as fast as others. All of us have special needs, but we all have things to offer one another. My friends help me walk to school and back home; sometimes I help them with their lessons.

When I travel with my mother to other churches for meetings I meet other young people who have special needs, but who don't have a school like Hidden Treasure to go to. I hope this book will encourage others to start schools like Hidden Treasure.

—Becky Vaughn

Foreword

*G*od privileged the John Vaughn family to suffer literal fiery trials for His glory. While undoubtedly they would not have chosen to experience some of the things they have, in retrospect they clearly see the good hand of God on their lives, preparing them for a unique ministry with disabled children.

It is clear throughout the Scriptures that God has a particular interest in children.

> Except ye be converted, and become as little children, ye shall not enter into the kingdom of heaven. Whosoever therefore shall humble himself as this little child, the same is greatest in the kingdom of heaven. And whoso shall receive one such little child in my name receiveth me. But whoso shall offend one of these little ones which believe in me, it were better for him that a millstone were hanged about his neck, and that he were drowned in the depth of the sea. (Matthew 18:3- 6)

But Jesus said, Suffer little children, and forbid them not, to come unto me: for of such is the kingdom of heaven. (Matthew 19:14)

For nearly three decades we have seen the modern Christian school movement blossom and develop fruit. Notably absent for most of this time period has been a recognition of the unique needs of disabled children. When they were acknowledged at all, the response was generally, "We would like to help but we do not believe that is our calling." Pastor John Vaughn and Faith Baptist Church believe God has called them to this type of ministry.

For some ten years Faith Baptist Church has operated Hidden Treasure Christian School as a unique ministry to the children of the Greenville area who, in God's sovereignty and love, have disabilities that call for individualized educational programs. While most Christian day schools have no outreach to disabled students, Hidden Treasure Christian School stands as one of the few commited solely to a ministry with disabled students.

The ministry of Hidden Treasure Christian School has not been without its difficulties, but God has given it His blessing, and it has had the privilege of providing *Christian* special education to many children who otherwise would have had to attend secular educational institutions. *Special Education: A Biblical Approach* seeks to share with others its burden for disabled children and to impart to other Christian educators many of the lessons it has learned in its first decade of ministry.

James W. Deuink, Ed.D.
Dean, School of Education
Bob Jones University

Acknowledgments

We gratefully acknowledge a number of persons who have contributed substantially to this work. Their assistance and expertise throughout the various phases of this project have allowed us to produce a more successful and effective resource.

To Dr. A.A. Baker we offer our sincere thanks for his prepublication advertising services and for securing the grant that underwrote the development expenses of this project. In like manner, we thank William Baddorf for his assistance in the establishment of the financial budget for this project and for his guidance throughout the development stages.

We owe a great deal of gratitude to both Debbie Vaughn and Julie Wingate for their excellent and diligent work in typing chapter manuscripts, producing charts, tables, and figures for the various chapters, and serving as mediators for all of us involved in this project. We also thank Carol Fichter for her assistance in the first draft of the learning disabilities chapter.

We also wish to thank Dr. Bill Maher, founder and director of God's Handi-Work, Ocala, Florida, for his continued involvement, encouragement, and friendship. His vision for a Christian school that could provide a Christ-centered special education to students with disabilities was instrumental in prompting Dr. John Vaughn to found Hidden Treasure Christian School.

Finally, we offer sincere gratitude to Dr. Grace C. Collins, chairman of the Departments of English Education and Linguistics, Bob Jones University, who undertook the task of editing the voluminous copy for this book. Her expert polishing has undoubtedly enhanced the quality and ministry of this work.

Special Education:
A Vision
and a Ministry

John C. Vaughn

The Purpose of This Book

*A*s its title states, this book presents a Biblical approach
to special education. Although it does assume some understanding of general educational techniques and of the methodology of special education, it has been prepared for those with a
limited knowledge of the need for and management of special
education programs in Christian schools. It is neither an exhaustive analysis of the topics it addresses nor an encyclopedia
of resources, but rather a place to begin. The authors hope and
expect that others will build on the philosophy presented here
and its application in Christian special education.

In preparing this book, we have not set out merely to glean from the best secular writing nor to duplicate usable material from secular special education, making it adaptable for Christian schools. Rather, our primary objective has been to articulate, above all else, a Biblical philosophy of Christian special education, and to report those well-researched techniques and methodologies that have proved successful in our work with disabled children in the last 10 years at Hidden Treasure Christian School. Obviously, there will be parallels in the practical application of a Biblical philosophy of special education to that observed in the secular classroom. Christian school administrators, teachers, and parents should be careful to avoid the philosophical corruption that can occur when methodologies are adopted without understanding. Although technique alone does not necessarily communicate philosophy, using technique without a guiding philosophy is contrary to the Biblical approach.

In the history of learning, public tax-supported education is a relatively new concept (Johnson, Collins, Dupuis, and Johansen, 1988), and public school special education is one of the latest innovations. Special education is a relatively young field (Sutton, 1990b), and carefully planned programs for disabled students in public schools have been around only since the passage of the landmark special education law, Public Law (PL) 94-142, in 1975 (Johnson et al., 1988). The field of special education in America has realized significant achievement and growth during the present century and particularly since the 1960s (Haring & McCormick, 1990; Hallahan & Kauffman, 1988). Prior to the 1960s, special education was very limited in scope, and there was little commonality among public schools that did provide programs. Before the sweeping legislation of the 1970s (see Chapter 4), which mandated appropriate education for all disabled students, programs were clearly inadequate. In addition, G. Cartwright, C. Cartwright, and Ward (1984) suggest that inappropriate placements were also prevalent.

Students were often placed in whatever schools or institutions were available, even if they addressed problems unrelated to those experienced by the child. For example, it would not have been unusual to find a child with cerebral palsy enrolled in a school for blind persons, if that was the only special education program available. Some children with other disabling conditions ended up in nursing homes or asylums or were neglected altogether. Cartwright et al. (1984) aptly describe the inappropriate placements and services allotted to some disabled children:

> As late as 1958, a local court (with or without parental permission) could place a mildly retarded student in a residential institution when the court felt that lower intelligence rendered the child unlikely to profit from public school classes. Consequently, handicapped children were denied a classroom in which to learn, and schools were made to feel no responsibility to create programs for these children. (p. 9)

In a very real sense, special education is still in its infancy. Most of the writing on secular special education has been done within the last fifteen years. A plethora of articles and books emerged in the late 1970s in response to federal legislation mandating special education in the public schools. Moreover, Hallahan and Kauffman (1988) indicate that the knowledge base on how to educate disabled students is "considerably more today... than [it was] ten or fifteen years ago" (p. 3). The secular special education teacher must develop his own approach as he sorts through scores of volumes on the subject. These volumes are often contradictory in philosophy and methodology, because there is no common conviction on the nature of man or his basic spiritual needs. Some teachers are led into special education through a frustrated search for workable answers to students' problems in general. Through a sort of analytical inertia, well-meaning persons dig deeper and deeper and become more narrow in their focus, without realizing that a specialized view of education can still miss the main point: we are God's creatures. God made us as we are, and we are responsible to Him for what we do with what He has given us. We do not belong to ourselves, and education is not merely the training which allows us to do what we want. As one frustrated parent declared in an exposé of fraudulent claims in public school special education, "It is often neither special, nor education" (Granger & Granger, 1986, p. 101).

It would be easy for those of us with a conviction for Christian education to dismiss the efforts of public schools because of conflicts in philosophy. But until recently the public schools, regardless of the motivation of those involved, were the only schools which provided much-needed and heretofore neglected compassionate care and services for disabled people. What Christians must realize is that if special education is a relatively new development in public schools, it is practically unheard of in Christian schools. Although some might think the contrary, the record shows that Christian education to date has done very little in meeting the needs of students with disabilities. For example, a number of recent reports by Christian educational researchers (e.g., Carver, 1989; Sutton, 1990a, 1990b, 1991, 1992; Sutton J., Everett, & Sutton C., in press) have found that only about 5-10% of private Christian schools in the United States have special education programs. Furthermore, the legitimacy of some of these programs is in question (Sutton et al., in preparation). A God-given call to a ministry is a call to prepare (I Timothy 3:2—"apt to teach" means "prepared" to teach). We are finding that the few Christian schools that do have minimal programs in special education generally do not have qualified teachers (Sutton, 1991, 1992; Sutton et al., in press).

This book is, in part, a response to these findings. Our objective is to stimulate a vision for the broad field of Christian special education, not to criticize secular special education. There will necessarily be comparisons. Through a two-fold approach of defining both what Christian special education is and what it is not, we strive to present, for Christian educators and parents, a Biblical approach to this subject. Because of this purpose, there is much that we cannot include. Other volumes will be needed, which may be produced by us or others. Curricula and educational materials must be developed, or adapted, for Christian special education. The task before us is enormous but essential. It must not be seen as something to distract Christian educators, but rather as part of the core of Christian education. We maintain that Christian education itself is a type of special education; and because this is true, the Christian school is uniquely qualified to provide leadership in this important field. Our challenge is to lay aside our fear that we are neither qualified nor equipped to provide special education and to acknowledge that in a sense we are already in the business of special education. We provide education which focuses on individual responsibility to God—a principle at the very heart of true special education. What secular experts have been learning experimentally and verifying through good research, we know intuitively and verify through God's revelation. Since all Christian education is special education, it is incumbent upon us to provide leadership in a field where most of us have so far been reluctant even to follow.

On the practical level, Christian special education is a developing field. For now, it may be that our school is in the lead among conservative Christian schools in developing special education per se, but we acknowledge that there are many others who are doing things that we have not yet learned. There is much known by others that is not known by us, and we issue a strong appeal for the sharing of ideas; for those in leadership to provide forums for this exchange; and for workshops and general sessions at Christian school conventions to address, above all, the Christian philosophy of special education, as well as its techniques. But especially, we appeal to those key spokesmen for Christian education—our pastors—to have vision for those who received priority in the ministry of Christ: disabled persons who were poor, maimed, halt, or blind.

This book is in no way offered as the final word on Christian special education. It comes from a sincere desire to help, to insist upon the truths that we are learning in our special education program. Christian special education is not an option; it is an obligation. It can be done. It must be done, and we want to help.

The People of Special Education

Our burden is for disabled students—not so much as recipients of our extra effort but as recipients of God's special attention. The student is not just a person to be pitied humanistically, but an individual to be encouraged spiritually, so that he might see himself as a channel of God's blessings to others. Moreover, disabled students must understand that God wants them to learn that their limitations can be turned into assets for His glory and service (Jones, 1954). A Scriptural burden for special education does not grow out of mere sympathy for unfortunate children, but rather from a mature understanding that limitations are another expression of the love of God. It is His love that constrains us to this ministry, as to all others. In view of our focus on special education students, we must give particular attention to the three key groups without whom special education cannot exist: parents, teachers, and administrators.

Parents

There are a number of helpful books available to parents who suspect their child needs special education. We know of no book that specifically addresses Christian parents who seek Christian special education for their children. Such a book may be needed, but a comprehensive study on this subject is beyond the scope of our present effort. We are dedicating one chapter to the role of parents in Christian special education. Although the existing helpful books lead the parent through a step-by-step identification of his child's learning difficulties, they also have a heavy emphasis on defending the child's rights, so that these texts tend to become child advocacy manuals rather than parent guidebooks. They should not be dismissed altogether because of this, for we are indebted to the valuable work these concerned writers have done for us; but parents should be alert. Christian parents can spend valuable years and considerable sums of money trying to help a child, only to come to the conclusion that no one knows for sure what the child's needs are or how to help him.

This frustration can be relieved somewhat by acknowledging a fact that should be self-evident: next to the Lord Jesus Christ, no one—not the teacher, not the administrator, not the public education system in its entirety—knows as much about the child, cares as much about the child, or has as much responsibility for the child as his parents. They are the primary teachers. They bear the primary responsibility to God, and they have the greatest opportunity to influence their child for God. Any educational system is, at best, a supplement to the home. Rather than presenting an educational format that competes with the home or substitutes for the home, we begin with this simple truth and build on it.

Teachers

Granting the fact that parents are the true teachers of their child, we further acknowledge that Christian special education includes teachers and a formal program in the classroom. (We will often refer to Christian special education by the simple term *special education*, reserving for ourselves that right since we will distinguish it from public or secular education when necessary.) No single chapter addresses only special education teachers, but this book should be used by teachers as well as parents and administrators. It is futile for parents and administrators to have a sound philosophy of special education unless the teacher in a special education classroom understands and believes that philosophy. Likewise methodology is of no value unless the teacher has the ability (and equipment) to utilize it. It might be appropriate here to define what we mean by a special education teacher.

A special education teacher is not merely a technician with education credentials. A Christian teacher with a certificate in learning disabilities does not, by that qualification alone, ensure an effective Christian special education program. We believe certain additional spiritual qualities characterize an effective teacher of disabled students. For example, the Christian special education teacher will be called of God to lead students to an understanding of their potential in Christ. He must be a deeply compassionate Christian teacher, one who thoroughly understands the Biblical concept of individual responsibility and who sees himself and his students as responsible to God above all. Without this understanding, no training or certification will prepare the teacher for Christian special education.

We are not suggesting, however, that teacher preparation and training in special education are not important. Just as the credentialed special education teacher who lacks these spiritual qualities would be ill-prepared to work with disabled students in a Christian school, Christian teachers who possess these qualities but lack the appropriate professional preparation in special education would be equally deficient.

The importance of formal teacher preparation cannot be overemphasized, since Christian schools historically have shown major weaknesses in this area. Even though the Christian school movement is now approaching a half century of maturity, the lack of professionally prepared teachers continues to be one of its biggest problems. For example, in data collected as recently as 1991, Sutton and Watson (in press) found that 46% of a nationwide randomly selected sample of Christian school teachers did not have bachelor's degrees in teacher education.

An effective Christian special education teacher will have both the needed preparation and the essential qualities for this high calling. With these qualities, however, it will be almost impossible for a Christian special education teacher to be overtrained or overeducated. He will realize that special education is simply individual education; and, therefore, special education can be as varied as the individuals who need it. He will be less likely to rely on a few proven techniques that are effective within normal parameters. He will continue to develop unique tools and approaches for the unique individuals with whom God allows him to work. He will receive the special rewards that come to a teacher who has been able to "break out of the mold," who is no longer simply comparing one student with another or one student with the norm. Instead, he will be truly helping the student come to an understanding of his own unique calling and helping the student to be equipped to pursue it. A Christian special education teacher is, in the truest sense of the word, a discipler, not just one who imparts knowledge.

Administrators

The qualities that characterize special education teachers must characterize administrators as well. The administrator has the additional responsibility of managing the unusual expenses and equipment needs of special education. He is responsible for developing and articulating responses to the standard arguments against special education, the same arguments that have long produced a reluctance to underwrite Christian education in general. He is responsible for keeping these truths before pastors, parents, and Christian colleges. If a Christian special education program is ultimately successful, it may well be because the administrator finds the way to make it work. He has a big job to do, but he will find that diligent management of a special education program in a Christian school will enhance the entire program of the Christian school. Administrators are urged not merely to purchase this book and other resources for their special education teachers, but to familiarize themselves thoroughly with the philosophy and basic techniques involved, so that they can insure the effectiveness of the program.

The Components of a Ministry

This book does not offer Christianized special education, but special Christian education for individuals. There are four Scriptural components that have guided us in the development of this book. The first and most significant of these components—that which makes up philosophy—is **principles.** Before we explain what needs to be done and how to do it, we must understand thoroughly why it should be done. In Chapter 2 we discuss our Biblical philosophy. Pastors and administrators, who may not all need the detailed information in succeeding chapters, should at least become familiar with these principles. On them the whole field of Christian special education rises or falls.

The second Scriptural component is **people;** and since the most important people in the life of a special education student are his parents and teachers, we have included a chapter that provides an orientation for them (Chapter 3). Discipleship cannot occur until there are truths being exchanged between a teacher and a learner. This commitment to people must precede the organization of any special education program. Conviction about principles must be accompanied by compassion for people.

Program, of course, is a Scriptural component that cannot be ignored. It will be seen that a special education program is, in essence, the application of principles to the people involved. Finally we will consider the fourth component, **property.** In this introductory book we cannot address every physical concern of special education programs. As with Christian education generally, we often find ourselves torn between utilization and utopia—between making do with what we have and wishing we had what we need. There are some aspects of special education that are beyond the financial resources of the average Christian school. However, there is much that can be done in an existing Christian school, once the philosophy is understood and the proper people are employed.

These four components will appear throughout this book, representing as they do the four essentials of any ministry. Furthermore, as in II Timothy 2:2, the order of **principles, people, program,** and **property** will be seen to be proper for implementing a ministry.

References

Cartwright, G. P., Cartwright, C. A., & Ward, M. E. (1984). *Educating special learners* (2nd ed). Belmont, CA: Wadsworth Publishing Co.

Carver, J. A. (1989). *The status of special education in fundamental Christian schools.* Unpublished doctoral dissertation, Pensacola Christian College, Pensacola, FL.

Granger, L., & Granger, B. (1986). *The magic feather: The truth about "special education."* New York, NY: E. P. Dutton.

Hallahan, D. P., & Kauffman, J. M. (1988). *Exceptional children: Introduction to special education* (4th ed.). Englewood Cliffs, NJ: Prentice-Hall.

Haring, N. G., & McCormick, L. (1990). *Exceptional children and youth* (5th ed.). Columbus, OH: Merrill Publishing Co.

Johnson, J. A., Collins, H. W., Dupuis, V. L., & Johansen, J. H. (1988). *Introduction to the foundations of American education* (7th ed.). Boston, MA: Allyn & Bacon.

Jones, R. R. (Speaker). (1954). *The secret to success* (Cassette Recording [no number]). Greenville, SC: Bob Jones University.

Sutton, J. P. (1990a). *Prevalence of special education programs in private Christian schools: The ACSI study.* Unpublished manuscript, Bob Jones University, Greenville, SC.

Sutton, J. P. (1990b). The forgotten sheep: Ministering to handicapped individuals. *Bob Jones University Voice of the Alumni, 64*(6), 7, 22-23.

Sutton, J. P. (1991). Special education: Meeting the spirit of Public Law 94-142 in Christian schools. *Balance, 11*(8), 1-2.

Sutton, J. P. (1992). Educating students with disabilities: A new item on the Christian school agenda. *Journal for Christian Educators, 9*(3), 7-8.

Sutton, J. P., Everett, E. G., & Sutton, C. J. (in press). Special education in private Christian/ fundamentalist schools: An investigation of programs, prevalence, and personnel. *Journal of Research on Christian Education.*

Sutton, J. P., & Watson, T. G. (in press). National profile of the Christian school teacher: Do we have cause for contentment or concern? *Christian Educators Journal.*

God's Mandate for Special Education

John C. Vaughn

The Great Commission

Christian educators often trace their Scriptural mandate to the Great Commission. Matthew tells us that we are to teach all nations. Mark states it more personally: this mandate includes "every creature." Disabled persons are not excluded. We could stop with this simple statement, but our purpose is not merely to *state* the mandate but to *understand* it. The Great Commission's context begins, for our purposes, in Matthew 27:62. Reading from that verse through Matthew 28:20, we clearly see that the Great Commission is presented in a context of unbelief. Thus, we find ourselves charged with "educating every creature in a context of unbelief." A brief study of this passage will be helpful here.

Education is not merely imparting information. It is not simply training. The Scriptural goal of education is understanding. Luke 2:52 tells us that Jesus increased in wisdom, not mere knowledge or ability. The Biblical philosophy of special education is not unlike the Christian philosophy of education. In the New Testament, the church derives its name from a Greek word which means the "called-out assembly." *Education* is based on a Latin word which means "to lead out." Thus, Christian education can be said to be "leading out the called-out." In Christian special education, we seek to lead students out from unbelief to the wisdom of God's truth—as individuals. *Special* means specific or individual. Thus, the Great Commission's mandate to preach the gospel to every creature includes Christian special education.

The Context and the Conflict

Not only does the mandate for Christian special education find its roots in the Great Commission, but a further analysis of the context in Matthew 27:62–28:20 also points up the conflict within education. The conflict in education grows out of the context of unbelief. The Pharisees, who sought to eliminate the competition they perceived to their own ministry from the Lord's miraculous appearance on earth, called Him a deceiver (v. 63). Unbelief begins with a rejection of God's revelation. Because the Word of God is the only inspired book in existence, it is also the most important book in existence. Any system of instruction, or any educational pursuit, which does not find its foundation in the revealed Word of God reinforces unbelief. Christian education has, since its inception as a modern movement, struggled against the tendency to Christianize traditional education, rather than beginning with the Word of God. To try to Christianize traditional education is to build on the unbelief and to ensure failure.

Just as Christian special education must be based on the

Bible, it must also be based on insight rather than mere sight. The Pharisees' continued unbelief was intended to be based on sight—they "set a watch" (v. 66) to guarantee the general acceptance of what they had already chosen to believe. Christian special educators must always approach statistical studies, test scores, and evaluations with a healthy suspicion that unbelief prepares men to find the wrong thing. Although there is much to be learned from secular sources and from experts who have studied widely and written extensively, the problem of unbelief can never be ignored. There will always be a conflict within education because of this problem of unbelief. The highly technical nature of special education makes it doubly important that this conflict be recognized early and watched for intently.

The *preparation* of unbelief, illustrated in the Pharisees' refusal to believe what Jesus said, led to the *problem* of unbelief in the beginning of Matthew 28. The soldiers, who were assigned to insure the validity of the unbelievers' explanation of things, saw the angel roll the stone from the Lord's tomb, saw that He was no longer there, and presumably heard the angel speaking to the two women who came to the sepulchre. They later reported these events to the Pharisees but received "large money" to give a false report. We should not expound this portion of Scripture with prejudice to conclude that the modern educational system is totally corrupt and deceitful in spending its money to keep us in the dark. But there is a principle here about the motives and methods of unbelief that Christian educators must remember while understanding their mandate in the Great Commission. The mandate for Christian education was delivered immediately after these events.

We must not forget that facts are not accepted simply because they are true. The fact that a mandate comes from God does not mean it will be obeyed. This problem afflicts not only unbelievers but believers as well. The disciples had a hard time believing the report of the women who had seen the empty tomb, almost like the Pharisees rejecting the report of the soldiers. The context continues in Matthew 28:12-15, speaking of well-financed opposition to God's truth that continues, as the text says, "until this day" (v. 15).

The Commission Itself

Let's look now at the actual statement of the Great Commission.

> All power is given unto me in heaven and in earth. Go ye, therefore, and teach all nations, baptizing them in the name of the Father, and of the Son, and of the Holy Ghost: Teaching them to observe all things whatsoever I have commanded you: and, lo, I am with you alway, even unto the end of the world.

The four components of this commission are rich in application for special education.

First, we are to *go;* or "having gone," we are to make disciples. Thus, wherever we are, we are to be content and seek to serve the Lord. The word *go* assumes that we will live and move about on this earth in the natural course of human life; and as we go, we do so with whatever physical and mental abilities the Lord has given us. We are not to excuse ourselves from making disciples because of where we go or how we get there. We are to use our "going" as the basis for making disciples. Thus, disabled persons, regardless of their limitations, whether physical, mental, emotional, or behavioral, are to use their circumstances to make disciples just as nondisabled persons are to do.

Second, we are to *make disciples.* The assumption is that we will go; the command is that we will make disciples. To disciple means to make a follower. The Lord discipled His followers by literally leading them as He walked. To disciple means to lead people as they learn. When Becky Vaughn was one of only two students at Hidden Treasure Christian School in the first grade, she was not able to walk well, nor could she hold a pencil in her fingerless hands. Her teacher developed a creative way to teach her the alphabet and help her physically at the same time. Beginning with A, and throughout the alphabet, the letters were taped to the classroom floor in large scale, four feet long and three feet wide. Becky would struggle with her little walker up the first stroke of the A, then turn and walk down the second stroke, turn again and walk the crossbar. Again and again, she did this until her legs were somewhat strengthened and she had learned the letter A. And so it was that Becky was "discipled" into learning the alphabet.

Obviously, to make disciples means to make believers in Jesus Christ, but the principle of leading a person as he learns applies to education as well as evangelism. There is also a principle for education in the word *baptize*, the third step in fulfilling the Great Commission. As we go and make disciples, we are to baptize. Of course, this literally means to immerse them in water as a testimony of their identification in the death, burial, and resurrection of Jesus Christ. But we can also apply it to immersing them in the doctrines of the Father, the Son, and the Holy Spirit. Our curricula center on these doctrines—the doctrine of the Father, who provided salvation and thus freedom; the doctrine of the Son, who demonstrated and called us to submission and thus to fellowship; and the doctrine of the Holy Spirit, who empowers us for service and thus gives us fruit. Christian education is a process of immersing a student in these truths, which will lead him through salvation into service.

The final responsibility stated in the Great Commission is to *teach them to observe* all things. The word *observe* means to watch out, or to obey; and they learn greater obedience by observing an obedient leader. We teach them not only to watch *out*, but to watch *us*—we encourage them to do as we do, while they listen to what we say. It is certainly true that those we influence do not merely become what we ask them to be, nor do they do what we tell them to do. They become what we are, and they do what we do. As we seek to educate in obedience to the Great Commission, we must be able to say with Paul, "Be ye followers of me, even as I also am of Christ" (I Corinthians 11:1) and "Those things, which ye have both learned, and received, and heard, and seen in me, do" (Philippians 4:9).

Thus, in whatever circumstances we find ourselves (having gone), we are to teach our students to believe God's truth (make disciples) by immersing them in the doctrines that find their basis in the person of God (baptize), as we teach them through precept and example until they are able to develop the abilities they have, to do the same for others (teach them to observe). When these responsibilities are applied, we find the distinctions between special education and regular education.

Application to Individuals

The limitations of disabled individuals and the demands placed on teachers make it difficult, if not impossible, for each to get the other's full attention in a regular classroom setting. The teacher of disabled students must apply specially designed instruction, sometimes in a separate learning environment, to get beyond the limitations that make it difficult for students to observe their teacher in the normal sense of the word. Similarly, the teacher finds it difficult to give his own attention to students who have unique needs while meeting the demands of 25 or 30 other students. Special education is, in its simplest definition, *individual education*—doing exactly what the Bible mandates that we do for every other student, but in an environment where the student can give attention and receive the needed attention.

As we state in Chapter 1, a Biblical philosophy of special education is dependent on a Biblical philosophy of education;

and we are not seeking here to repeat all that has been written on this subject. Deuteronomy 6 is where Christian education begins, and arguments can then be made for special education. We must realize that every obedient parent is in a sense a special education teacher; but what we are calling for here is special education in a church-sponsored school. Thus we concentrate on the church's commission.

The Great Commission was indeed given to us in the context of unbelief, but it is also the antidote for unbelief. We are no less responsible to fulfill the Great Commission for those with limitations because it is harder or because we have not made the necessary investment in training to discover how it must be done. The Great Commission obligates us to "every creature."

The Great Comparison

Again, Deuteronomy 6 makes it very clear that parents are given the primary responsibility to educate their children. Special education in the Christian school must find its impetus in God's mandates and Biblical principles, rather than in an attempt to Christianize the secular special education philosophy. Interestingly, when properly understood, the Biblical philosophy of special education will provide valuable help in understanding the Christian philosophy of education generally. This is so because as Christians we seek to help each individual to come to a saving knowledge of Christ and to fulfill God's purpose for his life. This goal presupposes the belief that God has a will or purpose for every *individual.* Thus, in this respect, every individual student is "special" to God and must not be seen only in a comparison with other children. II Corinthians 10:12 warns us against the danger of "the great comparison."

For we dare not make ourselves of the number, or compare ourselves with some that commend themselves: but they measuring themselves by themselves, and comparing themselves among themselves, are not wise.

Although standards of scholastic achievement are necessary and helpful, they are not absolute; and they are often very difficult to apply in a special education setting.

Distinctions Among Individuals

When Becky Vaughn was a preschooler, she was diligently striving to overcome the severe physical disabilities to her body caused by a major body burn at the age of two. After about ten minutes of struggling to turn the page of a little book with her weak and fingerless hands, in childlike curiosity she asked her mother, "Mommy, when I get bigger, will I have hands like Debbie [her big sister]?" Her mother very wisely replied, "Becky, Debbie has the hands that God has given her to do her job in life, and you have the hands that God has allowed you to have to do your job in life." In this loving response, there is a tremendous illustration of the basic principle of Christian special education. **Every child has everything he needs in order to do God's will for his life.** That does not mean he should not be trained, educated, and informed as far as possible, nor that he just needs to be polished by his education. Certainly, there will be changes and the gaining of new skills and insights. What we mean by this statement is that within the promises of Scripture every child can find the hope of accomplishing God's will, regardless of the God-given circumstances or limitations that he must face.

We believe that every child should strive to overcome, as far as possible, every physical and mental limitation that would hinder his service for the Lord. But if there is an insurmountable and therefore God-given difference between that child and others, he should be taught to graciously accept that limitation as from the Lord and find some way to compensate for it or use it for God's glory. Every effort should be made to avoid the exploitation of these distinctions for the personal benefit of the individual or his family, but using the limitation publicly for the glory of God should not be thought of as selfish exploitation.

We fall into the trap of "the Great Comparison" when we fail to have a Biblical understanding of the distinctions among individuals. Obviously, individuals are different both in appearance and in ability. It is neither practical nor usually possible for every child to receive individual attention from a teacher in a classroom setting. However, children do need individual attention for their education and development into adults, and God has ordained that they should receive it from their parents. It is impractical to expect teachers to do for children in a classroom what only parents have the time and obligation to do. On the other hand, the more attention a child needs, the more parental the teacher's role becomes. Special education teachers will, therefore, be focusing more on the distinctions of the individuals in the classroom, as parents must do at home.

It must always be held in mind that special education is individual education. Greatly reduced teacher/pupil ratios will, therefore, be essential. Specialized equipment, often used by only one student in a classroom, may have to be purchased. Curricula will be intensely personalized. The individual needs of students in special education will dictate the development of an individual education plan (IEP). All of this will be time-consuming and sometimes expensive. But there is a great blessing in store for all involved in this process. It is a new understanding that we are "fearfully and wonderfully made"—we are individuals in the sight of God. Just as we are saved individually, we are used individually by God. Students in special education, whose teachers wisely recognize their uniqueness, often have the advantage of hearing again and again that God has a plan for their lives and that they must discover it and submit to it. Nondisabled children who simply have to score a passing grade on a standardized test in a Christian school may not hear this as often.

A disability is an exclamation point in the student's life message. Persons who live for self, instead of God, reveal their message more emphatically if there is some limitation which attracts attention to their selfishness. Similarly, disabled children who give their lives to the Lord, seriously seeking to serve God with their whole heart, will be seen to do so far more easily since they are more noticeable.

Distinction Between Christian and Secular Education

Just as there are distinctions among individuals, there are differences between Christian and secular education. Although this sounds like a truism, it needs to be understood. The distinction between Christian and secular education may be overlooked without instant penalty in a Christian school without special education. But the special education program that fails to maintain the distinction between Christian and secular education does so at its immediate peril.

Some have seen the distinction between Christian and secular education as merely the difference between "traditional" and "progressive" education, when in fact traditional education was the foundation of progressive education. Curricula and philosophy are not necessarily Biblical because they are old. Humanism did not begin with the *Humanist Manifesto* of 1933, nor did progressive education demonstrate the first attempt by man to lead children to self-sufficiency without God. Although there is frequently a tendency in Christian education to get "back to the basics," the real emphasis should be to get back to the *Bible*.

If we look to the "tradition" in secular special education, we find progressive education well established before the public schools became involved in special education (Johnson, Collins, Dupuis, & Johansen, 1988). One may observe that the legislation which mandated public special education may be more closely linked with the civil rights movement. Accordingly, Hallahan and Kauffman (1988) note that during the years of President Johnson's term, "there [was] a recognition of the rights of handicapped individuals" (p. 23). Minorities that were experiencing discrimination in other segments of society were often disproportionately represented in special education classes in the 1970s (Hallahan & Kauffman, 1988; Salend, 1990). There is much in the literature of the period to suggest that mainstreaming was not only an educational philosophy but a social policy (Salend, 1990). This does not mean that we should reject the concept of mainstreaming itself, but that we should recognize that the secular tradition, especially as illustrated in special education, has been largely influenced by personal *rights*—a humanist concept—rather than personal *responsibility*, a Biblical concept. A Biblical approach will not lead us to the conclusion that disabled persons are just part of another minority group.

The distinction between Christian education and secular education is that the first is Christ-centered and the second is man-centered. A Christian education is mandated by the pre-eminence of Christ, not the student. Thus, a true Christian education helps a child to become *like* Christ; it does not merely tell him *about* Christ. We have seen that the church, which the Bible calls the body of Christ, is a "called-out assembly." We acknowledge the responsibility of individuals to assemble themselves in *local* churches for the purpose of accountability and discipleship, but we use the term in its largest sense here to include Christian families and Christian schools (the body of Christ) that have responded to the call out of sin into fellowship with God. We have also seen that Christian education in one sense is "leading out the called-out." This will necessarily be a Christ-centered task, rather than a man-centered task. We do not just lead the student; we lead him to Christ.

Those who claim to educate children out of the darkness of ignorance often stop short of God's mandate to lead them into the light of the knowledge of God. Secular education, in spite of its positive qualities and contributions to society, is at best a sophisticated form of accommodation: a man-centered enterprise which seeks to help the student become that which will best serve himself, rather than directing him into the purpose of his creation, which is serving God. A good secular education is like good shooting—without taking aim. Nowhere do the distinctions between Christian and secular education become more apparent than in special education.

Compare the concept of mainstreaming (keeping disabled children in the "mainstream" of the regular classroom as much as possible) with the better concept of genuinely meeting needs. We are not arguing for segregation of disabled children, but rather warning of the dangers of incorporating popular secular concepts into Christian special education. As we will show in Chapter 4, Public Law 94-142 calls for disabled children to remain in the "least restrictive environment." This concept grew out of a commitment to equal opportunity and is obviously man-centered. Christian special education, on the other hand, should be Christ-centered with a focus on individual responsibility. This truth derives from Psalm 139:14, where David declares, "I will praise thee; for I am fearfully and wonderfully made: marvelous are thy works; and that my soul knoweth right well." The Hebrew word translated *fearfully* speaks of God's concern for us as individuals, and the word *wonderfully* reveals His individual design for each of us. Thus, the concept of mainstreaming is not necessarily wrong—in fact, there is much that is right about including a disabled child in his peer group—but mainstreaming does not go far enough. It offers a disabled child only the same opportunity for selfishness and mediocrity that is offered to other children. It is irrelevant who comes in first, when no one wins.

Obligation and Opportunity

As surely as there are distinctions among individuals and distinctions between Christian and secular education (particularly special education), so are there distinctions in our obligation and our opportunity. God's mandate for us to disciple every creature is not mere accommodation of disabled students. Discipling is a definite Scriptural obligation. We often speak of Christian education as though it were a type of education, rather than the education of Christians. We speak of a "philosophy of Christian education," rather than a "Christian philosophy of education." These distinctions must be made clearer. Our Christian obligation to disabled students must stand above that perceived by the world. If we are motivated only out of pity for these children, we miss the point.

The commands of Scripture reveal the balance we must maintain. Galatians 6:5 commands us to bear our own burdens, but verse 2 commands us to bear one another's burdens. Part of what we must do is to help others do what they must, but cannot, do. Our obligation to disabled students grows out of *their* obligation to God. If we are motivated only by a sense of guilt because we are more fortunate than they are, we are un-Biblical. The "Great Comparison" affects our thinking at this point. We must be careful not to think that we have satisfied our obligation to God simply because we are doing better than someone else. Nor must we allow ourselves to think that we have met our obligation to disabled students because we have included them in a substandard program.

The key to this argument is found in II Corinthians 4:7, "But we have this treasure in earthen vessels, that the excellency of the power may be of God, and not of us." The treasure is not the vessel. The vessel is the physical life—the realm of limitation, where disabilities are seen. Tenderhearted people must look beyond the limitations of the vessel to find the "treasure" in every child. But, again, we err if we think that the treasure is something about the child himself. That is the man-centered approach. The preceding verse, II Corinthians 4:6, tells us that the treasure is "the light of the knowledge of the glory of God in the face of Jesus Christ." All of us have the opportunity and therefore the obligation to put our faith in Jesus Christ and to reflect Christlikeness in our lives, so that through Christ in us, others can see the glory of God. The treasure is not us; it is Christ in us. And because we must look beyond the physical man, the hidden treasure of disabled students is often easier to find than the hidden treasure of nondisabled persons. Simple human kindness forces us to overlook a disability, and so any polite person is already looking for something else on which to focus in a disabled child. The secular philosophy of God is confused by the notion that He cannot love us and still allow us to suffer. When disabled children demonstrate the grace of God in their hearts and are trained to the best of their ability to speak for Christ, they are in a powerful position to correct this confusion. Thus we have not only an obligation *to* disabled students, but a tremendous opportunity *through* them.

The Christian message is not a message of temporal life; it is a message of eternal life. Disabilities find their proper meaning only in the context of eternity. When we succumb to the Great Comparison, we find that some are disabled when compared with others; but when we reject the tendency to compare ourselves with one another, disabilities disappear. We all have something wrong with us; and as we get older, we have more things wrong with us than when we were younger. The average Christian sympathizes more with a young person who suffers limitations than with an elderly person. Senility is much like the mental condition of a child with a mental disability. Arthritis, glaucoma, baldness, and a host of other physical ailments that attack us with advancing age are heart-rending when seen in children. This does not mean that we should not sympathize with children who suffer these things, but it simply points out the contradiction in our compassion when we are more brokenhearted with children who suffer than with elderly people who suffer. Our concern is often not so much for human suffering as it is for the loss of human opportunity, which is a chief concern of humanism.

There is a vast mission field that we have overlooked by neglecting the education of disabled children. Approximately one out of ten children of school age is disabled (U.S. Department of Education, 1986) and will need special education—a tithe of our younger generation. Each of these children represents a family that potentially could be reached if we would include their children in our schools. Every church school that incorporates special education into its program exposes itself to a potential community 40% the size of its current enrollment. A church school with one hundred students that begins special education can expect potentially to reach ten students, therefore ten families or approximately forty new people that might be brought into the church.

It does not seem inappropriate to apply the lesson of Luke 14:16-24 to these days. We expect the soon return of the Lord. We will rejoice with Him at the Marriage Supper. Those who become involved in Christian education will find that although materialism and the distraction of the modern entertainment media have provided ready excuses for most prospects for evangelism, disabled persons are still very largely reachable. Perhaps the Lord is saying to us today in Christian education, "Go out quickly into the streets and lanes of the city, and bring in hither the poor, and the maimed, and the halt, and the blind."

A Call for Christian Special Education

A Personal Perspective

Admittedly, "Hidden Treasure" is an unusual name for a school. This term offers a variety of mental images. Some have thought of a pirate's treasure chest; others refer to our students themselves as "God's hidden treasures." Many people mispronounce the name of our school, calling it "Hidden Treasures," because they think the term refers to the students themselves. In fact, it is a Bible term and provides an insight into our purpose. We are to seek wisdom as hidden treasure (Proverbs 2:4); this is the key to special education. Disabled children often cannot merely accumulate knowledge and meet minimum standards to verify their education. They must necessarily go beyond mere knowledge to get understanding, or wisdom, the true hidden treasure. Often, they cannot participate in the athletic programs so popular in most schools, for they "have this treasure in earthen vessels," and their physical bodies are often broken by physical disabilities.

We believe that these broken vessels are uniquely suited to reveal the treasure within, not just their childlike qualities of sweetness and innocence, but the true value of a human soul to God—the indwelling Holy Spirit in the heart of a Christian child. The knowledge that every one of us has everything he needs to do the will of God for his life is truly the hidden treasure. This is what we seek to develop and to reveal in the lives of our students. Thus, the name of our school is Hidden Treasure Christian School. A brief review of our history may be helpful in understanding our approach to special education. The beginning of Hidden Treasure Christian School can be traced to a sermon on I Peter 4:12-13, preached at Faith Baptist Church on April 23, 1978:

> Beloved, think it not strange concerning the fiery trial which is to try you, as though some strange thing happened unto you: But rejoice, inasmuch as ye are partakers of Christ's sufferings; that, when his glory shall be revealed, ye may be glad also with exceeding joy.

God often raises up unusual ministries in unusual ways. The Bill Rice Ranch in Murfreesboro, Tennessee, was founded because God blessed the Rice home with a daughter who was deaf. The Shepherd's Home in Union Grove, Wisconsin, grew out of the concern of a small Sunday school class for mentally retarded persons within a local church. In the same way, the vision for Hidden Treasure Christian School began during the invitation after that message in 1978. That night, my wife Brenda and I dedicated our lives anew to being used of God in any way that He saw fit, without realizing that a fiery trial lay in our immediate future. On May 20, less than a month later, our home was the scene of a freak accident involving a gasoline explosion, in which Brenda and our two-year-old daughter Becky were severely injured. For many months, it was uncertain whether Becky would survive. After it was evident that God had spared her life, it was still unclear what the future would hold regarding Becky's education. By the time Becky reached school age, we were searching for an educational program suitable for her. Although there were a number of Christian schools interested in special education, and some that had begun resource rooms for those with learning disabilities, there was nothing available for the specialized help that Becky was going to need because of her physical limitations.

A continued search for an educational program suitable for Becky revealed nothing but numerous other cases like hers, where there was a need for special education in a Christian school but none provided. In 1981 Brenda and I began to meet with a local fellowship group called Mothers of Handicapped Children. There I shared my burden for a special education school. From that group grew a task force of parents who began to study the feasibility of a Christian school for disabled children. From II Corinthians 4:7, the Lord led us to call it Hidden Treasure Christian School, and it was begun as a ministry of Faith Baptist Church in Greenville, South Carolina. In the 1981-82 school year, classes began with just two students. The next year, there were 4, then 12, then 18, with increases each year until the facilities were filled up with 40 students.

It was not our intention at first to concentrate on students with moderate/severe learning disabilities or other mental disabilities, but rather to provide an educational environment for those with physical disabilities. But as the philosophy of the school began to develop, it would not allow us to exclude students with special education needs of all kinds. The often-told story about Becky "having the hands she needs to do the job that God has given her" illustrates the key to the burden of the founders.

Because of that memorable event, the Hidden Treasure principle was recognized. Each of us has everything he needs to do God's will for his life. We must simply focus on appropriating from God all that we need to perfect, as well as possible, what He has given us. It is one thing to have a sincere desire to help disabled children, but it is another matter altogether to know how to do it. The biggest hurdle we had to get over was in evaluation and assessment—simply knowing what the child's needs really were. Frustration was compounded by not knowing where to go to get the help that was needed and by not knowing whom to trust when help was offered. Many expensive test runs were made to develop an evaluation process. Some who wanted to help lacked the education experience necessary. Many Christian special education experts were found to be simply secular special education certificate holders who happened to be Christians. An entirely new philosophy would be needed whereby we could evaluate accepted assessment instruments.

Based on the principle of individual responsibility—that we have "hidden treasure in an earthly vessel"—our philosophy was developed. Psalm 139:14 was the guiding principle behind the concept of individual needs. We are all fearfully and wonderfully made, made differently, and made with a purpose. God makes no mistakes. If He made us the way we are, He must have something for us to do the way we are. But we did not stop with individual needs. It is humanistic and un-Biblical merely to accommodate students in a special education environment. Romans 14:12 tells us that "every one of us shall give an account of himself to God." Luke 12:48b clearly teaches that our accountability is based on our opportunity:

> For unto whomsoever much is given, of him shall be much required: and to whom men have committed much, of him they will ask the more.

Disabled children often attract a lot of attention. They must be helped to direct that attention to their Savior. This has been and remains the prime objective at Hidden Treasure Christian School.

A Pastor's Perspective

Before we strive to understand what *special* education is (particularly Christian special education), it is helpful to have a working understanding of what *education* is. That seems self-evident, but many people use a definition of education which is more properly a definition of training. As we have seen, the church has a mandate from God to educate—it is a part of the Great Commission. Education is part of the discipleship process. Again, we affirm that true education is "leading out the called-out." Leading someone requires knowledge of the place or point to which they are being led. Many educators would find it difficult to give an answer if asked where they are trying to lead their students. The most common objective of public school students seems to be "to graduate," which originally meant something like "to take another step"; but very few people know or are willing to consider where that step is leading them.

Before we chastise the public educators too severely, we should ask Christian educators where they are trying to lead their students. Many would eventually come up with the answer "Christlikeness"; but it is often difficult, if not impossible, to relate standardized scores, grades on report cards, and athletic programs to that goal. If education is "leading someone somewhere," and if that education is sincere, then it should lead the person to the place where God wants him to be.

Christian schools are often little more than nonpublic schools. Their identity exists, not in what they are, but in what they are not. We in Christian education are not "doing it right" merely because we are not doing it in the same wrong way as others are. The fallacy of this kind of thinking cannot be hidden for long in a special education school. If a Christian school fails to conform its nondisabled students to the image of Christ, we can hide that failure behind our academic product, our athletic prowess, or our fine arts performance. But we cannot usually offer disabled children the opportunity to become homecoming queen, captain of the basketball squad, or members in the honor society. We are faced with a decision when we have disabled children: we must either help them or hide them. Our motives come to the surface obviously and quickly.

Underlying the problem of comparing ourselves with the public schools is the more damaging problem of continuing to allow our students to compare themselves with one another. "An A student is better than a B student." No state wants to be last in SAT scores, and no student wants to be last in his class; but a student can be head of his class and still fall short of his responsibility to God. The Bible clearly tells us that if we compare ourselves among ourselves, we are not wise; yet if education is going to occur at all, there must be some sort of standardized expectation for us to know whether we are getting anything done. Special education keeps this in balance. Our Christian schools do not exist to offer equal access to mediocrity. If they do not exist to aid parents in helping their children to be conformed to the image of Christ, they have no right to exist. If that is indeed the reason for their existence, there is absolutely no basis whatsoever for excluding disabled children; for with that objective, all Christian education becomes special education.

A school with a goal of Christlikeness for its students should be Christlike in its approach. Christ consistently sought disabled individuals to use as illustrations of His compassion and power. The more helpless they were (sometimes they were dead!), the more powerfully and clearly His message was heard.

We challenge pastors whose ministries include Christian schools to consider that all Christian education is indeed a form of special education. If we graduate students who are not able to answer a question about the will of God for their lives—with an understanding that He has a will, some understanding of what it is, and a determined intention to submit to it—then we have failed. Reading, writing, and arithmetic must be learned, and we have started our schools because the public schools do not teach these subjects so that the students may be better equipped to glorify God, but rather to glorify self. We are not Christian educators if we seek only to teach more effectively to the goal of self-gratification.

We often hear the term "academic excellence" as though it were our goal, but our excellence is often defined merely by comparison with someone else's incompetence. Excellence is not our goal; excellence is our method. Christlikeness is our goal. Christ Himself lives today in a disabled body, and we do not refer to the nailprints in His hands; we refer to the Church, which is His body. He has committed to that body the same Commission that He illustrated by His life when He walked this earth physically. Like a child with cerebral palsy, this body does not receive or respond properly to the signals from the "head." The spasticity and lack of coordination within the body of Christ often makes the church and its related ministries the subject of the kind of ridicule often experienced by disabled children. Our prayer is that the thoughts on Christian special education offered here will work toward a correction of this tragic situation.

A Professional Perspective

Just as God has called us into special education, He must call you. Special education is much too involved, too expensive, and too important to be taken lightly or tried as an experiment. We do not need special education teachers who have entered the field because they want to treat children the way they wish they had been treated when they were growing up, teachers who perhaps have unresolved conflicts in other areas of their lives. Nor does Christian special education need secular special education teachers with the wrong philosophy who are tired of teaching in a public school. This does not rule out the possibility of those with unfortunate backgrounds or un-Biblical philosophies correcting their own thinking and becoming effective servants in special education. Certainly, we should have the same compassion for these hurting people as for anyone else. But we cannot simply transplant people into our Christian schools without a calling from God.

Administrators and pastors who have been challenged to begin special education programs often respond that our colleges should take the lead in providing special education teachers trained with the same Biblical philosophy of education as our other teachers. We must remember that colleges cannot dictate our needs, but they can respond to them. A number of our fine Christian colleges have, in recent years, begun degree programs in special education, because the need has been evident in our Christian schools. There must be a balance between preaching these principles to our young future teachers and providing special education opportunities for them. Then the undergraduate and graduate programs that will equip these teachers will, no doubt, be provided by our colleges.

This book has been prepared in part because our small

school and staff have been overwhelmed in recent years with inquiries about the questions that we seek to answer here. Frankly, Christian schools across America have demanded from us this response. Although we do not accept at face value all of the statistics being compiled today regarding the need for special education, the need is obvious. Our prayer is that our sincere attempt to share with others what we have been learning will, in some way, help the cause of Christian special education. There is a vast mission field here, since those 10 students represent 10 families with 40 to 50 potential church members in those homes. Although we do not propose special education as an evangelistic tool primarily, its evangelistic potential should not be ignored.

We believe that for too long, those invited to the "banquet" that the Lord offers in salvation have been distracted with other concerns. It is indeed time to go out and bring in hither the poor, the maimed, the halt, and the blind. We pray not only that Christian schools across America will respond to their obligation to those with disabilities, but that they will also receive renewed vision for the unique needs of all the students in their "normal" Christian schools as well.

Frequently Asked Questions

Can't we have a conviction for Christian education without taking on the education of disabled Christians?

1. *Let's first consider: What is Christian education?*
    Christian education is not just a type of education. It is the education of Christians, leading those that do not know Christ to a saving knowledge of Christ, and discipling them in the doctrines of the Word of God into Christlikeness. It is "leading out the called-out"—obeying the Bible mandate to make disciples of every creature.

2. **What is a conviction?**
   A conviction is a strongly held belief. It is a belief held by one who has been convinced, by the evidence, of the truth or need in question.

3. **What is special education?**
   Special education is "specifically designed instruction that meets the unique needs of an exceptional child [and which may include] special materials, teaching techniques, equipment and/or facilities" (Hallahan & Kauffman, 1988, p. 6). In its simplest form, special education is individual education. *Special* means specific, particular, different from a group or a class in an identified way. Special education is, therefore, education that focuses on the individual needs of a child to a far greater degree than is typical in a regular classroom.

4. **Why have we neglected Christian special education?**
   Perhaps our real conviction has not been for Christian education, but for nonpublic education. Perhaps we have failed to recognize that Christian education itself is a type of special education. Our main objective should be to identify and prepare the student for the will of God for his life, rather than simply trying to teach basic information in a civilized environment. We have further neglected Christian special education for the same reasons that we resisted Christian education a few decades ago. We have failed to properly define it. We feel that we cannot afford it. We are ill-prepared for it, and often those in decision-making roles are not affected by it. In essence, we have put too much emphasis on the "how" of education, instead of the "why."

How can we hope to educate disabled students when it costs so much?

1. *Can we afford it?*
   The premise of this question must be rejected. If we ask the same question about Christian education, it is very easy to

find a reason why we should close our schools. We cannot afford Christian special education any more than we can afford the tuition for Christian education in general. But if there truly is a Biblical mandate for it and we obey the Lord faithfully, He will make it possible for us to have it.

2. *Should every Christian school have a special education program?*
The answer is "yes" if there is a need. Furthermore, it is inevitable that, as Christian schools grow and begin to use a referral system (i.e., regular education teachers request that some students be evaluated for a possible disability), disabled students will be identified and become eligible for special education services. As the Lord allows students within a Christian school population to be classified and as other students with existing disabilities apply for admission, the Christian school has an obligation to provide a special education program; otherwise they in essence are closing their doors of ministry to these students (Sutton, 1991, 1992). Thus, every Christian school may need some type or types of special education. Providing a full range of special education services to all types of disabled students from mildly to severely disabled may be difficult or impossible, however, for smaller Christian schools. Therefore, there will be some specialized, self-contained schools that will emerge in the years ahead, where the full range of limitations can be addressed; but these schools are going to have to specialize in special education, for the most part, and be funded as missions projects that will not ever be self-sufficient.

3. *Should we just have a special education teacher?*
This is often the place to begin. That special education teacher can be a tutor or can head up a resource room where those with learning disabilities or other disabling conditions can spend part of their day getting the special help that they need. In the meantime, it may be found that some teacher

on the present faculty of the Christian school has an interest, or even training, in special education and can assume some of the duties of the special education needs already represented within the school. Sometimes a teacher will see the need and be willing to go and get the additional training in special education.

4. *What about volunteers?*

For a time, until a special education teacher and/or resource room can be incorporated into the school, volunteer tutors may be incorporated. Church members associated with the Christian school family may have experience in special education. These people may be willing to consider tutorial help of disabled students as a ministry. At the very least, the Christian school should find a way to provide help to those parents who have children with special needs. Often, the parents will already have learned much about meeting the needs of their child, and it could be that a parent can bring the child to school and function as an aide under the direction of a teacher while learning more about how to help the child at home.

5. *What about those that you cannot help?*

Residential programs are available for more severely disabled persons, although these are limited and often hard to get into. A family may need to relocate to an area where a school is available. But often within a community there are several good churches and/or Christian schools, none of which have a special education program. It would seem more reasonable for these to work together for the implementation of a special education program within one of them, than for each of them to feel individually that nothing can be done. Experience has shown that those who have the greatest need have the greatest burden. Parents who need help must shoulder much of the responsibility to persuade educators and pastors to begin these programs.

6. *What are the costs?*
A good rule of thumb, although not to be rigidly applied, is that special education costs approximately twice what regular education does, plus the expenses of the faculty. These costs too will be greatly increased over those of the regular Christian school because of the lower teacher/pupil ratio. For the more severely disabled students, buildings, furnishings, equipment, and textbook materials are all more expensive because of their unique design and function and their limited use, but there are benefits. If special education is prescribed by a licensed psychologist or medical doctor, the expenses associated with that education are often tax-deductible. Further, there are some circumstances in which a family's health insurance plan will pay the cost of special education. Parents should also be familiarized with the various possibilities of public assistance for special education. On the other hand, resource special education programs for students with mild disabilities will not require extra furnishings or expensive equipment.

What are the greatest challenges?

1. *Grasping the Bible philosophy*
Those involved in special education must remember that it is individual education. They must remember that each student has an individual responsibility because he is an individual creation. God's mandate for Christian special education is inherent in the mandate for Christian education. The same philosophy that demands we provide education for our nondisabled children also demands that we include those who are disabled. We must build our programs on the Bible philosophy, rather than adopting the secular philosophy.

2. *Keeping our terms and definitions straight*
We must guard against the tendency to refer to "special

education vs. traditional education," since traditional education refers to a type of secular education which preceded what has come to be called progressive education. It would be better to refer to special education as distinct from general education or "the normal classroom," even though the latter term seems to be somewhat prejudicial. We should further remember that, in fact, secular special education is a contradiction in terms. Secular education does not recognize the true individuality of God's creatures. Because it is humanistic, it seeks to elevate mankind, rather than seeing individual persons in relation to God. It focuses on equal opportunity rather than individual responsibility; therefore, secular special education is a form of humanitarian accommodation, rather than *true* individual education.

3. *Being directed by principle rather than pressure*
In Christian special education, we will constantly be pressured to "mainstream" our students. Our willingness as Christian educators to mainstream our disabled students should never go beyond transferring them from a Christian special education classroom to a regular Christian school classroom. The ultimate wrong application of mainstreaming would be to put our Christian children back into the public schools, into what is in fact the true mainstream. But in the same way that we have taken them out of the public system and started our own schools because they have unique needs and are headed in a different direction, there is a sense in which we will have to separate our disabled children, at times, to meet their unique needs. We must not be weak when accused of "sheltering" our children. The same argument is used against Christian education. In a sense we are sheltering them—from error—as surely as the secular system shelters them from a knowledge of God. We cannot expect disabled children to become what God wants them to be if

we are motivated more by humanistic pity than by Biblical conviction. The Biblical conviction includes compassion, but also a determination to put Christ first.

Distinctions Among Individuals: A Biblical Philosophy of Special Education

It is our conviction that God is directing the Christian school movement into special education to refocus its main mission—to reach individuals with the gospel and disciple them to the glory of God.

Too often, our Christian schools are merely nonpublic schools that bear all the markings of compulsory education. In his controversial and hard-hitting book, *Dumbing Us Down,* award-winning teacher of the year John Taylor Gatto (1992) indicts the government monopoly on education as having produced schools where mediocrity exists in a caste system of classes. He attacks the banality of curricula and schedules designed more to produce conformity in emotional dependence and indifference than to truly educate. Nowhere is this problem seen more clearly than in special education.

Our concern is that even our Christian schools have borrowed so heavily from compulsory government education that we are producing mediocre Christians just as the public schools are producing mediocre citizens. A Biblical philosophy of special education will not only define the objectives and methods of Christian special education, but will help to clarify the real purpose of Christian education in its entirety. This Biblical philosophy is based on the fact that "every one of us shall give an account of himself to God" (Romans 14:12). Individual responsibility requires individual accountability. Individual accountability grows out of individual ability; and individual ability is fostered through individual education—special education.

Special education is not merely a branch of Christian education; rather Christian education is a type of special education. Whereas the philosophies of humanism and materialism seek to elevate mankind at the expense of individual liberty, truly Christian education seeks to lift individuals out of the bondage of sin into the liberty of salvation and spiritual growth. Whereas the so-called New Age offers a false hope that religious morality can be returned to the public school curriculum, the truly Christian school fosters Biblical morality through individual responsibility to God. Our disabled students are providing helpful pressure to Christian education because they do not fit into our existing programs. Even if it were possible to sanitize the system, add Bible classes, and enroll only Christians, these elements alone would not insure we were engaged in Christian education.

Christian education is not a type of education merely; it is the education of Christians—individual Christians. It is "leading out the called-out" from wherever they are to wherever God wants them to be. It is the recognition that "every one of us has everything he needs to do God's perfect will for his life." When properly defined, Christian education is, in its purpose, synonymous with Christian special education. When special education is a part of the Christian school program, it will help to keep that purpose intact. The Christian school is the ideal environment in which to implement Gatto's "congregational principle"—the truth that small, independent bodies tend to correct their own errors and work together more effectively than do standardized, centrally-controlled systems. God deals with us as individuals; He places us in local autonomous assemblies; He indwells us, thus enabling us to function as "His body." Unless we address the critical need for Christian special education, Christ's body will continue to live with a serious disability.

References

Gatto, J. T. (1992). *Dumbing us down.* Philadelphia, PA: New Society Publishers.

Hallahan, D. P., & Kauffman, J. M. (1988). *Exceptional children: Introduction to special education* (4th edition). Englewood Cliffs, NJ: Prentice Hall.

Johnson, J. A., Collins, H. W., Dupuis, V. L., & Johansen, J. H. (1988). *Introduction to the foundations of American education* (7th edition). Boston, MA: Allyn and Bacon.

Salend, S. J. (1990). *Effective mainstreaming.* New York, NY: MacMillan.

Sutton, J. P. (1991). Special education: Meeting the spirit of Public Law 94-142 in Christian schools. *Balance, 11* (8), 1-2.

Sutton, J. P. (1992). Educating students with disabilities: A new item on the Christian school agenda. *Journal for Christian Educators, 9*(3), 7-8.

U. S. Department of Education. (1986). *To Assure the Free Appropriate Public Education of All Handicapped Children. Eighth Annual Report to Congress on Implementation of the Education of the Handicapped Act.* Volume 1. Washington, DC: Government Printing Office.

CHAPTER THREE

Orientation for Parents and Teachers

John C. Vaughn

Introduction

*A*lthough we are trying to make this book as comprehensive as possible, we must reiterate again that it cannot
address in detail everything that the special education teacher,
or even the parent of disabled children, will need to know. In
addition, this resource should not be thought of as a "how-to
book" for homeschoolers of disabled children; nor is it the only
resource a special education teacher in a Christian school needs
to have in order to be effective. With this book in hand,
however, Christian parents and teachers of disabled children
will find suggested resources that will help them obtain other
necessary materials. They will also be made aware of the things
that they need to learn more about.

More specifically, what we are offering here are guidelines for parents and teachers to help them get started with their disabled children. A number of the chapters in this book deal with philosophy and the Biblical and legal requirements for special education. They also present in some depth the specific special education needs of disabled children and how these are treated in the special education classroom; parents and teachers alike will profit from this information.

The purpose of this chapter is to orient the reader to some of the most important needs in Christian special education. It would be useful reading for pastors or administrators, in particular those who will not be working on a day-to-day basis in special education classrooms but who do need to understand the needs and some basic information about Christian school special education. A thorough reading of this material should allow them and others who will work directly or indirectly with disabled students to be more knowledgeable and effective in their service to these children.

This chapter, therefore, will concentrate on three critical needs for all Christians, whether teachers, parents, or administrators. First, we believe that everyone should be more aware of the characteristics and needs of students with disabilities; hence there is a need to keep oneself informed through reading available books and articles. Second, we must realize that Christian schools have very few special education textbooks, materials, and other references that are dependable and Biblically based. Thus, for the time being, Christian special education teachers and parents must learn the skill of making modifications and accommodations for our students. Finally, we have established the fact that special education is a novel idea in Christian education today. Therefore, it is extremely important that Christians gain a clear, accurate understanding of basic concepts in special education.

Keeping Informed Through Reading

The legislation related to special education discussed in Chapter 4 is important to know if parents and teachers of disabled children are going to understand much of the literature currently available on special education. New legislation continues to impinge on special education; and no doubt there will be future legislation with which parents and teachers will need to become familiar. Much, if not most, of the current legislation, however, does not relate to Christian schools, with their disabled students and special education programs, but to those in public schools. This is most evident in the Education of All Handicapped Children Act, Public Law (PL) 94-142, where the official wording reads "free appropriate *public* education" for all disabled children.

Helpful publications are available for parents, but not as many volumes are available as have been written for teachers. Texts and references for teachers are listed elsewhere in this book, but one volume that would be particularly helpful to parents is *The Special Education Handbook: How to Get the Best Education Possible for Your Learning Disabled Child* (Shore, 1986). Shore, who has written from a secular viewpoint, deals particularly with the rights and responsibilities of parents and students in the public school system. We do not advocate everything that Shore has written. It is interesting, however, that this book like so many others seems to suggest (at least in its title) that special education is only for "learning disabled" students. The typical lay person may perceive special education as a school or class for those with mental or learning disabilities, when it is actually much broader than that. In fact, in one of the premier textbooks today on special education co-authored by Hallahan and Kauffman (1988), eight exceptionalities are delineated: communication disorders, emotional disturbance /

behavior disorders, giftedness, hearing impairments, learning disabilities, mental retardation, physical impairments, and visual impairments.

The value of Shore's (1986) book for Christian parents is its focus on the concerns of parents. Although this is not the only book of its kind, it is one of the more recent and most comprehensive. It should be kept in mind that secular books often have a strong emphasis on child advocacy and rights; but if a parent suspects his child has a learning disability and has limited information to guide him, he should begin with this volume and then obtain Shore's book and study it well. The parent who arms himself with this kind of information will be far better prepared to communicate with special education teachers, testing and evaluation professionals, and others who would be involved in his child's education.

The alternative to the parents being informed is often tragic. Many students who have applied at Hidden Treasure Christian School in their early to middle teens should have had intervention in their educational program years earlier. Often these children have been in four or five "special education programs" dealing with problems unrelated to the one the child is experiencing. The parent has taken the child to these schools on the recommendations of friends or teachers, only to find—after two or three wasted years—that the school either did not understand the child's need or did not know how to help him. Two or three more schools like this were sought for help, until finally the parents, in frustration, took matters into their own hands and found a school that was properly prepared to help their child. This is what the parents should have done in the first place—accept complete responsibility for their child.

We suggest that another reference work is needed to provide Christian parents with a resource on special education, much like Shore's (1986) handbook, but one that is based on a Biblical philosophy and addresses the specific concerns of the

Christian school instead of the public school. Until such a volume is available, there is another book that would be helpful to the Christian parent. Wood and his colleagues at the Shepherd's Home in Union Grove, Wisconsin, have prepared a small volume called *Unto the Least of These: Special Education in the Church* (Wood, 1984). Although it deals primarily with the ministry to retarded people in the local church, there is a chapter on "Initiating a Program in the Christian School." The fourth section of the book presents "Principles of Working with the Mentally Retarded," which is applicable both in the church setting and in the Christian school. Although limited in scope (dealing almost exclusively with mentally retarded people), it contains valuable material and should prove helpful to parents and teachers who are making their initial inquiries into special education.

Making Modifications and Accommodations in Teaching

Perhaps it would be helpful to explain why we refer to and recommend secular materials from time to time. We do so, not because we prefer these materials to dependable, Biblically based sources, but because there are so few dependable or Biblically based materials that we know of in existence at this time. It is easy for Christian educators to criticize secular sources, even though they are often well researched, well written, and getting the job done to some degree, albeit often contrary to Scripture. But until Christians accept the challenge of a ministry in special education and produce the necessary textbooks and reference materials, we will have to work with what is available. It is our conviction that it is better to improvise what we presently have rather than to use an ungodly or philosophically corrupt secular book unnecessarily. For example, children would be better off learning to decode from reading Biblical Sunday school literature that has been adapted and designed for their chronological or mental age group, than from sophisticated special education readers that are keyed to word decoding but clearly teach humanism or ungodliness. But modification is possible, and we must learn to adapt dependable materials for now.

Special education is individualized education. This means that more attention must be given to each child in the special education classroom than is possible in the regular classroom. A godly, competent special education teacher in a Christian school may be in a far better position to modify and/or adapt the available materials than a regular teacher. Because each child will have an individual educational program, the special education teacher will have many more opportunities to scrutinize the material. Also, some material is philosophically neutral. Some people may take issue with that statement, but we are referring here to material like spelling word lists, math facts, and handwriting workbooks. Christian special education teachers are in a position to correct subtle errors in the content or presentation by teaching and applying Biblical principles. Many of the resource books we refer to in this book describe appropriate and effective techniques and methods to use with disabled children, without discussing philosophy at all. For these reasons, we refer to these resources. Parents and teachers in special education, then, must avail themselves of materials currently available in special education and modify other materials when needed. Parent handbooks and teacher resources— at this time primarily secular—are available and easy to find. These materials are improving as secular special education comes to maturity.

Several good resources (e.g., Bauer & Shea, 1989; Gearheart & Weishahn, 1980; Lovitt, 1989) describe how to make modifications and accommodations for students with disabilities. Marsh, C. Gearheart, and B. Gearheart (cited in Gearheart & Weishahn, 1980) explain:

> Accommodation . . . refers to a process whereby the learning environment of the student, either some of the elements or the total environment, is modified to promote learning. The focus is on changing the learning environment or the academic requirements so that the student may learn in spite of a fundamental weakness or deficiency. This may involve the use of modified instructional techniques, more flexible administrative practices, [or] modified academic requirements. (p. 184)

Lovitt (1989) indicates that adaptations and modifications of teaching materials can occur through use of audio tape recordings, advance organizers, and microcomputers. Bauer and Shea (1989) add that teachers can provide modifications for disabled students by giving careful attention to how they present or teach content to students during a lesson, explain directions on completing tasks, and give extra support and assistance in completion of those tasks.

Understanding Basic Special Education Concepts

Since special education is individual education, the minimum components of special education that parents and teachers must understand include: (a) the evaluation process that takes the child from recognition of his need to placement in a special education classroom; (b) the development and implementation of the individual education plan (IEP); and (c) the challenge of mediating problems and finding ways in which to support both the child and the school in which he is enrolled.

When parents must determine whether their children need special education, especially parents of children in Christian schools, answers are often given in complex terms or in terms that lack standard definition among educators. Chapter 5 of this book deals in detail with recognition of the need for special education and placement of students in the special education classroom. What we offer in the present chapter, based on our experiences at Hidden Treasure Christian School, is information that answers some of the common questions about the testing procedures used to determine whether special education is appropriate for a particular child.

Recognition to Placement

The following terms and definitions will help to clarify the terminology that the parent or teacher must understand to proceed through the recognition and placement process.

1. **Psychological evaluation** does not refer to psychoanalysis of the child. It refers to a comprehensive battery of tests that determine the child's mental abilities, achievement, and other behavioral characteristics.

2. **Physiological examinations** are tests administered by the family doctor or other medical specialists to determine whether the child has adequate sensory and motor skills.

3. **Diagnostic testing** involves "analyz[ing] or locat[ing] an individual's specific areas of weakness or strength to receive attention in future instruction" (Vergason, 1990, p. 50).

4. **Assessment** refers to "special diagnosis that may include mental, social, psychological, and educational evaluations, used to determine assignment to programs or services; a process employing observation, testing, and task analysis to determine an individual's strengths and weaknesses for educational and social purposes" (Vergason, 1990, p. 15).

5. **Referral** is a term used by educators to indicate that a teacher, administrator, physician, or other professional has recommended the student for further evaluation and possible placement in a special education setting.

6. **Evaluation** refers to the entire process of determining a child's specific difficulty and appropriate placement in the special education setting. It includes, but is not limited to, psychological evaluation, physical examination, parental and family interviews, and local assessment by the teacher or other school staff member.

Once a child has been identified as disabled, school personnel must determine a special education placement. There are many different types of placements where students may receive special education services. For a number of years at Hidden Treasure Christian School, we were able to meet all the requirements of our students with just three types of special education placements. Our school seeks to provide a Christian education for any student that can be trained or educated beyond basic hygienic and life skills. Therefore, we found it most effective during the early years to organize our students into one of these classes: (a) a multi-grade class; (b) a resource class; or (c) a practical Christian training class. These were classrooms where students received direct special education services on a separate, self-contained campus, not sheltered workshops or vocational rehabilitation programs.

Our multi-grade class includes physically disabled children and others who, for primarily physical reasons, cannot function effectively in a regular classroom. Individual attention is ensured to these children by low pupil/teacher ratio and utilization of teacher's aides qualified to carry out the teacher's instructions, and/or occupational therapists who help accommodate for physical limitations.

Our resource class (on a self-contained school campus) is designed for students with moderate to severe learning disabilities. Students should receive comprehensive evaluation through professional diagnostic testing prior to enrollment in a resource class, since there are many types of disabilities that manifest similar symptoms. In this class, an individual education plan

(IEP) should be developed for each student, based on accurate information from several sources. These include the professional psychological evaluation and diagnostic testing conducted by the local public school, by a private testing agency such as a speech, hearing, and learning center, or by other qualified professionals such as educational diagnosticians trained to administer the appropriate tests and examinations.

In addition to psychological testing, other forms of assessment should be administered, such as physiological examinations, parental interviews, and local assessment through tests administered by the teacher; these will ensure proper placement and development of the IEP. A thorough professional evaluation should be completed every three years, and local diagnostic assessment and testing should be performed at least at the beginning and end of each school year, or during the year as necessary. These comprehensive evaluations are required to ensure that the IEP is actually meeting the student's needs and that his continued enrollment is necessary.

Our practical Christian training class is designed for educable and trainable mentally disabled students (see Chapters 9 and 10 on educable mentally retarded and trainable mentally retarded students respectively). Every effort should be made to follow the same procedure of evaluation for the practical Christian training students as for those in the resource room.

Parents and teachers not trained in special education should become familiar with Figure 3.1 to understand the possible routes to be followed from initial recognition to eventual placement in a special education classroom. Figure 3.1 illustrates typical facets of the evaluation process, which consists of five basic stages. Step 1 is the **recognition** of the problem, in which a variety of observers of the child will come together to discuss and determine whether referral is necessary. Step 2 is administration of several **prereferral interventions** to determine whether the child's problem can be resolved before formal testing and possible subsequent placement in special education occur. Step 3 is **referral** to the appropriate testing agency to determine whether there is an identifiable need for special education. Step 4 is the **formal assessment** of the student. It is during this step that the tests are administered to the individual. Step 5 is the **evaluation** of the specific data collected in the steps taken above. Step 6 is the **placement** of the child in a special education classroom by the school authorities. This diagram is similar to others in secular special education guidebooks, with the important exception that it includes a track on which ministry to the family can occur. This is critical, and it is one of the main distinctions between Christian special education and public special education.

For example, a child may be diagnosed by a certified child psychologist as having an "attention deficit disorder," which means that for some reason the child does not pay attention well in class. The term "attention deficit disorder" implies that there is something wrong with the child's *ability* to pay attention, which may be true, but this does not necessitate a special education placement. In fact, a child's classification by a psychologist as having only attention deficit disorder does not by itself entitle him to special education under federal guidelines. There has been much confusion and misinformation regarding attention deficit disorder in Christian circles. Parents must realize, however, that attention deficit disorder is not a legitimate disabling condition. The only way an attention deficit disordered child can receive special education services is to have a concurrent classification in a disabling area like learning disabilities or emotional disorders.

Yet children with attention deficit disorder do have troubling behaviors. A godly, qualified counselor, such as a pastor, should be able to determine in an interview with the family whether there have been frequent and obvious displays of

Figure 3.1

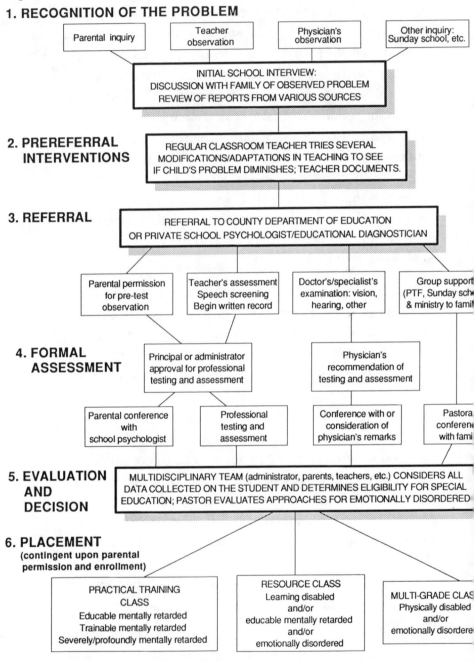

1. RECOGNITION OF THE PROBLEM

| Parental inquiry | Teacher observation | Physician's observation | Other inquiry: Sunday school, etc. |

INITIAL SCHOOL INTERVIEW:
DISCUSSION WITH FAMILY OF OBSERVED PROBLEM
REVIEW OF REPORTS FROM VARIOUS SOURCES

2. PREREFERRAL INTERVENTIONS

REGULAR CLASSROOM TEACHER TRIES SEVERAL
MODIFICATIONS/ADAPTATIONS IN TEACHING TO SEE
IF CHILD'S PROBLEM DIMINISHES; TEACHER DOCUMENTS.

3. REFERRAL

REFERRAL TO COUNTY DEPARTMENT OF EDUCATION
OR PRIVATE SCHOOL PSYCHOLOGIST/EDUCATIONAL DIAGNOSTICIAN

| Parental permission for pre-test observation | Teacher's assessment Speech screening Begin written record | Doctor's/specialist's examination: vision, hearing, other | Group support (PTF, Sunday sch & ministry to fami |

4. FORMAL ASSESSMENT

| Principal or administrator approval for professional testing and assessment | Physician's recommendation of testing and assessment |

| Parental conference with school psychologist | Professional testing and assessment | Conference with or consideration of physician's remarks | Pastora conferen with fami |

5. EVALUATION AND DECISION

MULTIDISCIPLINARY TEAM (administrator, parents, teachers, etc.) CONSIDERS ALL
DATA COLLECTED ON THE STUDENT AND DETERMINES ELIGIBILITY FOR SPECIAL
EDUCATION; PASTOR EVALUATES APPROACHES FOR EMOTIONALLY DISORDERED

6. PLACEMENT
(contingent upon parental permission and enrollment)

| PRACTICAL TRAINING CLASS Educable mentally retarded Trainable mentally retarded Severely/profoundly mentally retarded | RESOURCE CLASS Learning disabled and/or educable mentally retarded and/or emotionally disordered | MULTI-GRADE CLAS Physically disabled and/or emotionally disordere |

parental anger in the home, and whether the child is demonstrating learned behavior. On a practical level, there is not much difference between passive-aggressive behavior on the part of the student and anger on the part of a parent. Passive-aggressive behavior can easily be diagnosed as an attention deficit disorder. But in the final analysis, it may be the parent who needs intervention, just as much as the student. The public education system cannot offer this to the family, but the Bible-believing local church can, and it must.

Counseling with the pastor should help the parents deal with their anger Scripturally, and it may correct the problem that the child is experiencing in school, completely eliminating the need for an attention deficit disorder label and possible subsequent placement in a special education class. It is a tragedy that we are spending so much time and money and accomplishing so little in the lives of students who do not have real special education needs, but who are currently being placed in special education classes because of problems like this. The Biblical approach to special education compels us to consider the needs of the entire family during the evaluation process and not just the surface academic needs of the student. As the field of Christian special education develops, it is imperative that we balance the extensive writing on the legal rights of children with a greater emphasis on the loving responsibility of parents.

Understanding the IEP

As we have said before, special education is individual education. Education is individualized in special education through the IEP, or individual education plan. The IEP is used throughout the process of special education, and so parents and teachers should be thoroughly familiar with what an IEP is, how it is developed, and how it is implemented in the student's classroom activity. The most effective IEP is one that includes long-range goals, as well as the specific objectives that will help reach the long-range goals. It is more effective to begin with the long-range goals and work toward the specific objectives.

In Christian special education, long-term goals are synonymous with what the parents, the teachers, and the student have discovered is God's will for the child. A good starting point to help identify those God-given goals is Luke 2:52. Figure 3.2 is a long-range goals worksheet based on Luke 2:52. This verse identifies the components in the education of our Lord from the age of 12 to adulthood.

> And Jesus increased in wisdom and stature, and in
> favour with God and man.   (Luke 2:52)

The four components identified here—wisdom, stature, favor with God, and favor with man—can also be called mental development, physical development, spiritual development, and social development. There may be other areas of development in the child's life which should be considered by the parents, but the activities which take place in the Christian school can all be included in these four broad categories. As Figure 3.2 illustrates, the academic disciplines comprise the subdivisions of these four categories; under them, specific areas are listed with a brief definition for each. There is space on which the parent and teacher can write a goal to be realized in the child's life at some point in the future. This long-range goals worksheet can be updated as necessary in parent-teacher conferences. Entries should be made in pencil, but the document should be kept on file as part of the IEP.

Report cards are a challenge in special education. They usually provide an indication of the child's academic and/or behavioral accomplishments and efforts. Just as an IEP is used as a guide to teach the child in an individualized way, a report card must also represent an individualized measure of the student's performance. Some subjects can be standardized, but others must be individualized. The report card can easily be adapted to reflect progress toward the long-range goals. Figure 3.3 shows how this can be done through a sample report card.

We recommend that the goals worksheet (Figure 3.2) and the IEP lesson plans sheet (Figure 3.4) be used together. The IEP itself will not tell the teacher what to teach the student on a daily basis in order for him to end up where he is supposed to be. Yet IEP lesson plans can be developed and used daily by the special education teacher, reflecting the larger, more global goals and objectives on the IEP (Mercer & Mercer, 1988). Substitute teachers will not be able to step in and teach several students working from IEPs unless these coordinated lesson plans are clear.

Working from the long-range goals worksheet, the teacher establishes specific goals and short-term objectives to be achieved in a period of time not to exceed one academic school year. These can be arranged by academic subject, and starting and ending dates can be included (see Figure 3.4). A short-term objectives worksheet should include space for identifying materials, methods, techniques, and special resources to be used by the teacher and/or parent in reaching the objective.

These two documents, the long-term goals worksheet and the short-term objectives / lesson plan worksheet will also provide information necessary to determine teacher workload and student class assignment. The feasibility of categorization and grouping within specific academic subjects—reading groups, history study groups, and the like—will be easier to determine. The special education teacher will probably find it necessary to prepare coordinated lesson plans for the entire class, plans that graphically illustrate how the IEPs flow together during the daily schedule. This is one of the main reasons for a low pupil/teacher ratio in a special education classroom. Administrators should be careful not to assume that if a special education teacher can easily handle 8 students in a given classroom, that

Figure 3.2

Individual Education Plan
Long-Range Goals

Student: _____

Date: _____

This form provides working definitions of each item or subject listed on the Individual Education Plan/Report form used at Hidden Treasure Christian School. The subjects are categorized under four major areas of personal development seen in Luke 2:52:

> "And Jesus increased in wisdom and stature, and in favor with God and man."

After each standard definition, space is provided for recording the specific goal established in that item or subject by the teacher. These goals are projected after careful consideration of the psychological evaluation, the academic record, the parents' recommendation, the physical examination, and personal observation.

Only those items or subjects actually to be taught will have specific goals projected for the current year.

100 MENTAL DEVELOPMENT (WISDOM)

101 Bible

101.1 Content includes Bible words, verses, characters, and events.

_____

101.11 The story/lesson is an individual or group activity presented through various media.

_____

101.12 Memory work requires accurate reproduction of the words (spelling if written) and references of verses from the King James Version.

_____

101.2 **Doctrine** identifies the fundamentals and beliefs of true Christianity.

101.21 **Catechism** teaches doctrine through the memorization of questions and answers.

101.22 **Bible class** teaches Bible stories/lesson/content by lecturing or preaching.

101.3 **Practical theology** develops skills to communicate a personal life message.

101.31 **Devotions** teaches practical skills for daily Bible reading and prayer.

101.32 **Testimony training** helps the child express his own salvation experience and unique message.

101.33 **Witnessing instruction** develops skills in personal evangelism.

102 **Language Arts**

102.1 **Thinking** is mentally processing facts and ideas—absorbing, organizing, and utilizing abstract concepts.

102.11 Study reference skills include knowledge of Bible divisions and references; reading maps, charts, graphs, etc.; and using the dictionary, encyclopedias, and other reference and library materials.

102.12 Problem solving is the application of facts and ideas in decision making—the use of academic knowledge in practical matters.

101.2 Speaking refers to accurate oral communication of thoughts.

102.21 Word usage is the ability to use words properly in speaking.

102.22 Articulation includes both pronunciation and vocal expression.

101.3 Listening is directing the attention to audible instruction.

102.31 Attentiveness refers to the effort expended in listening.

102.32 Responsiveness communicates the act of listening and the ability to follow directions.

102.4 Reading includes visual recognition, comprehension, and oral reproduction of the printed word.

102.41 Vocabulary consists of the words understood by or available to the student.

102.42 Phonetics is the study of the written representation or production of speech sounds.

102.43 Comprehension is the mental grasp or understanding of an idea.

102.5 Writing refers to accurate graphic representation of thoughts.

102.51 Penmanship is the proper formation of graphic symbols in standard form; it includes letter shape, consistency, and neatness.

102.52 Spelling measures the ability to reproduce words with the proper combination of letters.

102.53 Grammar is the system of rules used in speaking and writing language.

102.54 Expression in writing is the accurate communication of the thought intended.

102.55 Machines for writing include the alphabitor, the typewriter, the word processor, and the computer.

---

103 Fine Arts

103.1 Music includes instruction in singing, basic theory, and development of personal talents.

103.2 Art includes various forms of creative expression using form, line, and color.

103.3 Public speaking develops poise, projection, and verbal communication.

---

104 Mathematics

104.1 Content is the "language" of mathematics expressed in numbers, fractions, symbols, and sets.

104.11 Numeration is the number system.

104.12 Fractions include whole number portions expressed in decimals, geometric shapes, or numerators and denominators.

104.13 Symbols are mathematical signs used to indicate operations to be performed.

104.14 Sets are groups of numbers, shapes, or objects representing quantities.

104.2 Operations involve the combination and functions of numbers and sets.

104.21 Arithmetic includes addition, subtraction, multiplication, and division.

104.22 Algebra is a mathematical system used to generalize certain arithmetical operations by use of letters or other symbols representing numbers.

104.23 Geometry deals with properties, measurements, and relationships of points, lines, and solids.

104.24 Trigonometry deals with relations between the sides and angles of triangles.

104.25 Mental computation is the mental performance of operations given orally.

104.26 Numerical reasoning is the computational process—the ability to express and determine quantities in mathematical language.

104.3 Applications are the functional use of math content and operations.

104.31 Word problems express required operations in a combination of verbal and mathematical language.

104.32 Money illustrates arithmetical operations expressed in quantities represented by the face value of currency.

104.33 Measurement involves relative quantities of standard units of length, weight, or volume.

104.34 Time is the identification of time intervals and their functional use, including clocks and calendars.

104.35 Machines for mathematical computation include the calculator, digitator, and computer.

---

105 Science

105.1 Physical science is the study of nonliving creation.

105.2 Biology is the study of living creation.

105.3 Health/safety includes basic instruction in maintaining personal hygiene and avoiding danger.

---

106 History

106.1 History is the study of past human events.

106.2 Geography defines and differentiates the physical features of regions on the earth.

106.3 Civics is the study of our governmental and citizenship responsibilities.

---

200 PHYSICAL DEVELOPMENT (STATURE)

201 Physical Education

201.1 Fitness training promotes the optimum physical condition appropriate for the student.

201.2 Therapy is a medically approved program of rehabilitative or adaptive physical activities.

---

202 Self-Help Skills

202.1 Table etiquette is the development of proper manners and eating habits.

202.2 Hygiene includes personal cleanliness and application of personal health science.

202.3 Grooming stresses personal neatness and appearance.

202.4 **Mobility** encourages independent, graceful bodily movement and gestures.

---

300 SPIRITUAL DEVELOPMENT (FAVOR WITH GOD)

301 Bible Action Truths (Understanding)
These reveal the balance between God's authority and man's responsibility. These BATs are not subjects taught, but principles woven into every other subject. (Source: *Elementary Bible Truths Handbook* [Greenville, SC: Bob Jones University Press, 1981], pp. 3-7.)

301.1 Principle of Mental Development

301.11 The salvation/separation principle is the basic truth of God's grace—obedience follows salvation; it doesn't earn it. (Understanding of Jesus Christ, repentance and faith, and separation from the world.)

301.12 **The grace/gratitude principle** balances man's behavior—we love Him because He first loved us. (Grace, exaltation of Christ, praise, contentment, and humility.)

301.2 Principle of Physical Development

301.21 **The uniqueness/unity principle** relates the student's individuality to his responsibility in the body of Christ. (Self-concept, mind, emotional control, body as a temple, unity of Christ and church.)

301.22 **The power/preparation (prevailing) principle** balances the sources of the believer's strength—we are strong as we trust Him in our weakness. (Faith in promises, power of the Word of God, fight, courage.)

301.3 Principle of Spiritual Development

301.31 The holiness/habit principle guides the development of Christian purity—He declares us righteous; we develop righteous character. (Sowing and reaping, purity, honesty, victory.)

301.32 The communion/consecration principle guides the development of devotional life—He speaks to us through the Bible; we speak to Him in prayer. (Bible study, prayer, Spirit-filled life, clear conscience, and forgiveness.)

301.4 Principle of Social Development

301.41 The sonship/service (servant) principle guides development of Christian behavior—He makes us His sons; we make ourselves His servants. (Authority, servanthood, faithfulness, goal-setting, work, enthusiasm.)

301.42 The love/life principle guides development of personal relationships—He loves us; we love others. (Love, giving, evangelism and missions, communication, and friendliness.)

302 Christian Living (Action)

302.1 Service is the use of God's gifts to the individual for the benefit of others and the glory of God.

301.2 Attitude involves the student's heart response to providential circumstances and Bible Action Truths being learned.

301.3 Conduct identifies the student's outward demonstration of attitudes.

400 SOCIAL DEVELOPMENT (FAVOR WITH MAN)

401.1 Relationships with authority measures progress in the development of submissiveness.

401.2 Relationships with peers measures progress in the development of social adjustment and brotherly love.

401.3 Relationships as a leader concerns the development of skills required to motivate others to do right.

---

402 Social Skills

402.1 Etiquette is common courtesy—the conventional rules for behavior in polite society or professional life.

402.2 Independent living skills include those activities required to function without physical help.

402.3 Home economics is principles for maintaining the order and physical aspects of the residential environment.

402.4 Vocational skills include a variety of practical skills required for employment.

IEP Lesson Plans

Specific Objectives (Short-Term Goals)

Subject: _____

Student: _____

Date: _____

Specific objectives	Project Start Finish	Materials, methods, techniques, special resources

Figure 3.4

Sample Report Card

Please sign this report below and return it with your child on the next regular school day. Thank you.

Report for
_____

School year _____

Division (or grade) _____

"And Jesus increased in wisdom and stature, and in favour with God and man."
— Luke 2:52

The four areas of development identified in this verse provide the outline for this Individual Educational Plan/Report. You will find here a sketch of our goals for your child and our evaluation of his progress in these four areas:

Mental development
Physical development
Spiritual development
Social development

A more detailed explanation of the specific steps being used to reach these goals is on file at the school.

Grading Period 1
Comments:
_____
_____
_____
_____
_____
_____

Parent's Signature

Grading Period 2
Comments:
_____
_____
_____
_____
_____

Parent's Signature

Grading Period 3
Comments:
_____
_____
_____
_____
_____
_____

Grading Period 4
Comments:
_____
_____
_____
_____
_____

& SOCIAL DEVELOPMENT (favor with man)

	1	2	3	4

300.1 **Obedient** – Inwardly accepts and outwardly acts on the wishes of God and others in authority.

300. **Patient** – accepts without complaint a difficult situation as from God without giving God a deadline to remove it.

300.3 **Cooperative** – works together with others in order to achieve a common goal.

300.4 **Self-Controlled** – recognizes future consequences of present actions and acts accordingly.

300.5 **Neat** – keeps himself and his belongings clean and in good order.

300.6 **Responsible** – is capable of being relied on and is answerable for his own behavior.

300.7 **Respectful** – is considerate of peers and shows honor to authorities.

300.8 **Punctual** – shows respect for other people and their time by not keeping them waiting; starts assignments promptly.

ATTENDANCE RECORD

QUARTER	1	2	3	4
Days Present				
Days Absent				
Tardy				

This report should always be considered in the context of the student's IEP. Grade levels are not defined for every student in every subject. Except in reading, writing, and math, where the appropriate level is given, the student is working at his chronological or mental age level shown on the IEP.

GL 1 2 I 3 4 II YR.

101 Bible
_____
_____

102 Language Arts
102.1 Reading
    Oral reading comp.
    Silent reading comp.
102.2 Phonics
102.3 Spelling
102.4 Grammar
    Spoken
    Written
102.5 Penmanship

103 Fine Arts
103.1 Music
103.2 Art
103.3 Public speaking

104 Math

105 Science

106 Heritage Studies

200 PHYSICAL DEVELOPMENT (Stature)

201 **Physical Education**

The student will receive a grade or rating in those subjects he is actually studying according to the goals in his IEP. Grades or ratings may not always be meaningful in each item on the IEP; these are included on this report in the subject category which includes the minor item.

Grade/Rating Key

A	90-100	D	60-69	E - Excellent
B	80-89	F	Below 60	S - Satisfactory
C	70-79			I - Improving
				N - Needs Improvement

same teacher could handle 16 students with the addition of a teacher's aide. Preparing, coordinating, and updating 16 IEPs is a demanding task, for which time and skill are essential. In our state, the public schools allow as many as 18 students in a special education resource room over the course of a school day and up to 24 if a teacher's aide is present! Our experience reveals that these children will receive inadequate education in academic subjects if these classes are any more than six to eight students in any one class period.

The Greater Challenge: Finding Solutions To Unexpected Problems

Meeting problems head-on is a challenge for every area of the ministry—and particularly so in special education. To provide a classroom for no more than eight students seems economically impossible. But again, the question is not whether it is affordable, but whether it is required. Many of the things that God commands do not seem to be affordable; but if He ordains it, He will meet the need. We have not fulfilled our responsibility to the Lord merely by providing a classroom or a set of books to a student and then telling him to do the best he can. Education for the Christian is but one component of discipleship. Special education is personalized discipleship. It is difficult to place a price on such a responsibility.

Beyond the problem of cost is the more difficult problem of facing up to family difficulties, which often surface when special education is being considered. We hold that there are legitimate emotional disorders which may require a student's placement in a special education class or school, but our approach to these disorders marks the greatest departure from established procedures in the field of special education. Emotional disorders are not as often individual problems as they are family problems. Parents of children diagnosed with emotional disorders must be transparent and submissive to Biblical truth if they are to see progress in their struggling student. We refer readers to Chapter 7 for a more detailed discussion of emotional disorders.

Frequent evaluation of every student's progress is always necessary. Special education is not just a process of identifying a problem and then working diligently at correcting and/or compensating for that problem. This may be true with physical disabilities, which are easily recognized. But it is not so simple with mental retardation, learning disabilities, or emotional disorders. These problems, as well as the psychological aspects of a disability, are dynamic. Children, for instance, do not care as much about their appearance as teenagers do. A learning disability in math may not bother a child emotionally when he is in grade school if most of his peers "hate math"; but when he is a teenager unable to get a job in a fast-food restaurant because he cannot make change, new problems arise. There must be constant interaction between parents and teachers—the home and the school—to provide the necessary evaluation of the student's progress and encouragement to see that it is on schedule. Compassionate, God-called teachers are needed to face the challenges that Christian special education will be confronted with in the years ahead. But the greatest need is for compassionate and determined parents who will persist in seeing their children, not as learning to be "just like everyone else," but as being conformed to the image of Christ.

As we face the future in Christian special education, it is important for us to establish goals for our students and to determine the lesson plans that will guide our daily activities; but it is just as important for us to know where our schools are headed. Any family or school that embarks on a program of special education to meet the needs of disabled students should clearly define what they are trying to do and whom they are trying to help. A final illustration is seen in Figure 3.5, the

Figure 3.5

Student Profile Statement

Name _____ Birthday _____ Grade _____
Address _____ Phone _____

Test Results

Tests Given

	Present	9 Weeks	18 Weeks	27 Weeks	Final
Spiritual Development					
Salvation					
Character					
Service					
Emotional Development					
Peer Relationships					
Adult Relationships					
Behavior					
Physical Development					
Height					
Weight					
General Health					

Specific Recommendations

_____

_____

Figure 3.5

	Present	9 Weeks	18 Weeks	27 Weeks	Final

Academic Development

English _____

Math _____

Social Studies _____

Science _____

Specific Educational Objectives

English _____

_____

_____

Math _____

_____

_____

Social Studies _____

_____

_____

Proposed Access to Learning Aids

Tape Recorders _____

Reading Tutors _____

Computers _____

Manipulatives _____

Student Profile Statement. This is not offered as a standard for every Christian school, but it illustrates how our school has developed its objectives in written form so that problems can easily be identified and dealt with in the lives of those students we feel qualified to help.

Summary

Special education is individual education. Although much good is being done and many valuable resources are available from secular sources, Christian parents must remember to focus on the goal of God's will for the child. The student must be encouraged to grow into Christlikeness and not merely be defended in his right to be like everyone else. When secular sources are used, these qualifiers must be kept in mind.

Parents should assume full responsibility for seeing to it that their children get through the evaluation process from the initial recognition of a problem to eventual placement, if needed, in a special education class or school. They should work with teachers and administrators in an ongoing relationship to evaluate the progress that the child is making. They should also be willing to consider the possibility that the child's problem may be a reflection of larger problems in the home and they should be submissive to spiritual counsel to correct these problems for the glory of God and the good of the child. They should become thoroughly familiar with their student's IEP and make it the central focus of the parent-teacher conference when discussing the student's progress and in determining his future objectives.

Problems should be met squarely, whether they are spiritual problems in the home or educational problems at the school. Parents and teachers should enter into a commitment for special education with determination and patience, realizing that it is a long, tedious, and expensive process, but one that is necessary if we are to be obedient to the Lord.

References

Bauer, A. M., & Shea, T. M. (1989). *Teaching exceptional students in your classroom.* Boston, MA: Allyn and Bacon.

Gearheart, B. R., & Weishahn, M. W. (1980). *The handicapped student in the regular classroom.* St. Louis, MO: C. V. Mosby Co.

Hallahan, D. P., & Kauffman, J. M. (1988). *Exceptional children: Introduction to special education* (4th ed.). Englewood Cliffs, NJ: Prentice-Hall.

Lovitt, T. C. (1989). *Introduction to learning disabilities.* Boston, MA: Allyn & Bacon.

Mercer, C. D., & Mercer, A. R. (1988). *Teaching students with learning problems.* Columbus, OH: Charles E. Merrill Publishing Co.

Shore, K. (1986). *The special education handbook: How to get the best education possible for your learning disabled child.* New York, NY: Teachers College Press.

Vergason, G. A. (1990). *Dictionary of special education and rehabilitation* (3rd ed.). Denver, CO: Love Publishing Co.

Wood, A. H. (1984). *Unto the least of these: Special education in the church.* Schaumburg, IL: Regular Baptist Press.

Man's Mandates
for Public Special
Education

John J. McCormick

Introduction

*F*or many years the needs of disabled people have been greatly misunderstood and neglected. Mentally retarded persons, especially in years past, have been institutionalized under less than humane conditions. Persons with cerebral palsy whose minds were sharp but whose bodies did not reflect their intellectual capabilities were also isolated and labeled as having "no hope." Emotionally disabled persons whose problems may have been the result of a chemical imbalance or other legitimate environmental factors, or who may not have been able to cope with the emotional scarring of a personal trauma, have been placed in insane asylums only to become the brunt of vicious ridicule by those on the outside.

Physically disabled, blind, and/or deaf persons also faced obstacles which hindered them from functioning within the areas of their potential. In the recent past, and unfortunately sometimes even now, those who appear able to function in a normal classroom situation but cannot because of an unseen dysfunction in their mental processes or cognitive abilities are labeled "lazy," "stupid," "rebellious," and "apathetic."

Fortunately, there have been family members, teachers, medical personnel and other professionals who would not accept the conditions imposed on these persons. They also would not accept the suggestion that a disabled person had nothing to offer. As concerned individuals began to work with various disabled people, they began to see changes taking place in the lives of these unique individuals. Hidden potential was uncovered. Stifled creativity emerged, and repressed behavior became active involvement.

As disabled people were given opportunities to exhibit their talents, their supporters worked to provide them with additional opportunities to develop the gifts they had been given. As a result of those efforts, Congress has put into effect laws that require states to give all disabled persons the opportunity to participate in educational programs consistent with their abilities and consistent with the programs of their nondisabled peers.

Major Legislation

Rehabilitation Act of 1973

The Rehabilitation Act of 1973 was one of the first laws to deal with the education of disabled persons. Section 504 of this law states:

> No otherwise qualified handicapped individual in the United States . . . shall, solely by reason of his handicap, be excluded from the participation in, be

denied the benefit of, or be subjected to discrimination under any program or activity receiving federal financial assistance (*United States Statutes*, 1974).

Public Law 94-142

Since 1973 there have been several amendments to this law as well as the establishment of other laws guaranteeing all disabled persons the right to a free public education. The most significant of these laws is Public Law (PL) 94-142, The Education for All Handicapped Children Act.

"Since this act provides the basic framework for all subsequent acts and since it is the most noteworthy legislative landmark [in special education] of recent years" (Hallahan & Kauffman, 1988, p. 28), it is recommended that those interested in special education be familiar with its contents. The following discussion provides answers to many of the questions asked regarding this law and the benefits received. The information is not intended to be exhaustive but provides general guidelines as to the definitions and related services delineated in PL 94-142. For further information regarding its interpretation, procedures, and additional benefits, the best source is the Protection and Advocacy for the Handicapped, Inc., in one's state or the national office located in Washington, DC (address listed in Appendix 4).

1. What is PL 94-142?

PL 94-142 is the major special education law in our country today. While the Rehabilitation Act of 1973 stated that no person could be excluded from any program receiving federal assistance, PL 94-142 provides the funds to make certain that no disabled person is excluded from receiving a free appropriate public education. It sets up a strict system of accountability between the school system and the parent(s) in order to provide appropriate education for disabled children.

2. What is the purpose of Public Law 94-142?

The law itself states:

The regulations include provisions which are designed (1) to assure that all disabled children have available to them… a free appropriate public education; (2) to assure that the rights of handicapped children and their parents are protected; (3) to assist States and localities to provide for the education of all handicapped children; and (4) to assess and assure the effectiveness of efforts to educate such children. (Federal Register, August 23, 1977, p. 42474)

In short, the purpose of PL 94-142 was "to make certain that handicapped children are given an appropriate education" (Lerner, 1989, p. 33). To assure that the above stated objectives are carried out, this act provides the necessary funds for the supervision of and implementation of the objectives. The Rehabilitation Act of 1973 had not provided the necessary funding.

3. In what way are the funds associated with PL 94-142 used?

In order of importance, these funds are used to:

    a. Identify, locate, evaluate, and provide special education and related services to disabled children who are not enrolled in an educational program (called "first priority")

    b. Provide the same services to disabled children who are enrolled in an educational program but whose specific needs are not being met by that program (called "second priority")

    c. Insure that all other requirements of the Act are being met (Rauth, no date, p. 2)

4. If my child is attending a private school, what benefits might my child receive from this law?

That would depend on the degree of your involvement in securing these benefits for your child. As stated above, the state must make provisions to identify, locate, evaluate, and provide special education and related services. You can help the state to identify and locate your child by simply calling your local school district and informing the appropriate person that you have, or you believe you may have, a child eligible for special education services. Once this is done, you have the right to request the school district to perform a psychological evaluation of your child in order to confirm or deny your suspicions.

5. What is a psychological evaluation?
A psychological evaluation is simply a battery of tests that is administered to your child to determine strengths and weaknesses in the physical (fine and gross motor skills, vision, and hearing), academic, behavioral, and social areas. The purpose of this evaluation is to determine whether or not your child qualifies for special education services and to identify problem areas in order to provide recommendations for strengthening those areas.

6. After the initial request for this evaluation, how long might I expect to wait until the testing is actually performed?
You should hear from the school district within a reasonable time (15 days), informing you of a testing date. The law stipulates that actual testing should take place within 30 to 45 days of the request.

If you are not contacted within a reasonable time, make your request again, stating that it is your second request. If no action is taken, put your request in writing, send a copy to the school district and a copy to your state's Protection and Advocacy for the Handicapped, Inc. By using a "Copy to" line at the bottom of the letter, make it clear to the school district that a copy has gone to this organization.

7. If it is determined that my child qualifies for special education services, what do I do next?
By law, you have the right to request an IEP (individual

education plan) meeting. If your child is enrolled in a private school, you should inform the principal of your school and your child's teacher that this testing is being done and then let them know the results once the testing has been completed. Since both of these persons are involved in the education of your child, you might request that they accompany you to the IEP meeting. Their presence will help them better understand the problems your child is experiencing, and they might be able to contribute information to be incorporated into the IEP.

8. *What information might I expect to receive as a result of the IEP meeting?*

You should receive a written statement explaining the following:

a. The grade and age level(s) at which your child is performing

b. Annual goals, broken down into short-term objectives for reaching those goals

c. The specific special education program (resource room, self-contained special class, etc.) and related services (transportation, physical therapy, etc.) that the child will receive

d. The extent to which your child will be able to participate in a regular classroom situation (the law requires that the child be placed in "the least restrictive environment")

e. The anticipated dates for starting these services and an estimated period of time in which these services will continue

f. The procedures and schedules for determining, on at least an annual basis, whether or not the short-term objectives are being met according to specified evaluation criteria (Federal Register, Vol. 42, No. 163, August 23, 1977, p. 42491).

9. What is meant by the "least restrictive environment"?
This means that whenever possible the child would be educated in the same environment as his nondisabled peers. The law states that "to the maximum extent appropriate, handicapped children, including children in public or private institutions or other care facilities, are educated with children who are not handicapped, and that special classes, separate schooling, or other removal of handicapped children from the regular educational environment occurs only when the nature or severity of the handicap is such that education in regular classes with the use of supplementary aids and services cannot be achieved satisfactorily" (Federal Register, August 23, 1977, p. 42497)

10. Who will insure that these recommendations and procedures are followed?
If the public school system recommends placement in a private school, the public system is responsible. If, on the other hand, you place your child in a private school against its recommendations, the public system waives its responsibility. You along with your child's school principal and teacher may choose to follow the recommendations but are under no legal obligation to do so.

11. Are there any other benefits that my child might receive from this law?
Yes. You are entitled to "related services," but this is where the real work begins. Federal regulations define related services as "transportation and such developmental, corrective, and other support services are required to assist a handicapped child to benefit from special education, and includes speech pathology and audiology, psychological services, physical and occupational therapy, recreation, early identification and assessment of disabilities in children, counseling services, and medical services for diagnostic or evaluation purposes" (Federal Register, August 23, 1977, p. 42479).

If your child's IEP includes any of the above services, you have the right to request and expect your local public school district to provide these services. Two students in our own program at Hidden Treasure Christian School needed speech therapy which we could not provide; consequently, the parents contacted their local school district and requested this service. It took several weeks for the therapy to begin, but they are participating in this program two hours a week. Provision of related services may mean adjusting the child's educational program somewhat, but these services can be of real benefit to the student. It is recommended that you call your local school district's special education department or the attorney for your state's Office for Special Education Services to determine other related services that are available and the steps you need to take in order to secure these services.

12. *If testing indicates that my child does not qualify for special education services or if I disagree with specific recommendations, do I have any recourse?*

Yes. You have the right to request a due process hearing, which is a hearing conducted for the purpose of appealing any decision made by the local school district. This hearing may not be conducted by an employee of the school district involved, but by an impartial hearing officer not involved with the education or care of your child. Both you and the school district representative may attend the hearing; you both may be represented by legal counsel and by professionals who are familiar with the needs of disabled students. Your child may also attend the hearing. The activities which take place closely resemble the activities that take place in a court of law. The hearing includes (a) submission of evidence, (b) the calling forth of witnesses to be questioned and cross-examined, and (c) the tape recording and stenographer's recording of the hearing. Both recordings are made available to either party for future reference, and any evidence submitted must be disclosed to each party five days before the hearing takes place (Federal Register, August 23, 1977, p. 42503).

The decision made at the hearing is not necessarily final. If the initial hearing is conducted by the local educational agency and either party disagrees with the local agency's decision, an appeal may be made to the state agency which is responsible to conduct an impartial hearing. If disagreement continues after the state agency rules, then again either party may appeal and bring a civil action suit at the state level. Cases concerning definitions, recommendations, and various aspects of services provided have gone as far as the Supreme Court for final rulings (e.g., *Board of Education v. Rowley*).

13. Has a decision ever been made requiring the State to pay the tuition and related expenses to a student attending a private school?
Yes. These situations, however, are more the exception than the rule. If the public school is able to provide a "free appropriate public education" to a disabled child, it would not recommend a child be placed in a private school or any other alternative program. Since such a recommendation would not be made, it would be up to the parent to prove that the child's placement is inappropriate. A number of court cases reflect suits filed by parents with regard to reimbursement of tuition to private schools and/or alternative placements in private schools (e.g., *Angelvine v. Jenkins,* 1991; *Block v. Sobol,* 1991; *David D. v. Dartmouth School Committee,* 1985; *Hall v. Vance County Board of Education,* 1985; *Hudson v. Wilson,* 1987; *Muth v. Central Bucks School District,* 1989; *Rapid City School District 51/4 v. Vahler,* 1991; *Shirk v. District of Columbia,* 1991). It is unfortunate, however, that the ultimate result of these legal proceedings has tended to take us away from our primary concern—

addressing the individual needs of disabled students. As Zirkel (1989) has noted regarding the *Muth* case in particular, the "financial focus and legal finagling in [these] special education cases [are] preoccupations that divert attention and resources from direct educational services" (p. 251).

14. What is a "free appropriate public education"?

"Free appropriate public education" is one of the major provisions of PL 94-142. In the Supreme Court decision *Board of Education v. Rowley,* Judge Rehnquist stated that the education provided had to be sufficient to confer some educational benefit on the student (Osborne, 1988). Realistically speaking, this leaves the term "appropriate" open to interpretation. "Appropriate" does not mean the best. It does not mean that if there is a better program available for your child the program he or she is enrolled in is not appropriate. Nor does it mean the program that you as parents desire for your child. A "free appropriate public education" is made up of special education and related services which: (a) are provided at public expense, under public supervision and direction, and without charge, (b) meet the standards of the State educational agency, including the requirements of this part, (c) include preschool, elementary school, or secondary school education in the State involved, and (d) are provided in conformity with an individualized education program (Federal Register, August 23, 1977, p. 42478). "Appropriate" does mean that the IEP must be developed to meet the unique needs of the individual. If the conditions agreed upon in the IEP are not being carried out, the educational program would be deemed inappropriate and you would have the right, once again, to petition the courts in order to provide your child with an appropriate education. If the public school system cannot meet the conditions of the IEP, it must provide the necessary funding for a private organization to do so. The private organization, however, is subject to the approval of the public agency (National Association of State Directors of Special Education, 1989), and the public agency will review the IEP on an annual basis to be certain the conditions are being meet. Funding will continue only if continued placement in the private organization is recommended.

15. I have a strong conviction for educating my child in a Christian environment and feel that the only "appropriate" education is a Christian education. Will this personal conviction have any bearing on my child's school placement or the public system's responsibility to fund my child's education?

If the primary effect of special education and related services is the advancement of religion, then the Establishment Clause (separation of church and state) is being violated. In the case of *Board of Education v. Wieder* (1987) the court withdrew services "not because of the nature of [the children's] handicaps, but because of their Hasidic faith and socio-cultural background" (Data Research, Inc., Vol. III, No. 9, May 1988, p. 3).

There seems to have been a precedent set in situations involving college-level students. The following is one such case. The U.S. Supreme Court ruled unanimously on the issue of state aid to disabled students at private religious schools in *Witters v. Washington Department of Services for the Blind* (1986). The Court held that the First Amendment to the U.S. Constitution does not prevent a state from providing financial assistance to a disabled person attending a Christian college. The plaintiff in this case, a blind person, sought vocational rehabilitative services from the state of Washington's Commission for the Blind pursuant to state law (Washington Rev. Code sec. 74.16.181, 1981). The law provided that visually disabled persons were eligible for educational assistance to enable them to "overcome vocational handicaps and to obtain the maximum degree of self-support and self-care" (Data Research, Inc., Vol. II, No. 8, April 1986, p. 1). However, because the plaintiff was a private school student intending to pursue a career of service in the church, the Commission for the Blind denied him assistance. The Washington Supreme Court upheld this decision on the ground that the First Amendment to the U.S. Constitution prohibited state funding of a student's education in a religious college.

The U.S. Supreme Court took a different, much less restrictive view of the First Amendment and reversed the Washington court. The operation of Washington's program was such that the commission paid money directly to the student, who would then attend the school of his choice. The fact that the student in this case chose to attend a religious college did not constitute state support of religion, because "the decision to support religious education is made by the individual, not the state" (Data Research, Inc. Vol. II, No. 8, April 1986, p. 1). The First Amendment was therefore not offended.

Although the requirements of PL 94-142 do not seem very favorable toward Christian schools and private schools in general, there are services available to all children that would be beneficial. The psychological evaluation, the establishment of an IEP, and the availability of related services all help to supplement any child's educational program. As mentioned earlier, the services and benefits Christian parents receive will be a direct result of their willingness to pursue these services and benefits. The information provided here barely scratches the surface of all that is incorporated in The Education for all Handicapped Children Act.

Other Legislation

Other significant legislation has followed the passage of PL 94-142 in 1975. For example, in 1986 another law was passed concerning services provided to disabled preschool children and their families. PL 99-457, The Handicapped Children's Protection Act, extends full rights and protections to disabled children aged 3-5 years by the 1990-91 school year. It also establishes a new state grant system for infants and toddlers from birth to 3 years old. The child's IEP will be replaced by an Individual Family Services Plan (IFSP) which requires that "a case manager be named who will give guidance to the family and will be responsible for the implementation of the plan" (Lerner, 1989, p. 133). Additionally, on July 26, 1990, President George Bush signed into law the Americans with Disabilities Act (ADA), PL 101-336, which "gives civil rights protection to individuals with disabilities in private sector employment, all public services, public accommodations transportation and telecommunications (Council for Exceptional Children, 1990, supplement). Finally, the Individuals with Disabilities Education Act (IDEA), PL 101-476, which represents a renaming of the EHA or PL 94-142, was passed on October 30, 1990. Along with replacing the original EHA term *handicapped* with *disabled,* the IDEA includes a number of major changes (Johns, 1991). For example, the individual education plan (IEP) must now include a clear statement of transition services (i.e., activities that facilitate the movement of disabled students from one community or school environment to another) along with the other required components delineated earlier in this chapter. Parents and Christian educators of disabled children would be do well to become familiar with these laws.

Implications for Christian Parents and Educators

The fact that these laws now exist should bring two questions to the mind of Christian parents and educators. First, "Why is the government insisting that the public educational system make all these provisions for disabled students?" Second, "What is my responsibility to disabled persons who are a part of the body of Christ?"

The government is insisting upon these provisions because the general public has, in essence, given it the responsibility to educate their children. The government is viewed as the "great provider and meeter of our needs." It has wholeheartedly accepted this position as well as the responsibility. However, in delegating our responsibilities, we have also given to them the authority to perform as they believe is best. This generally does not coincide with what Christian parents believe is best. Since this education is "free," those that now have the authority dictate the content and the implementation of the education.

In providing for the educational needs of disabled students, federal, state, and local governments are simply enhancing their position as compassionate caretakers. The humanistic philosophy of having the right to have one's needs met has replaced the Biblical philosophy of trusting God to meet one's needs. Since these rights have been provided to disabled persons, the government has issued a subtle statement—"We know you have needs. You have a right to have those needs met. We are concerned about those needs. And we are willing to help you meet them when no one else has." The government, though established by God, wants no credit given to God for what it is providing. In a very real sense it is vainly attempting to take away opportunities through which God can be glorified.

This is not to ignore the fact that something had to be done for students with disabilities. The circumstances in which disabled students were placed and the treatment they received, in times past, should not have been allowed to continue as long as they did. These services should have been and should continue to be provided to disabled persons, not to hold man or man's programs in high esteem "but that the works of God should be made manifest" (John 9:36).

Scripture clearly teaches that the responsibility for a child's education rests primarily on the shoulders of the parents (Deuteronomy 6:7, Proverbs 22:6, Ephesians 6:4). The parents, in turn, may elect to delegate that responsibility to others who will educate their children in a manner consistent with their religious beliefs (Galatians 4:1-2). This is the basis of Christian education. It is not that we dislike or are dissatisfied with the public education, but that we are convinced that a Christ-centered education is what God demands we provide for our children. The Christian school, being the instrument through which parents choose to provide this education, is acting *in loco parentis* (in place of the parents) in carrying out the educational responsibilities.

Christian educators do have a responsibility to meet the needs of disabled students. It is incumbent upon Christian educators to view Christian disabled persons as "necessary" (I Corinthians 12:22) and provide for them the services that would allow them the opportunity to glorify God rather than man. In recent research, Sutton (1990) found that, out of approximately 2700 Christian schools surveyed nationwide, only about 8% of these schools indicated that they had any type of special education program. Although the government has taken on the responsibility to educate disabled students, God has not relieved the church of its responsibility to insure "that the members should have the same care one for another" (I Corinthians 12:25).

References

Angelvine v. Jenkins, 752 F. Supp. 24 (D.D.C. 1991).

Block v. Sobol, 748 F. Supp. 97 (S.D.N.Y. 1991).

Board of Education v. Rowley, 102 S. CT. 3034 (1982).

Board of Education v. Weider, 522 N.Y.S. 2nd. 878 (A.D.2d. Dept. 1987).

Council for Exceptional Children. (1990). Americans with Disabilities Act of 1990: What should you know? *Exceptional Children, 57,* supplement.

Data Research, Inc. (1988, May). *Special Education and the Handicapped* (Vol. III, No. 9). Rosemount, MN: Data Research, Inc.

Data Research, Inc. (1986, April). *Special education and the handicapped* (Vol. II, No. 8). Rosemount, MN: Data Research, Inc.

David D. v. Dartmouth School Committee, 775 F.2nd. 411 (1st Cir. 1985).

Federal Register. (1977). *Implementation of part B of the Education of the Handicapped Act.* Washington, DC: Department of Health, Education, and Welfare, August 23.

Hall v. Vance County Board of Education, 774 F.2nd. 629 (4th Cir. 1985).

Hallahan, D. P., & Kauffman, J. M. (1988). *Exceptional children: Introduction to special education* (4th ed.). Englewood Cliffs, NJ: Prentice Hall.

Hudson v. Wilson, 828 F.2nd. 1059 (4th Cir. 1987).

Johns, B. (1991). Highlights of the new IDEA (Individuals with Disabilities Education Act). *DLD Times, 8*(2), 5.

Lerner, J. W. (1989). *Learning disabilities* (5th ed.). Boston, MA: Houghton Mifflin.

Muth v. Central Bucks School District, 839 F.2d. 113,122,126 (Pa. 3d. Cir. 1989).

National Association of State Directors of Special Education. (1989). A guide for cooperation between public and private schools in the provision of a free appropriate public education. *NASDSE Liaison Bulletin, 15*(7), 2.

Osborne, A. G. (1988). *Complete legal guide to special educational services.* West Nyack, NY: Parker Publishing Co., Inc.

Rapid City School District 51/4 v. Vahler, 922 F.2d. 476 (C.A.S.D. 1991).

Rauth, M. (no date). *A guide to understanding the Education for All Handicapped Children Act (PL 94-142): Questions and answers on the federal law and regulations.* Washington, DC: American Federation of Teachers, AFL-CIO.

Shirk v. District of Columbia, 756 F. Supp. 31 (D.D.C. 1991).

Sutton, J. P. (1990). *Prevalence of special education programs in private Christian schools: The ACSI study.* Unpublished manuscript, Bob Jones University, Greenville, SC.

United States Statutes at Large. (1974). Washington, DC: United States Government Printing Office.

Witters v. Washington Department of Services for the Blind, 106 S.Ct. 748 (1985).

Zirkel, P. A. (1989). The latest Supreme Court special education case: Not moot but Muth. *Phi Delta Kappan, 70,* 250-251.

Recognition, Identification, and Placement in Special Education

John J. McCormick
Joe P. Sutton

Introduction

*M*ost parents have high expectations for their children as they progress through each developmental stage. Parents talk about the age at which their child first walked (motor stage), talked, and learned the alphabet (cognitive), and they mention that he or she has grown appropriately in height and weight compared to other children the same age. It is natural for parents to take pride in the progress of their children. But what if a child is not walking, talking, understanding, or growing in accordance with the children in the nursery, toddlers, or walkers class, or in accordance with the developmental charts that hang in the physician's office? Is there cause for concern, and what actions, if any, should be taken in order to confirm or negate these concerns? The purpose of early problem recognition is to identify problems at the earliest stage possible in order to develop and implement a program that would provide a child the opportunity to enhance his strengths while making the necessary adjustments to compensate for his weaknesses.

Some disabling conditions are recognizable at birth, such as Down's syndrome, orthopedic disabilities, and blindness. Treatment or remediation for these can begin almost immediately. Other conditions (e.g., autism and mental retardation) can go unnoticed for months after birth. Still other conditions (e.g., neurological impairment and specific learning disabilities) may go undetected until the child enters school and is called upon to perform academic functions that are beyond his capability. Early recognition of these latter conditions will provide a child with a better opportunity to function within his abilities as he progresses through school.

This chapter provides information about the process that leads to ultimate placement of a child in special education. When a parent or teacher suspects that a child may have a disability, certain steps must be taken before the child is actually classified and labeled as disabled in some way. Initially, parents and teachers must recognize that a problem exists. After recognition, certain prereferral interventions (or strategies) must be implemented by the teacher in the regular classroom in an effort to accommodate or compensate for the child's needs. If these interventions are not successful and the child's problems persist or worsen, then a professional evaluation should be conducted to determine whether the child has a disability. After completion of the professional testing, the parents, along with school personnel, become part of a multidisciplinary team which renders a formal decision on whether the child is disabled or not. If the team determines that the child is disabled, they recommend placement of the child in an appropriate special education setting. A number of special education placement options are available depending on the severity level of the child's disability.

103

*Recognition,
Identification,
and Placement
in Special
Education*

Recognition

Infants

The Denver Developmental Screening Test (Frankenburg, Dodds, Fandel, Kazuk, & Cohrs, 1975) is a screening tool often referred to by physicians, psychologists, and educators (Widerstrom, Mowder, & Sandall, 1991). It provides basic guidelines for the functions or growth patterns that a child should be involved in at specific points in time. While these guidelines are helpful, a parent should not be concerned if a child does not meet these conditions at the precise time the charts indicate. It must be remembered that these figures are averages, and that children vary in their rates of development.

At the same time, these charts do provide information that is useful in determining normal development. For example, 90% of all children by age 1 will say "Mama" or "Dada," play "peek-a-boo," wave "bye-bye," and respond to their name. By age 2, 90% of children can name a few of their toys, can imitate their parents, and can identify their ears, eyes, nose, and mouth (Dobson, 1983). When a delay is suspected, if a reasonable amount of time has passed and a child is still not performing a certain function, parents should seek the counsel of a pediatrician to help diagnose whether there is a problem. There are programs available that will assist parents with a child's unique needs if it is determined that a child qualifies for special educational services. PL 99-457 provides for a free appropriate education to all eligible children from 3 to 21 years of age. This law also mandated that a state-wide system of intervention for all eligible children from ages 3 to 5 was to be in place by the 1990-91 school year (Hallahan & Kauffman, 1988).

Preschoolers (Ages 3-5)

Besides the developmental charts, there are other indicators that a child may be experiencing difficulty in motor control or in information processing. By age 3, a child will usually repeat simple rhymes, enjoy playing alone with toys, understand simple stories, and climb stairs. At age 4, a child will generally talk in short, syntactically correct sentences, enjoy playing with other children, give correct answers to simple questions, and be able to balance on one foot. At age 5, his speech is normally understood by people other than his family members. He is more willing to share and take turns. He understands the terms *yesterday, today,* and *tomorrow* and is capable of throwing over-hand or catching a large ball (Dobson, 1983). Again, the fact that the child is not performing these activities exactly at this age should not cause a person to think that the child is not developing normally. Many of these characteristics are often present in those without disabilities, but if efforts to perform one or more of the activities seem to be laborious, or tend to frustrate the child, then it may be appropriate for the child to see a physician.

Primary and Secondary School Children

Ideally, the time to recognize and begin to deal with children's disabilities is before they enter a school environment. Unfortunately, this is not always possible. Many disabilities are not manifested until a child is called upon to perform academic activities. Some parents who have denied that a problem exists may feel that a school environment will "straighten their child out" by providing structure, organization, and an opportunity to mature. More often than not, however, academic demands only serve to bring out the presence of a disability. A number of leading authorities (e.g., Dobson, 1983; Hallahan & Kauffman, 1988; Lerner, 1989) have discussed persistent problems in children that may necessitate further evaluation:

1. Difficulty in understanding spoken directions
2. Trouble with pronouncing a word until someone says it for him
3. Treating others well, but often saying something inappropriate

4. Difficulty in following written instructions
5. Leaving out or reversing words or letters while writing
6. Mismatching clothes
7. Extreme disorganization
8. Short-term memory problems—forgetting where his belongings are placed
9. Trouble naming familiar people or things
10. Poor gross motor skills, often evidenced by clumsiness
11. Poor fine motor skills, often evidenced by poor letter formation or drawings
12. Extreme overactivity or underactivity
13. Short attention span
14. Impulsivity

If a disability is suspected, parents should not procrastinate. They should immediately contact their local school district or other qualified professionals to request a psychological evaluation of their child. This evaluation will do one of two things: Either it will confirm their suspicions and provide a plan to help the child compensate for the areas of weakness, or it will negate their suspicions and allow for the investigation of other possible causes for the difficulties.

Regardless of when a child is found to have a physical, mental, or other disabling condition, it is up to the parent to make certain that educators and related professionals design and implement an appropriate program that will meet the specific needs of the child. For further details regarding recognition of learning disabilities, see Chapter 8 and Appendix 3.

Prereferral Interventions

Today, most states require prereferral interventions prior to recommending a child for psychological assessment. Educational interventions might include something as simple as a change in seating in the classroom. On the other hand, a modification in teaching techniques or even a change of teachers could make a difference. For example, public schools in North Carolina are required to implement prereferral interventions that are "designed in consultation with other staff members and may include, but not be limited to, changes in the student's class schedule, curriculum, teachers, instructional techniques, and interventions by student services personnel" (North Carolina Department of Public Instruction, 1984, p. 3).

Bowman (1987) addressed some issues concerning current intervention practices. She indicated that teachers should use "preventive interventions for low achievers who could conceivably be labeled as handicapped if not helped properly" (p. 5). Her discussion of intervention practices includes four areas:

1. Teacher-student strategies
   - Reciprocal teaching, with a sharing of information between teacher and student
   - Cognitive behavior modification, using self-statements to change behavior
   - Making use of learning styles (perceptual, auditory, tactile, and kinesthetic)
   - Metacognitive strategies
2. Student-peer strategies
   - Peer support groups
   - Peer tutoring
   - Cooperative learning
3. Teacher-peer strategies
   - Interaction between teachers and colleagues
4. School-organized strategies
   - Parent support groups

Some states require written records of prereferral interventions with documentation of results, whether positive or negative. The number of interventions required varies from state to state. For example, North Carolina (North Carolina Depart-

107

*Recognition,
Identification,
and Placement
in Special
Education*

ment of Public Instruction, 1984) requires at least two, and Virginia (Virginia Department of Education, 1987) requires at least three. If prereferral strategies fail to produce satisfactory results, the next step would be initiation of formal and informal assessment procedures (Salvia & Ysseldyke, 1988). These would include referral for a psychological evaluation.

Identification

Testing

Proper identification of disabled students must include testing and evaluation. A psychological assessment (or evaluation) consists of a battery of tests administered by professionals. These tests include not only individual tests of intelligence and achievement, but also tests for a wide range of behaviors. The tests are necessary to confirm the presence of a suspected disability and to give more specific information about the nature of the child's problem. Professionals (e.g., licensed psychologists and educational diagnosticians) evaluate the test results and make general conclusions and recommendations about the child's problem and report their findings to the multidisciplinary team. Except for the parents and school personnel who comprise the multidisciplinary team, these test results must remain confidential.

As discussed previously, many parents are skeptical of the validity of test findings. Nevertheless, assessment is a major means available to us to determine whether a student will be eligible to receive special education services and to establish a base from which to start assessment for teaching. The test results also indicate the main problem areas that need to be targeted for help.

Salvia and Ysseldyke (1988) have indicated that an appropriate evaluation will include both formal and informal assessment data. Furthermore, it is important that evaluators gather both current and historical information about a child. Examples of current information would include (a) observations of a student's behavior in the classroom; (b) intelligence test results; (c) parent evaluations of the child's behavior at home; and (d) rating scales completed by teachers. Historical information might include (a) observations of the child by previous teachers; (b) results of the annual achievement tests given the preceding year; and (c) previous medical and psychological records. Of all the test data gathered, however, the results of individually administered intelligence tests probably have received more attention in the literature and by professionals and lay persons than any other.

Intelligence Tests

Wechsler (cited in N. A. Sprinthall & R. C. Sprinthall, 1987) has defined intelligence as "the aggregate or global capacity of the individual to act purposefully, to think rationally, and to deal effectively with his environment" (p. 395). The purpose of giving an intelligence test is to determine the IQ, the Intelligence Quotient, of an individual. This quotient is then used to predict a child's potential to learn and to achieve in an educational setting. Many people erroneously equate IQ score and intelligence. An IQ score is simply a good predictor of academic success, which is one facet of intelligence.

An IQ score is found by dividing a person's mental age (MA), which is determined by the test itself, by his chronological age (CA) and then multiplying that answer by 100. For example, if a child's MA is 12 years old, and his CA is 10, then the calculated IQ would be $12/10 = 1.2 \times 100 = 120$. Thus a person with a mental age of 12 years and a chronological age of 10 years is said to have an intelligence quotient of 120 (N.A. Sprinthall & R. C. Sprinthall, 1987).

There are several factors that must be considered when arriving at an IQ score: (a) the student's unfamiliarity with the

109

*Recognition,
Identification,
and Placement
in Special
Education*

testing situation; (b) his possible lack of motivation in taking the test; (c) the difficulty experienced with the way in which test items are presented; (d) the conditions under which testing takes place; (e) the student's rapport with the examiner (lack of rapport could create a reluctance on the part of the student to participate); (f) the student's emotional state (he may be anxious or excited); and (g) the student's difficulty in understanding instructions or in communicating accurate responses to the questions asked.

Parents and teachers should be aware of a number of individually administered aptitude and intelligence tests frequently used today. They include (a) WPPSI (*Wechsler Preschool and Primary Scale of Intelligence* [Wechsler, 1967]); (b) WISC-R (*Wechsler Intelligence Scales for Children—Revised* [Wechsler, 1974]); (c) *Stanford-Binet Intelligence Scale* (Thorndike, Hagen & Sattler, 1986); (d) WJ (*Woodcock-Johnson*) Test of Cognitive Ability (Woodcock and Johnson, 1989); (e) K-ABC (*Kaufman Assessment Battery for Children* [A. Kaufman & N. Kauffman, 1983]); and (f) DTLA-II (*Detroit Test of Learning Aptitude* [Hammill, 1985]). One popularly used test, the *Slosson Intelligence Test* (Slosson, 1981), has been determined by investigators to be an inadequate measure of intelligence in classifying students for special education (Harris & Reid, 1991).

Intelligence Testing in the Light of Scripture

In II Corinthians 10:12, the Scripture says, "For we dare not make ourselves of the number, or compare ourselves with some that commend themselves: but they measuring themselves by themselves, and comparing themselves among themselves, are not wise." Discussing testing in light of this verse places one in an awkward position, since intelligence and achievement tests are administered to determine how well an individual is performing in relationship to his or her peers. Yet we can view testing and evaluation in another way. Testing, in a sense, gives us a general idea of how much has been placed in an individual's care (intelligence/ability), and what he does with what has been placed in his care (achievement). I Corinthians 4:2 states, "Moreover it is required in stewards, that a man be found faithful." This verse implies that a person is to be found faithful concerning the things that he has been placed over or the things that have been placed in his care by someone else. If few things have been placed in his care, then he must account for those few things. If many things are placed in his care, then he must account for those many things. As illustrated in the parable of the talents (Matthew 25:14-30), the principle is not how much a person was given, but how the person took care of what he was given. Aside from the Lord, no one really knows the achievements that can be performed by a person who submits himself completely to the power of the Holy Spirit. While testing does provide guidelines as to what can reasonably be expected from a person, it does not take into account the indwelling work of the Holy Spirit in the life of a believer. A person's success, scholastically or otherwise, must be determined on the basis of the abilities that God has given him, not on the basis of the abilities that God has given to someone else.

Multidisciplinary Team

Aside from the development of the child's individual education plan (IEP), probably the most critical part of the identification process is the actual decision to classify or label the child as disabled. It is imperative that Christian parents and educators keep the following principle in mind as this decision takes place: The decision to classify and label a child as disabled should never rest with any one person. This idea is completely justifiable, given the fact that many different persons in reality influence and are responsible for the education of a child (parent, classroom teacher, principal). In deciding the educational fate of a child, each of these adults has a different view of the child and his behaviors, performance, and actions in school and home contexts. Therefore, it is important that the final decision to label a child as disabled reflect the observations and opinions of all these people.

The federal government recognized this idea of collective decision-making in the PL 94-142 mandate that a multidisciplinary team be responsible for determining the eligibility of a child for special education services. We believe that Christian school education programs should borrow this concept of the multidisciplinary team in identifying and labeling students for special education. The law stipulates that the membership of the multidisciplinary team shall consist of the following:

1. A representative of the ... [school] other than the child's teacher, who is qualified to provide or supervise the provision of special education [e.g., the school administrator];
2. The child's teacher;
3. One or both of the child's parents;
4. The child, where appropriate; [and]
5. Other individuals [e.g., person responsible for testing] at the discretion of the parent or agency. (*Federal Register*, August 23, 1977, p. 42490)

Two of the most important members of this team are the parent and the child (if he is mature enough to provide input about himself). It is easy for educators in general to forget the importance of parental involvement in this process and to yield almost entirely to the advice and judgment of the one who is actually doing the assessment on the child. As Christians, however, we hold that direct involvement of the parent is not only important in the identification process but absolutely essential. The Bible makes it clear that parents are the primary educators of their children. We can remain Scripturally obedient even in situations like this.

The legal responsibilities of this team may vary from state to state. Yet the duties of the team members, whether done individually or collectively, should allow for the most precise and accurate decision regarding the child's eligibility for special education services. For example, multidisciplinary team members in North Carolina public schools must (a) collect relevant data on the child; (b) observe the child in the regular classroom; (c) review all data and findings from observations; (d) make a collective group decision on whether the child has a disability; (e) write up a report of findings and conclusions; (f) recommend an appropriate educational program; (g) make recommendations on development of the IEP; and (h) decide the responsibilities of each team member when the child must be evaluated at the end of his third year in special education (North Carolina Department of Public Instruction, 1984).

Placement

Through a series of public laws (PL 94-142, PL 99-457, and PL 101-476), the federal government has mandated that educational services be provided for children needing special education. Although these services are available, parents need to remember that ultimately they themselves are the ones responsible for the education of their children (Deuteronomy 6:6-8). When parents allow their child to be placed in a special education program, they are delegating their God-given responsibility for education to those overseeing that particular program (Galatians 4:1-2). Any teacher or person involved in the education of a child is acting in place of the parent *(in loco parentis)*. It is important, therefore, to be familiar with the types of programs that a public or private school system may offer. Once the child's placement has been determined, the parents must make every attempt to work closely with those involved in the education of their child. The following services are provided

113

*Recognition,
Identification,
and Placement
in Special
Education*

by the public school system, and suggestions are offered to private Christian school personnel who desire to incorporate such special education services into their educational program.

Infant-Focused / Infant Stimulation Program

In this program, therapists provide a variety of patterning techniques that enhance motor skill development. These activities include swallowing techniques, visual and auditory stimulation exercises, and the manipulation of the child's arms and legs in such a way as to imitate the natural movement of a normal developing child. In addition, Widerstrom, Mowder, and Sandall (1991) note that some programs may focus on "a developmental care model, others on remediating perceived deficits by stimulating sensory modalities, teaching skills or facilitating infant interactions" (p. 235). The parent may take the child to a developmental center two or three days a week for approximately one hour each day or may have the option of having a case worker come into the home, work with the child, and teach the parents the patterning techniques so that they might be able to work with their own child during the times that the therapist is not available to do so.

Preschool Programs

A preschool program is generally a center-based program (i.e., the parent makes the arrangements for the child to travel to the facility). As opposed to a homebound program, the center-based program provides the child and the parents with many advantages. Staff members—including learning disabilities teachers, early childhood teachers, speech and language pathologists, medical personnel, psychologists, adapted physical education experts, physical therapists, and occupational therapists—are available to clarify procedures used in meeting the child's needs. Special equipment and other materials not normally found in the home are available. The three to five hours a day that a preschool child spends at the center also provide opportunity to develop much-needed social skills (Lerner, 1989, p. 238).

Resource Class

The resource class is the most widely used for serving mildly disabled students (Mercer & Mercer, 1981). It is designed for students with mild to moderate difficulties who are enrolled in a regular classroom but need additional assistance from a specially trained teacher. Students may spend from several hours a week to several hours a day in a resource room. A resource classroom has special materials and equipment available to support the academic area which is in need of remediation (usually reading or math). In order for the resource program to be effective, the resource teacher and regular classroom teacher must maintain close communication with each other. Advice, suggestions, and recommendations need to be shared in order to establish and maintain a pattern of successful progress. The room itself is a special room set aside to be used for teaching students with special needs in small groups. Ideally, it should have a desk for each child, some carrels for those that need a place free of distractions, a table for small-group instruction, and plenty of storage space.

Although there are many benefits of the resource class for the student and the teacher, perhaps the greatest advantage is that it allows the pupil to be mainstreamed for as many classes as he is capable of handling. In the resource room, he receives individualized instruction in his weakest academic areas. Yet he can receive instruction in other academic areas with his friends in the regular class the rest of the day. Another advantage of the resource room is that it can serve very young children who may have mild developmental problems.

Resource classrooms typically offer remedial/tutorial and supportive services to mildly disabled students on a part-time

115

*Recognition,
Identification,
and Placement
in Special
. Education*

basis (Cohen, 1982; Harris & Schultz, 1986; Wiederholt, Hammill, & Brown, 1983), and they usually allow students to continue on within the same general education curriculum (Harris & Schultz, 1986) or with slight adjustments and modifications within the general education curriculum (Wiederholt et al., 1983). In addition, the resource room setting allows the student to receive both direct and indirect special education services (Zigmond & Sansone, 1986). While in the resource room, the student receives direct special education services from the special education teacher in the form of special tutoring, alternative teaching methods and techniques, and other modifications and accommodations. The student also receives indirect services in the regular classroom, where he spends the greater part of his school day. Indirect services come as the special education teacher and regular education teachers collaboratively consult with each other (Idol, Paolucci-Whitcomb, Nevin, 1986) to decide how the mildly disabled student can best succeed in the regular classroom.

In discussing the scope of the resource teacher's duties, Barnes and Barnes (1989) note that the resource teacher "must be perceived as the person in the school who can serve as a resource to the principal, teachers, parents, and children" (p. 91). He has the responsibility to teach students in their problem areas, usually in math and reading skills, in a resource room. It is the resource teacher's duty to assess what to teach as well as how to teach and to make regular evaluations to determine when and if a child is ready for total mainstreaming. Some resource teachers even assist the child in the regular classroom setting. Barnes and Barnes recommend this method for primary students. Communicating with the parents and recommending ways they can help in the home is the resource teacher's job also. Finally, when the student enters the high school years, the resource teacher also becomes an advisor as to future work or vocational training.

The number of students served and the teacher-student ratio are important factors to consider in setting up resource classrooms. There is some agreement among authorities with regard to the number of disabled students that should be served in resource classrooms in a given day. For example, Zacherman (1982) says that the total student caseload of a special education resource teacher per day should not exceed 20 students. Similarly, Reger (1973) believes that the enrollment in an elementary resource classroom should be limited to 15 students, while a secondary level resource classroom should have a maximum of 20 students.

With regard to the number of students a special education teacher serves per class hour, Zacherman (1982) recommends that groups not exceed five students, which is a one-to-five teacher-student ratio. Reger (1973) says that a resource teacher should have only three to four students per class hour. Zimmerman (1982) differentiates between small groups and large groups in resource classrooms. She indicates that some mildly disabled students can function in small groups of five, whereas others can function in larger groups of seven to ten. Based on the information provided by these professionals, we believe that an ideal teacher-student ratio would be one teacher to five to eight students, depending on the collective nature of their disabilities. We also recommend that as resource classrooms are approaching seven and eight students per class hour teacher aides and/or volunteers be placed in these classrooms to assist the special education teacher.

Self-Contained Class

The self-contained class was probably the first attempt to meet the needs of mentally handicapped children in the public school system. At the turn of the century, compulsory education laws made these children more visible, and the first such classes served merely as a place for children who did not fit into a regular classroom. These first self-contained classes were not well orga-

117

*Recognition,
Identification,
and Placement
in Special
Education*

nized; but, in time, objectives and desires to help these children developed (Ysseldyke & Algozzine, 1984). Although some teachers may have used these classes just to remove a problem child from the regular classroom, the self-contained classes have their place in providing for the needs of these children.

A self-contained class is designed for students with moderate to severe disabilities who may need remediation in all subject areas. These children generally stay in the self-contained special education class for all academic instruction, but they may be mainstreamed into art, physical education, and/or music classes as well as lunch.

A special education teacher's total student case load per day in this setting is much smaller than in the resource classroom. For example, in Virginia, public school self-contained classroom teachers serve a maximum of eight to ten different students per day with a teacher's aide (Sutton, 1989). As in resource classrooms, however, it is advisable that teachers in self-contained classrooms serve no more than five to eight students per class hour. Given the severe problems of the disabled students in this type of setting, administrators would be wise to remain at the lower end of this range and to provide the teacher with a paraprofessional or teacher's aide.

Students in self-contained special education classrooms generally receive more intensive attention from the special education teacher. Instruction in these classrooms centers mainly on primary skills in basic academic areas and on social skills (Wallace & McLoughlin, 1979). Moreover, the teacher clearly has more control over the curriculum because the student receives most of his academic instruction in the self-contained classroom (Hallahan & Kauffman, 1988).

Itinerant Teacher

One of the least intensive and most integrative types of special education options for mildly disabled students makes use of the itinerant teacher concept. In this situation, the mildly disabled student spends most, if not all, of his school day in the regular classroom. The student does receive some special education services intermittently from an itinerant special education teacher. Such a teacher generally is responsible for serving students with mild disabilities (as well as students with mild visual, hearing, and/or physical impairments) who may be enrolled in several different school sites in a school district. Thus the itinerant teacher may do much traveling. Hallahan and Kauffman (1988) indicate that the

> primary role of the [itinerant] special education teacher [is] . . . to visit [the] classroom regularly and see that appropriate instruction, materials, and other services are provided; to offer consultation, demonstration, and referral for [the] regular teacher and assessment and instruction of [the] student as needed; to work toward total integration of [the] student. (p. 10)

Special Education Options in Christian Schools

Christian schools that do not receive federal funding are not required by law, as are the public schools, to provide the above-mentioned placement opportunities for disabled students (Sutton, 1991). Administrators, however, should give careful consideration to providing as many of these placements as possible, because they currently represent the best practice for providing appropriate special education services for disabled students. Not many Christian private schools can afford to provide such services, but there are alternatives that can allow disabled students to be educated in a Christian school environment:

1. A full-time special education instructor to work with individual students

2. A part-time special education instructor

3. A full-time reading and/or math teacher to work exclusively with disabled students

4. A part-time reading and/or math teacher

5. A full-time teacher's aide who would allow the head teacher to work with the disabled student

6. A part-time teacher's aide

7. A volunteer teacher's aide, such as a parent

8. A peer tutor or a higher grade-level student who, under the guidance of the head teacher, could work with the handicapped student

9. A contracted speech therapist, physical therapist, or occupational therapist to work with the disabled student and to give the teacher suggestions for working with the student when the therapist is not available

The parents of disabled children in a Christian school may be responsible to pay for these services. Depending on the particular type of health insurance, all or part of these expenses may be covered. If this possibility is considered, it would be good to negotiate the rates charged by the person(s) performing these services on a contract basis. Many times, a reduced rate is available where there is the potential of multiple clients from the same organization.

In light of the limitations of most Christian schools to provide these services, especially at the lower age levels (birth to age 5), one recommendation is to take advantage of the services provided by the public school system during the child's early age and to glean from those services that which would be appropriate to carry over into the child's formal educational program. Once the child is enrolled in a Christian school, if the therapy is still needed, the parent (in conjunction with the therapist and the enrolling school) should make the necessary arrangements to continue to have the therapy provided. An advantage to having the local school district perform the psychological evaluation is that the school district is aware of the need and will be more likely to help provide for the need. It has been our experience that most of the people involved in special education in the public school system are genuinely concerned with providing a child with the services he or she needs. Their willingness to assist extends to children in private schools as well as public schools.

Summary

For parents, one of the hardest questions to ask and to have answered regarding their child's limitations is whether or not he needs special education. The question itself brings about feelings and thoughts of inferiority, substandardness, and incompleteness. These feelings come about as parents compare their children with other children. II Corinthians 10:12 tells us, however, that those making these comparisons are not wise. Each person's responsibility is to determine what God's will is for his life and to perform it in accordance with the abilities God has given him. Likewise, parents should provide the proper guidance for their children to help them discover God's will for their lives and perform it in accordance with their abilities. Part of that guiding procedure is trying to determine the tasks that reflect their ability levels. The purpose of the recognition, identification, and placement process should be to find what our children are capable of, not in comparison to what others are capable of but simply looking at their own God-given abilities.

Once a general understanding of their abilities has been established, then it is our responsibility to take them from where they are and guide them into the tasks that they are capable of performing, focusing on their strengths while attempting to remediate their weaknesses. The sooner we are made aware of these areas, the more effective we can be in determining the proper environment and teaching methodologies through which our children can function and learn most

121
*Recognition,
Identification,
and Placement
in Special
Education*

effectively. The hardest truth for parents to remember is that God is concerned for and loves our children far more than we can ever expect to love them ourselves. Once we realize that God has "set the members every one of them in the body, as it hath pleased him" (I Corinthians 12:18), we can have the confidence that God will be glorified through each member as well as through the lives of those that have been affected by that member.

References

Barnes, D. B., & Barnes, C. K. (1989). *Special educator's survival guide: Practical techniques and materials for supervision and instruction.* West Nyack, NY: Center for Applied Research in education.

Bowman, J. E. (1987, April). *When is intervention an ounce of prevention?* Paper presented at the American Educators Research Association, Washington, DC

Cohen, J. H. (1982). The resource room: A real world context. In J. H. Cohen (Ed.), *Handbook of resource room teaching* (pp. 1-23). Rockville, MD: Aspen.

Dobson, J. C. (1983). *Learning difficulties fact sheet.* Arcadia, CA: Focus on the Family.

Federal Register. (1977). *Implementation of part B of the Education of the Handicapped Act.* Washington, DC: Department of Health, Education, and Welfare, August 23.

Frankenburg, W., Dodds, J., Fandal, A., Kazuk, E., & Cohrs, M. (1975). *Denver Developmental Screening Test Reference Manual Revised.* Denver, CO: LA-DOCA Project & Publishing Foundation.

Hallahan, D. P., & Kauffman, J. M. (1988). *Exceptional children: Introduction to special education* (4th ed.). Englewood Cliffs, NJ: Prentice Hall.

Hammill, D. D. (1985). *Detroit Test of Learning Aptitude–2.* Austin, TX: Pro-Ed.

Harris, K. R., & Reid, R. (1991). A critical review of the *Slosson Intelligence Test. Learning Disabilities Research and Practice, 6*(3), 188-191.

Harris, W. J., & Schutz, P. N. B. (1986). *The special education resource program.* Columbus, OH: Merrill.

Idol, L., Paolucci-Whitcomb, & P. G., Nevin, A. (1986). *Collaborative consultation.* Rockville, MD: Aspen.

Kaufman, A., & Kaufman, N. (1983). *Kaufman Assessment Battery for Children Interpretive Manual.* Circle Pines, MN: American Guidance Service.

Lerner, J. W. (1989). *Learning disabilities: Theories, diagnosis, and teaching strategies* (5th ed.). Boston, MA: Houghton Mifflin.

Mercer, C. D., & Mercer, A. R. (1981). *Teaching students with learning problems.* Columbus, OH: Merrill.

North Carolina Department of Public Instruction. (1984). *Specific learning disabilities definition and identification procedures.* Raleigh, NC: North Carolina Department of Public Instruction, Division for Exceptional Children.

Reger, R. (1973). What is a resource room program? *Journal for Learning Disabilities, 6*(10), 609-614.

Salvia, J., & Ysseldyke, J. E. (1988). *Assessment in remedial and special education* (4th ed.). Boston, MA: Houghton Mifflin.

Slosson, R. L. (1981). *Slosson Intelligence Test.* East Aurora, NY: Slosson Educational Publications, Inc.

Sprinthall, N. A., & Sprinthall, R. C. (1987). *Educational Psychology: A Developmental Approach* (4th ed.). New York, NY: Random House, Inc.

Sutton, J. P. (1989). *The effects of grade level and program type on teachers' instructional behaviors in learning disabilities classrooms.* Unpublished doctoral dissertation, Charlottesville, VA, University of Virginia.

Sutton, J. P. (1991). Special education: Meeting the spirit of Public Law 94-142 in Christian schools. *Balance, 11(8),* 1-2.

Thorndike, R. L., Hagen, E., & Sattler, J. (1986). *The Stanford-Binet Intelligence Scale (4th ed.) Technical Manual.* Chicago, IL: The Riverside Publishing Co.

Virginia Department of Education. (1987). *A position paper on the identification of students with specific learning disabilities in Virginia.* Richmond, VA: Virginia Department of Education, Division of Special Education and Pupil Personnel Services.

Wallace, G., & McLoughlin, J. A. (1979). *Learning disabilities: Concepts and characteristics.* Columbus, OH: Merrill.

Wechsler, D. (1974). *Manual for Wechsler Intelligence Scale for Children–Revised.* Cleveland, OH: The Psychological Corporation.

Wechsler, D. (1967). *Manual for the Wechsler Preschool and Primary Scale of Intelligence.* Cleveland, OH: The Psychological Corporation.

Widerstrom, A. H., Mowder, B. A., & Sandell, S. R. (1991). *At-risk and handicapped newborns and infants: Development, assessment, and intervention.* Englewood Cliffs, NJ: Prentice Hall.

Wiederholt, J. L., Hammill, D. D., & Brown, V. L. (1983). *The resource teacher: A guide to effective practices* (2nd. ed.). Boston, MA: Allyn & Bacon, Inc.

Woodcock, R. W., & Johnson, M. B. (1989). *Woodcock-Johnson Tests of Cognitive Ability–Revised.* Allen, TX: DLM Teaching Resources.

Ysseldyke, J. E., & Algozzine, B. (1984). *Introduction to special education.* Boston, MA: Houghton Mifflin.

Zacherman, J. (1982). Administration of a resource program. In J. H. Cohen (Ed.), *Handbook of resource room teaching* (pp. 253-273). Rockville, MD: Aspen.

Zigmond, N., & Sansone, J. (1986). Designing a program for the learning disabled adolescent. *Remedial and Special Education, 7,* 13-17.

Zimmerman, B. (1982). Developing an elementary school resource program. In J. H. Cohen (Ed.), *Handbook of resource room teaching* (pp. 115-138). Rockville, MD: Aspen.

Physical Disabilities

John C. Vaughn

Introduction

*P*hysically disabled people constitute a "large heterogeneous group...whose one common denominator is their be-
low-average physical ability" (Anderson, 1978, p. 15). Physical
disabilities can be simple or complex. They represent conditions which can be congenital or acquired. Depending upon
which bodily systems they affect, they can range from mild to
severe in nature. Often the causes of physical disabilities—birth
defects, injuries, and diseases—can also cause other types of
disabilities (e.g., mental retardation). For physically disabled
children whose intelligence falls within the normal range,
however, parents and educators must remember one very important principle when it comes to educating these children—
*overcome every disability if possible, and adapt to the
unchangeable.*

Early intervention often produces dramatic results in the life of a determined child who has a physical disability. With enough determination and practice, the human body can adapt amazingly to severe limitations. Severely crippled people can often walk; those with missing limbs can still perform complex tasks; and those with a variety of limitations in their motor skills have made priceless contributions to mankind. Without a miracle, however, those with physical disabilities are never healed. The key for these individuals is adaptation and education within the limitations of their physical disability.

Teachers should pursue academic subjects as much as possible with physically disabled students. That is, reading, writing, and arithmetic—basic academic subjects—should all be taught. Any limitation to the child's development in academic areas is defined by the child's particular disability, but accommodation may be necessary. Specialized equipment, technology, and innovation have made the education of physically disabled students a reality.

It is imperative, though, that educators and parents realize that adaptation is a chief goal, and that educational goals may need to be completely redefined for physically disabled students. In a world where beauty, success, and materialism are inordinately emphasized, discerning and doing the will of God is often one of the few things we can offer physically disabled students. In this limitation they are blessed indeed. They should be taught this truth, and those around them should realize it as well. Physically disabled students who love the Lord are perhaps the best illustration that we know of to show the truth of II Corinthians 4:7, "But we have this treasure in earthen vessels, that the excellency of the power may be of God, and not of us."

Educating physically disabled students requires a working knowledge of the physical difficulties that students must overcome. Innovative procedures vary for the different types of disabilities, and specific procedures must be learned. This chapter is a general introduction to physical disabilities along with certain interventions and techniques. Parents and teachers of physically disabled students will find a place to begin here, and they will find many other resources readily available at local libraries and bookstores and from the organizations listed in Appendix 4.

Definition and Prevalence

Approximately 200,000 students or an estimated 0.5% of the school-age population are physically disabled in some way (U.S. Department of Education, 1986). Hallahan and Kauffman (1988) define and characterize physically disabled students as those

> whose physical limitations or health problems interfere with school attendance or learning to such an extent that special service, training, equipment, materials, or facilities are required ... [and] whose *primary* characteristics are [not] visual or auditory impairments, although some physically disabled children have these deficiencies as *secondary* problems ... [and who] may also have mental retardation, learning disabilities, emotional disturbance, speech and language disorders, or special gifts or talents. (p. 358)

Clearly, what sets this group of disabled students apart from others who are served through special eduction is that their disability is due mainly to physical limitations or health problems. Yet these students may also have accompanying problems in learning, emotional stability, and the like that are characteristic of students with other types of disabilities.

Table 6-1

Physically Disabling Conditions

AIDS
Allergies
Amputations / limb deficiencies
Arthritis
Arthrogryposis
Asthma
Autism
Burns
Cancer
Cerebral palsy
Clubfoot
Congenital malformations:
— Heart
— Hip dislocations
— Extremities
— Craniofacial
Cystic fibrosis
Diabetes

Epilepsy/seizures
Falls resulting in injury
Heart conditions
Hemophilia
Multiple sclerosis
Muscular dystrophy
Nephrosis/nephritis
Osteogenesis imperfecta
Osteomyelitis
Poisoning
Poliomyelitis
Rheumatic fever
Scoliosis
Sickle cell anemia
Spina bifida
Spinal cord injury
Transportation accidents
Tuberculosis

Causal Conditions

The causes of physical disabilities among children and adults are numerous and varied. From more extensive discussions of physical disabilities provided by Hallahan and Kauffman (1988) and Haring and McCormick (1990), we have compiled a list of different causal conditions in Table 6.1. Some of the causes are neurologically based, yet others reflect musculoskeletal conditions. Still others reflect congenital malformations and chronic health problems. We will limit our general discussion to five of these conditions: (a) amputation and limb deficiencies; (b) cerebral palsy; (c) multiple sclerosis; (d) muscular dystrophy; and (e) spina bifida.

Amputation and Limb Deficiencies

Amputations include the loss of any extremity. The effect of this loss varies, depending on a number of factors: (a) the personality of the child; (b) the attitude of the parents; (c) the effectiveness of the prosthetic adaptation; and (d) the degree of limitation that results. All of these factors contribute to the ultimate problem that the amputation causes. Whether mild or severe, it must be dealt with, and the amputation often produces a permanent and significant limitation of the child's educational opportunity.

Generally an amputation is the result of some serious injury. Although older people often undergo amputations due to circulatory problems, this situation is not common in children. Another cause is disease or paralysis that may necessitate the removal of a useless limb, or portion thereof, to allow the individual to be fitted with a more useful prosthesis. The *Yearbook of Special Education* (1978-79), available in most local libraries, gives information on the specific needs of a person with a limb deficiency, as well as information on all types of physical and mental disabilities.

Various mobility aids are available to help such persons compensate. These include wheelchairs, crutches, canes, prostheses (artificial limbs), and many other types of mechanical or electromechanical devices. Television and movies have confused most people on the effectiveness of prosthetic devices. Artificial limbs are limited, still very much in the early stages of their development, and decades away from anything remotely resembling the "better than the original parts" that makes good science fiction. Children are often disappointed when fitted with some device that they find out is more bother than help. In the early stages of Christian education, the teacher may find himself disciplining the student simply to wear his prosthesis at school, instead of taking it off constantly, because the student complains, "it's too hot, it itches, it doesn't work," or simply, "I don't like it." Special education teachers would benefit from knowing how the family selected the physical devices that the child uses to help him compensate. They may have been appropriate for his extracurricular activities yet not function well at school. For example, some persons with very limited or no use of their legs function well in some circumstances in a wheelchair but could do much better in another circumstance with double crutches and leg braces. The needs of the student in his school environment should be brought to the attention of the family. The parents can then discuss these needs in greater detail with the physicians involved and together determine a program of intervention that is most effective for the child.

Well-meaning and compassionate Christian people often fail to understand the realities that amputees must face. There are ample illustrations in the Bible which could be misused to undermine the faith of a young amputee, if someone leads him to believe that God will "heal him" by replacing his amputated limb. Obviously, if God chooses to do that, He certainly has the power; but we have no Scriptural support to indicate that we should ever offer this to a child as an alternative for which he should pray. Christ healed physical infirmities to illustrate His more significant and eternal offer of spiritual healing. We can do far more psychological harm to a child than we realize by suggesting that the child have faith that God will heal him of a permanent physical disability, than by focusing on common-sense concerns for accepting, adapting, and incorporating this limitation into his life message.

Christian special education teachers should concentrate on the compensation that this child must learn in order to function properly. There are a number of limitations and other responsibilities that he must face.

1. He may not be able to perform functions that require the use of his missing or deficient limb, without some cost.
2. There may be some activities in which he will be a bystander and must be given some new opportunity to participate.
3. He will tire more easily until he develops the compensating strength, if possible, from the use of his other limbs or extremities.
4. He may always look different and may at times be extremely conscious of his different appearance.
5. He may be constantly aware of his missing limb, prosthesis, or orthosis (brace) even though others do not notice it. There may be unpleasant sounds or odors associated with the prosthesis or orthosis that will embarrass him.
6. He may be in physical pain and more than likely will frequently experience some discomfort.
7. He may fall, break things, or not be able to use the prosthesis or orthosis properly at times.
8. The child may not have an adequate prosthesis or orthosis, or proper equipment to help him compensate for his disability, because of his parents' lack of knowledge or resources. School officials may need to provide counsel or assistance to the family in learning about sources of help.
9. Depending on the age and activities of the child when the amputation occurs, problems will vary. A very young child who cannot remember life before the amputation will respond much differently to his problems than will a teenager who was the star

basketball player until he lost an arm or a leg in some tragic accident.

Some children with limb deficiencies may never have a need for special education. They can adapt to a regular classroom with few problems. But the Christian teacher with an amputee in his classroom should be alert to unique needs in the student's life. These include "depression, resentment, anxiety, defiance, resignation, indifference, perfectionism . . . aggression, or withdrawal" (Davis & Tindall, 1978-79). Other students may have some of these same behavioral or psychological problems for other reasons. The teacher must be alert to determine whether the hurdles this student is overcoming are related to the amputation or are caused by some other problem. Amputations, like all other physical disabilities, will introduce special concerns into the life of this student and into his education.

Cerebral Palsy

One out of 250 people have cerebral palsy—an estimated 1 million Americans (Davis & Tindall, 1978-79). Approximately 10% of these are mildly disabled and little remediation is required. Another 10% are severely affected; but 80% have the condition in varying degrees of limitation which call for some intervention.

In a sense, the term *cerebral palsy* is much like the term *stomach trouble*. It is very general and conveys very little specific information. Perlstein (1961) explains that the term *cerebral palsy* is an oversimplification that does not describe a single disease but covers a group of medical conditions. Hallahan and Kauffman (1988) explain that cerebral palsy is "part of a syndrome that includes motor dysfunction, psychological dysfunction, convulsions, or behavior disorders due to brain damage" (p. 361). In order to determine the effectiveness of an educational program, the specific effects of these conditions must be known and evaluated.

Cerebral palsy is a condition that results from brain damage. This brain damage, which occurs before, during, or shortly after birth, affects control over the voluntary muscles. The definition of the words explains the condition itself. *Cerebral* means brain, and *palsy* means paralysis of a voluntary muscle. There are a number of causes for the brain damage which may result in cerebral palsy, including insufficient oxygen to the brain before birth, the Rh blood factor, a brain hemorrhage at or before birth, severe prematurity, or German measles in the mother in the early months of pregnancy.

There are several ways to classify students with cerebral palsy. Keats (1973) describes five systems of classification: (a) physiological, by the type of uncontrolled movements; (b) topographical, by the number of limbs involved; (c) etiological, by the cause; (d) functional capacity, by the degree of severity; and (e) therapeutic, by the degree of treatment required. In the physiologically-based classification system, cerebral palsied persons would be classified as spastic, athetoid, ataxic, or mixed.

About half the people with cerebral palsy have the spastic type. They "walk with a lurching gait, fling their arms, and toss their heads, and speak in guttural voices" (Davis & Tindall, 1978-79, p. 301). Twenty-five percent are athetoid. These persons are observed to have "a constant recurring series of slow, involuntary movements of hands, feet, and trunk" characterizing their movement (p. 301). Approximately 7% of those with cerebral palsy are ataxic. They are characterized by a lack of balance, frequent falling, and tremors of the hands and feet. Others have a combination of these types. Different problems in movement are symptomatic of different portions of the brain that have been affected.

As with other disabling conditions, many people are misinformed about cerebral palsy. Those who know very little about cerebral palsy sometimes assume that all its victims are retarded. Others who know a little about it insist that none of them have any mental limitations. Both opinions are unfounded. The brain is the center not only of muscular control, but also of intelligence, behavior, and personality. There can be numerous dysfunctions in these areas as well. Students with cerebral palsy may be observed to have one or more of the following complications: "Speech/language disability; mental deficiency; convulsions; continued personality problems; deficiencies in visual, auditory, tactual, and position and movement senses" (Davis & Tindall, 1978-79, p. 302). Keats (1973) relates that 50% of children with cerebral palsy have visual impairment, and hearing impairments are reported in 16%. McDaniel (1969) notes that 33% of persons with cerebral palsy have speech problems.

It is entirely possible for students with cerebral palsy to have normal or superior intelligence. In many of them, there is no correlation between the severity of their motor disability and their intellectual capacity. Unfortunately, superior intelligence is the exception, not the rule. Robinault and Denhof (1973) explain:

> the mean IQ of cerebral palsy population varies from 70 to 75, as compared to 100 for the normal population. Mental retardation in about 50 percent of the cerebral palsy population further challenges therapists, educators, counsellors, and physicians. Approximately 25 percent [are] dull-normal, and about 25 percent tested normal, above average, [or] superior. (p. 305)

Many people with cerebral palsy lead normal lives. Perlstein (1961) points out that the decisive factor in the success of a person with cerebral palsy is not his ability to deal with intellectual or physical limitations but rather his emotional state. A study of cerebral palsied persons who had difficulty in securing and holding jobs revealed that 80% experienced more trouble from their emotional state than from their intellectual or physical state.

Choosing the right type of education for cerebral palsied students, especially if they are Christians, is important. Every child whose parents desire for him a Christian education should be afforded the opportunity to obtain it, if at all possible; cerebral palsy should not be the deciding factor. Except for children who are incapable of doing anything for themselves (those who would require one or more caregivers to attend to them at all times), some effort should be made to incorporate these students into the Christian school. Students who are able to overcome the physical limitations of the disability often go on to college, as many have. When a student has learned the necessary academic subjects to enable him to advance, we should encourage him to do so. Numerous resources are available to encourage cerebral palsied students vocationally, and many of these students could be competitively employed. For parents and teachers with an ongoing commitment to those with cerebral palsy, resources are available through the United Cerebral Palsy Association.

Multiple Sclerosis

A number of diseases can cause physical disabilities in children and adults. One such disease is multiple sclerosis (MS). Davis & Tindall (1978-79) describe this condition:

> Multiple sclerosis is a neurological disease which results when the insulation (myelin tissue) around the nerve fibers of the brain and spinal cord is destroyed. This disappearance of the insulation occurs in patches which often are widely scattered throughout the central nervous system. This is why the term "multiple" is used, where the insulation has disappeared, and hard semi-transparent scar tissue begins to form. The scar tissue is called *sclerosis*, which is derived from a Greek word meaning hardening. Thus, multiple sclerosis is a disease characterized by formation of hardening scar tissue

(sclerosis) in patches (multiple), throughout the central nervous system. The scar tissue eventually prevents nerve impulses from being transmitted properly. (p. 305)

When the neurological damage affects the voluntary muscles, the frequent result is mobility impairment. It is often quickly and severely disabling and sometimes progressively disabling. This disease is particularly frustrating, both to its victims and to their families. Its cause is unknown. It has a somewhat identifiable geographic distribution with more cases occurring in some areas of the country than in others. There is no cure known, and it is difficult to diagnose. Although it is technically a disease, the focus of our study here is the mobility impairments rather than the neurological disease itself.

Since this condition is neurological, any part of the nervous system can be affected. Depending on how and whether the cerebellum and/or spinal cord are affected, various types of disabilities are manifested in the person. Multiple sclerosis, like many other progressively disabling conditions, works at cross purposes with the educational goals of the student. While the student and his family are striving toward improvement, academically and socially, the child is regressing physically. Students with this condition will require tremendous spiritual intervention and ministry to keep from losing hope. Although individual cases see rapid progress in the condition with an early death for its victim, some persons live for a long period of time and are able to be remarkably productive. There is a very good possibility that 5 to 20 years, or even more, of productivity is possible. For the Christian student, all involved should realize that progress is made in the context of eternity and not just the few limited years of life expectancy. Thus there is every reason that a student should do his best to honor the Lord; after all, none of us have any idea how long we will live, or in what condition in the future.

Practical considerations for the student with multiple sclerosis include reduced activity and opportunities for adequate rest. The student may be required to have physical therapy. This may need to be incorporated into the physical education program of this student's IEP (individual education plan). Physical modifications may be required for these students, as with those experiencing various types of paralysis. Consideration for emotional needs discussed earlier also applies here, as do the environmental adaptations listed above. Additional information is available through the National Multiple Sclerosis Society.

Muscular Dystrophy

Muscular dystrophy is a hereditary disease (Hallahan & Kauffman, 1988) that causes physical disabilities in students. Davis & Tindall (1978-79) characterize this condition:

> Muscular dystrophy is a general term referring to a group of neuro-muscular diseases where there is a progressing weakening and wasting of the skeletal and voluntary muscles. As muscular dystrophy progresses, the person may need to depend upon a wheelchair for mobility and eventually may find it difficult to perform ordinary activities of life . . . there are degrees of severity depending upon age and onset, initial muscle groups affected, and rate of progression of muscle degeneration. (p. 308)

Nearly a quarter of a million men, women, and children have this condition. Two-thirds of these are children between the ages of 3 and 13 (Davis & Tindall, 1978-79). There is no known cure for any of the types of muscular dystrophy, but life expectancy can be extended and compensatory treatments are available, including antibiotics, physical therapy, and specialized equipment. For the typical Christian school, the likelihood of having a student with muscular dystrophy is remote. It is possible, however, and many of the guidelines that apply for the care and intervention of the other physical disabilities also apply here. Additional information is available through the Muscular Dystrophy Association of America.

Spina Bifida

Spina bifida is one of the most common birth defects, occurring in an estimated 0.1% of the population (Hallahan & Kauffman, 1988). Davis & Tindall (1978-79) provide a description of this condition:

> Spina bifida is a malformation of the central nervous system occurring between the fourth and sixth week of pregnancy, in which the vertebrae fail to develop around the spinal cord. More simply stated, spina bifida occurs when the spine fails to form properly. Terms such as "meningocele," "myelomeningocele," "spina bifida occulta," and "spina bifida manifesta," indicate whether a portion of the spine that protruded from the surface of the body was covered with a sac or goes unnoticed because of [there being] no outward physical characteristics. The labels are not important[;] more important are the outward symptoms caused by the undeveloped spinal cord. (p. 310)

Recent developments in surgical techniques have made it possible for these persons to overcome this disabling condition to a very large degree, and more and more of them are appearing in educational programs.

Spina bifida is not a newly discovered condition; it has been recognized since the 17th century. Only recently have treatments been developed that make a productive life possible for persons who have this condition. In 1963, the advantages of surgery shortly after birth were recognized. Shunting techniques developed in the 1950s also help these children. More recently, techniques have been perfected that offer the possibility of a more normal and rewarding life for children born with spina bifida.

Children with spina bifida experience varying degrees of paralysis or lack of sensation in the lower extremities, depending on the severity of the condition or the success of surgical repair. The guidelines that have been offered for intervention for other physically disabled students would apply to these students as well. Readers may obtain additional information from the National Spina Bifida Association of America.

Educational Considerations

Choosing Appropriate Educational Settings

Applying educational techniques specifically designed for physically disabled students poses an interesting set of choices for Christian educators. Many times it boils down to whether we should meet the needs of physically disabled students in a mainstream regular classroom or in a segregated special education setting. Even in the regular classroom, there will often seem to be a conflict between (1) the need for adaptation for either the student or his IEP and (2) the need to follow the demands of the regular academic curriculum. When the pendulum swings all the way toward adaptation, we are no longer involved in education, but in occupational therapy. When it swings completely to the side of academics, we are no longer concerned with appropriate adaptations. Whether in mainstreamed or segregated settings, appropriate special education attempts to maintain a proper balance between adaptations and academics. Parents and Christian educators must carefully evaluate which educational setting is best for a physically disabled child. A physically disabled child may need to be segregated from the mainstream for a time to learn compensatory techniques for his specific limitation. It then may be possible to reintegrate him into a regular program with his peers. Some limiting condi-tions, however, do necessitate segregation throughout the edu-cational experience of the student. Residential programs, separate special education schools, or even self-contained classes within a regular school campus may be available, or it may be necessary for the family to relocate to an area of the country where appropriate service providers and programs are available.

Enhancing Their Communication Skills

Christian educators should not overlook the value of music and art in an educational program for the physically disabled children. Communication through normal channels is often difficult for these students. Even if speech or the ability to manipulate writing instruments is not limited, perceptual problems may reduce the student's ability to express himself. Expressive communication goes hand-in-hand with receptive communication and should not be minimized in the develop-ment of the IEP. Every opportunity to participate in music and art should be offered. An entire section of this book could easily be dedicated to this subject, but it is beyond the scope of our present endeavor. Perhaps later there will be extensive material available on this subject. But for now, Christian educators may refer to secular sources mentioned elsewhere that provide spe-cial needs children with therapeutic opportunities for artistic expression (Anderson, 1978).

Of particular note to Christian educators should be the use of handbells at the Melmark School in Berwyn, Pennsylvania. The Melmark School has also demonstrated the effective use of animals in working with mentally retarded persons. Our own experience reveals the benefit of providing programs centered in nature such as horticulture and animal husbandry for physi-cally disabled students, as well as for mentally retarded students. The Shepherd's Home in Union Grove, Wisconsin, success-fully uses horticulture in their program for retarded persons. Christian educators should not overlook the wealth of illustrations of God's sovereignty in creation as they work with physically disabled students.

Making Necessary Equipment Available

Certain equipment may be necessary for an appropriately developed educational program for physically· disabled students. Two areas of equipment are personal and professional equipment. Personal equipment will usually be the responsibility of the family. It may be necessary for Christian educators to work together with occupational therapists or other therapeutic caregivers to develop the necessary compensatory tools to help the student with his education. Open lines of communication will be needed to ensure that the child receives the very best in personal equipment, so that he is not further disabled through a lack of knowledge or equipment on the part of his parents or teachers.

Professional equipment would include those items that are available to the school primarily and are beyond the budget or long-range need of the family. Electromechanical devices such as a chair lift can be purchased or manufactured; because they would be needed by a student only briefly, they would be retained at the school for use with other students later on. Academic equipment such as the Alphamaster, the Drillmaster, or the Skillmaster (see The Learning Center in Appendix 6), or other electronic teaching aids, computer equipment, or recreational equipment are easily obtained through donations or fund-raising drives. A Christian school could encourage memorial gifts for these items, and a special check-out library could be established with a "Book of Remembrance" in which to list the donors. Communication within the community will often uncover resources that otherwise might go unnoticed. Schools in our area have obtained valuable equipment through food label coupons and cash register receipt campaigns sponsored by local groceries, collected not just by the students' parents or members of the sponsoring church, but by friends all over the area who want to help the school and can do so through these means.

Although many helpful resources are listed in this book and others are available from local public libraries, there will be some conditions which challenge Christian educators: those on which no writing has yet been done or for which no equipment yet exists to help the student compensate. Teachers will need to exercise creativity, guided by common sense. Often there will be volunteers within the church or Christian school family who can step in to manufacture needed equipment. One student learned to walk with a walking device manufactured from PVC pipe. It was like the little walkers that infants use, only much larger and stronger for this school-aged child.

If the budget of the Christian school prohibits the purchase of educational equipment especially designed for physically disabled students, there are sometimes simple alternatives. Local libraries will often lend equipment. Parents can be encouraged to purchase items for their children themselves, or equipment on hand can be modified. Burkhart (see Appendix 6 for address) has prepared helpful material on various types of switches that can be controlled by physically disabled children. Usually these switches can be made from common household items. Use of these switches makes audio-visual equipment accessible to the student who is able to move only his head or who has very limited use of his hands or legs. Parents whose children may never be able to enroll in a special education program, but who want to do all they can to help their children enjoy an improved quality of life at home, should make use of Burkhart's material to see what helpful items might be available at very little expense.

Another resource which is growing in America, one that has been used for many years in Europe, is LEKOTEC, whose name comes from a loosely translated Swedish term meaning "play library." There are, at this writing, 52 LEKOTEC centers in the United States. Family services are provided in these centers where parents can be instructed on the use of toys and equipment designed or adapted specifically for physically disabled persons. These centers provide these items through a lending system to the parents. For information about the nearest LEKOTEC center, or the possibility of starting a LEKOTEC center in your area, contact the National LEKOTEC Center (see Appendix 6).

Ensuring Adequate Building Facilities

Facilities are one of the biggest limitations to education for physically disabled students in the Christian school. It is expensive to adapt or build facilities equipped for physically disabled students. Although special education for certain mildly disabling conditions such as learning disabilities, educable mental retardation, and mild emotional disturbance can be offered by most Christian schools with the addition of a special education teacher, it may often be necessary for several Christian schools within a given area to work together to provide educational opportunities in only one of those schools for physically disabled students. Thus, new facilities must be built; delays and expense may be great. Ministries considering construction of new schools and church buildings should not overlook the needs of physically disabled students. Facilities designed for access by disabled persons are generally accessible without interrupting the normal routing of nondisabled persons. Architectural considerations mentioned earlier are important and often required by law, especially in new construction. If a Christian school wants to offer Christian special education that does not exclude physically disabled students, one possibility would be the addition of a "play therapy" room in which can occur a wide range of activities specifically designed for physically disabled students. More information than can be quickly implemented can be collected by an afternoon's visit to a nearby children's hospital.

We cannot overemphasize the importance of providing adequate facilities for personal hygiene for physically disabled students. The same considerations that are given to restrooms should also be applied to food services. A powerful message to all nondisabled people in a ministry is conveyed through architectural implementation of equipment and points of access which reinforce our Lord's invitation and assurance, "Him that cometh to me I will in no wise cast out" (John 6:37).

Modifying Instructional Activities

What can a teacher do to keep the classroom from becoming an environment that further handicaps a student with a physical disability? Depending on the degree of limitation, the teacher will have to compensate through modifications to the classroom itself or the activity which occurs there. Although teachers may be unable to modify the classroom structurally, they can be concerned about the arrangement of desks and other furniture within the classroom, so that disabled students are able to get around easily. Modification of classroom activities is often necessary once all the possible physical modifications are in place. A number of ideas follow:

1. Activities with laboratory experiments that could be dangerous if not performed properly can be reorganized to allow team effort, or the disabled student can be only an observer.
2. If a student cannot physically perform required work in note-taking or examination, a teacher's aide may administer the examination orally or through some multiple-choice process that allows the student to select the information which will be written down by another.
3. Required written work can be done on a computer adapted for use by the disabled person. It is possible to combine the work of several students with compatible limitations, so that one student would dictate

his work to another student who could practice typing or word processing skills.

4. Physical strength and speed are factors that will affect the student's responses in class. The teacher should be careful not to impose a pass/fail requirement on a student where responses are affected by these factors.

5. Some students require frequent rest periods and may not be able to attend school during the normal hours of a given day. A different pace and tutorial help may need to be factored into that student's IEP.

These are just suggestions for the teacher to consider. Again, the biggest barrier that the physically disabled student faces is not usually his disability or the architecture of the building in which he studies or resides; it is usually his own attitude and the attitudes of his caregivers—their willingness to serve the Lord by helping these students. If that barrier can be overcome, the Lord will guide us into an understanding of ways to overcome the other barriers.

Letting the IEP Reflect Unique Needs

The individual education plan for physically disabled students in the Christian school must not only factor in the issues we have already discussed but must also anticipate unusual schedules. Physically disabled children may often be away from school for up to a month at a time for hospitalization and corrective surgical procedures. Lengthy periods of physical or occupational therapy may interfere with their academic progress. If at all possible, these considerations should be incorporated into the IEP, so that the child and the parents realize that those experiences are not interruptions of his schooling but integral parts of it. By creatively scheduling physical therapy to occur at recess time and near the other students if appropriate, it is possible to help the child understand that recess is a kind of therapy for everyone. If the therapy is painful or embarrassing, however, it would be wise to make other arrangements.

Homework loads may need to be adjusted, as well as special assignments and examinations. School officials should be alert and sensitive to difficulties in the home which might mean that the child will not get the same support and assistance there that he would at school. Special education provides an opportunity for the Christian school to intervene in problems in the home that the normal Christian school does not have. For example, in a regular school if parents lead an undisciplined life and do not help their children get their homework done, the child gets a poor education. Parents who have enrolled their children in a special education program have already acknowledged that their child needs extra help. There is, therefore, a precedent for continued accountability between the school and the home that is far more intense than would be realized in a regular education program.

Using Teacher's Aides and Volunteers

Teacher's aides and volunteers in a special education program are a rich source of help for the very busy teacher of the special education class. Christian school teachers with undergraduate degrees who are considering the field of special education might find it a demanding experience to work as a teacher's aide in a special education classroom. They will quickly learn that a teacher's aide in this classroom must often do many things for which they have not yet been prepared by their education and experience in a regular classroom. There is some latitude for Christian schools to employ teachers who are neither certified nor educated in special education to work as teachers' aides if there is a fully qualified teacher present. Our school has successfully employed disabled adults to work as volunteers or as paid teacher's aides in our school. This is not only a tremendous ministry for these disabled adults, but also an economic boon to the Christian school. Some disabled adults are receiving social security payments and are not able to work beyond a few hours a day because of their physical limitations. Such persons can volunteer to make themselves available to help students in remedial reading, to supervise independent work, or simply to be present during teachers' meetings or during lunch to give the staff a break. Teens and young adults in a church can assist with play therapy, recess, or field trips, helping to make sure that everyone is safe and receives proper attention. Of course, due consideration must be given to legal qualifications if the volunteer duties involve vehicles or specialized equipment.

Although most Christian schools seek to enlist parental involvement in some way in the school activities—certainly in each child's education—in the special education program parental involvement is essential. Because of the individualized program that each child is going through and because of the correlation between his physical needs and his educational limitations, parents may sometimes have to come to school with their children while new programs are being implemented. Some parents may be available to work as part-time teacher's aides, helping their own child. Other programs might be set up as tutorial programs in which the teachers guide the parents in the early stages of working with their own children. This is particularly effective with home schooling or physical intervention in Down's syndrome students, and it provides the additional benefit to the family of avoiding excessive tuition costs when they can take care of the work themselves.

School plays, music programs, or special programs at church should be planned for physically disabled students, so that they also have an opportunity to participate in the blessings of public ministry. Although care should be taken to avoid exploitation of the children, it is often a tremendous blessing to the entire body of believers when disabled children are allowed to participate in roles that are typically reserved for nondisabled children. We should be careful to avoid placing them in stereotyped roles as "crippled children."

Providing Encouragement on a Regular Basis

Nearly all writers who address the subject of education for physically disabled students stress the importance of emotional support. Christian educators are in the unique position of providing the only type of emotional support that is of eternal value. Jesus Christ healed the sick. He did so not only because of his compassion for them, but because of His commitment to declare conclusively, in a visible way, His intention to heal the spiritually sick above all. Physically disabled children should be encouraged to develop a life message, wherein their visible limitation becomes a powerful illustration of salvation. Some day they will indeed be delivered from the physical suffering of this present life. That hope, which will direct the life of a physically disabled child, is the hope that every saved person should have as he anticipates being delivered from the presence of sin and its ravages on mankind. Anyone who has ever heard a gospel witness from a physically disabled person knows that a sweet spirit guiding the testimony of such a person is one of the most powerful influences for Christ that we will ever see. This tremendous opportunity presents these children with an obligation that could overwhelm them without our help and encouragement.

Emphasizing Service and Personal Ministry

As we have stated, Christian educators are uniquely qualified to offer a complete education to disabled children. Whereas a secular or humanistic approach to special education can, at best, provide accommodation to improve the quality of human life for disabled children, the Biblical approach to special education offers investments in eternal life. Christian special education should go beyond mere compensatory techniques to stress service *from* as well as service *to* physically disabled students. They will necessarily be receivers of extra attention for much of their lives, but they should also be taught and held responsible to become givers, as much as possible. Physically disabled students do have something to offer, regardless of how severely they are limited. Even those completely restricted in mobility can still have a ministry of prayer. A ministry of correspondence, or writing, may be possible for physically disabled students. Furthermore, it could well be from the ranks of physically disabled persons trained in our Christian schools, that the next generation is offered a wide range of textbook materials and reference works dealing with the disabilities they have overcome.

Other students in the Christian school—particularly in the special education program—should be taught to serve by helping those with problems more severe than their own. An important concept of classroom management, one that should be incorporated in every Christian special education class, is the assignment of student partners. Over a period of time, some disabled students will prove themselves far more willing to assist other disabled students than will some of their nondisabled peers. Positive reinforcement and use of these students as an example will often encourage others to become involved, as these have. There will be times when it is necessary to meet with parents to explain why their child enrolled in special education is being required to help some other child. The concept of student partners not only teaches the children to serve but quickly identifies limiting attitudes in families—attitudes that compound the student's disabilities through overprotection or unnecessary sympathy instead of accountability.

Summary

This chapter has introduced the Christian educator to the various types of physical disabilities and how they affect a student's education. We have suggested ways to compensate and overcome these limitations to provide the best possible Christian education for these children. There is a need for a number of residential programs for physically disabled persons that are thoroughly Christian and Biblical in their approach. Until God raises up these programs, we must find ways to meet the needs of physically disabled students in our Christian schools. There will be expense and extra effort involved in responding to this need. Additional training will be required of our teachers and administrators. New equipment and expanded facilities will be included. The driving force behind these steps of progress will be the conviction that this is indeed a ministry, not only *to* physically disabled students, but *through* them.

References

Anderson, F. E. (1978). *Art for all the children: A creative sourcebook for the impaired child.* Springfield, MO: Charles C. Thomas.

Davis, K., & Tindall, L. W. (1978-79). Physically handicapped: It's about time physical disabilities came out in the open! Part I. In *Yearbook of Special Education* (4th ed.). Chicago, IL: Marquis Academic Media, Marquis Who's Who, Inc.

Hallahan, D. P., & Kauffman, J. M. (1988). *Exceptional children: Introduction to special education* (4th ed.). Englewood Cliffs, NJ: Prentice Hall.

Haring, N. J., & McCormick, L. (1990). *Exceptional children and youth* (5th ed.). Columbus, OH: Merrill Publishing Co.

Keats, S. (1973). *Cerebral palsy.* Springfield, IL: Charles C. Thomas.

McDaniel, J. W. (1969). *Physical disability and human behavior.* Elmsford, NY: Pergamon Press.

Perlstein, M. (1961). *Cerebral palsy: Dr. Meyer Perlstein answers questions parents ask.* Chicago, IL: National Easter Seal Society for Crippled Children and Adults.

Robinault, I. P., & Denhof, E. (1973). The multiple dysfunctions called cerebral palsy. In B. A. Cobb (Ed.), *Medical and psychological aspects of disability.* Springfield, IL: Charles C. Thomas.

U. S. Department of Education. (1986). *To assure the Free Appropriate Public Education for all Handicapped Children. Eighth Annual Report to Congress on Implementation of the Education of the Handicapped Act,* Volume 1. Washington, DC: Government Printing Office.

Yearbook of special education (4th ed.). (1978-79). Chicago, IL: Marquis Academic Media, Marquis Who's Who, Inc.

Emotional Disorders

John C. Vaughn

Introduction

*I*n spite of our desire to avoid the subject altogether in the present work, we believe that some discussion of emotional disorders is imperative. It is not our intention to deny the existence of emotional disorders altogether, nor to accept the standard secular definitions of emotional "disorders" and seek to offer Biblical solutions to them. Rather, we will discuss the difficulty of definition, offering a clarifying definition as far as possible; briefly introduce the educational approach to dealing with the generally accepted types of emotional disorders; and then provide a more comprehensive discussion of how the believer in Jesus Christ changes and grows and how the Christian school teacher and/or parent can facilitate that change.

An Unfortunate Approach

Many secular texts deal with emotional disorders as though they were exclusively behavioral disorders. In our view, defining emotional disorders as behavior disorders necessarily limits our evaluation to the environmental and biophysical factors that can be seen as causes for the inappropriate behavior. Christian education is uniquely suited to address behavior problems because it assumes that behavior grows out of the human will, which can be changed when under the control of the Holy Spirit. The typical educational approach for correcting emotional disorders or behavior disorders is to alter or adapt the environment, or to treat the biophysical causes with medication or adaptive techniques, without considering the spiritual implications of the student's struggle. The tendency of many professional educators and psychologists to dismiss the spiritual nature of man, coupled with the unwillingness of many spiritual leaders to acknowledge the existence of emotional disorders which require special education, has made dialogue on this particular educational challenge difficult if not impossible.

Most Christian educators will eventually be faced with the responsibility of meeting the needs of a student who has been diagnosed as emotionally disordered. Thus it is important for the Christian educator to learn the vocabulary of this field of special education, so that he can make informed decisions about what components of special education technique he can and should employ in his response. We are seeking in this section to provide the tools that the Christian educator would need in this situation, but we must qualify our approach with the acknowledgment that we disagree with much current writing on the subject of emotional/behavior disorders.

The secular approach that sees a close cause-and-effect relationship between social environment and social behavior, particularly with respect to "modeling"—the idea that children's behavioral patterns tend to demonstrate an imitation of the behavior of others (Kirk & Gallagher, 1983, p. 339)— leads us to some seemingly innocent conclusions which, in our view, can easily be misused. Although we agree that children learn behavior from observation and often imitate the behavior of their peers, we believe it is inappropriate to define Biblical discipline as a form of aggression which in turn produces aggression in the children under such discipline. Similarly, we reject the narrow conclusion that academic segregation in a Christian school environment in itself necessarily produces social withdrawal or isolation in the students enrolled in Christian schools. We do acknowledge the two primary emotional/behavior disorders of unacceptable aggression and debilitating withdrawal and we do not deny that excessive discipline or prolonged isolation, however well intentioned, can produce emotional disorders in the children subjected to such an environment.

It is also unfortunate that such a wide variety of terms is currently used for emotional/behavior disorders. Undoubtedly, there are duplications among these terms, which further complicate our attempt to bring the balancing truth of man's spiritual nature into play. As Hallahan and Kauffman (1988) have pointed out,

> Many different terms have been used to designate children who have extreme social inter-personal and/or intra-personal problems. For example, many terms have been used to designate students or problems such as: emotionally handicapped, emotionally impaired, behaviorally impaired, socially/emotionally handicapped, emotionally conflicted, personal and social adjustment problems, and seriously behaviorally disabled. These terms do

not designate distinctly different types of disorders. They do not refer to clearly different types of children and youth. Rather, the different labels appear to represent personal preferences for terms and perhaps slightly different theoretical orientations. (p. 160)

Just as there is a need for a common terminology in education generally, there is a need for more specific terminology in Christian education particularly. To label every child with an emotional or behavior disorder as a child with a sin problem, a child with an attitude problem, or "a rebel" is simplistic, inappropriate, and naive. Yes, the Bible has the answer to these problems, but it is un-Biblical and un-Christian for Christian educators to believe that a mere command to "stop it" will solve the problem.

It may not be incorrect to define discipline as enforced discipleship. Thus our Christian education program should be in a good position to offer substantive help to these children. But whereas discipline of the socially well-adjusted child consists of a program of working closely with the parents to change the behavior of the child to that which fosters rather than hinders his educational progress and character development, intervention in a disabled child's life will likely include intervention with the entire family. This will present costly and time-consuming challenges, especially for those families who are not members of the church sponsoring the Christian school or who are not quick to submit to the spiritual leadership of the school administration.

In the public sector, those with behavior disorders are easily categorized with others who need special education due to physical, sensory, or mental impairments, for the simple reason that their behavior falls outside the range of expected behavior. It will be difficult for Christian schools to incorporate into their programs those with special education needs due to mental, physical, and/or sensory impairments. It will be more difficult to include those who fall outside the norms due to behavior problems, for the simple reason that we perceive our schools to have a narrower standard for behavior than do the public schools. We are not appealing for the implementation of special education programs which provide nothing more than remedial discipline, or which provide an easy escape from the difficult behavior problems to which the teacher in the normal Christian school classroom must respond. We are, rather, calling for special education programs which include those students whose emotional adjustment and/or behavior has hindered or is hindering their education significantly, but who desire, as do their parents, a genuine change in behavior that will enable the student to do his best academically and spiritually.

Unfortunately, many Christian parents erroneously believe that the Christian school will correct the neglect of Christian character training in the home. The Christian school alone cannot correct behavioral problems. Our aim in special education cannot be to offer an ineffective educational environment in lieu of needed punishment for unacceptable behavior, nor should we merely warehouse children in special classrooms hoping that they will grow out of their problems. Thus, the focus of this chapter is limited to those legitimately defined emotional disorders which can be properly dealt with in the Christian school classroom, with an individual education plan (IEP) designed to provide the optimum environment and with due consideration to the biophysical/physiological and spiritual factors that can be altered to produce a change in the child's behavior.

We must acknowledge two current errors in order to make progress in this area. In addition to the above-mentioned denial of the problem on the part of many within the Christian community, there is the equally inappropriate response of Christianized secular psychology, which seeks to change human behavior through a mere alteration of environmental/physical factors. The approach that we advocate focuses on the student's will, which is provided with decision- making information through his mind. Thus we shall see that through accountability for individual responsibilities, along with appropriate educational intervention to help the student renew his mind, in many cases we can expect much progress.

A Very Real Problem

Although this particular area of special education is the greatest point of divergence between Christian and secular special education, here, as in every other area of special education, we can learn much from secular sources such as those used throughout this introduction. We differ, however, on this particular subject even with those with whom we have the greatest agreement. It has been asserted that "there is no sound scientific basis for belief in hidden causes; the child's behavior and ... social contacts are the problems" (Hallahan & Kauffman, p. 161). But there is a sound Biblical basis, reasonably accepted by faith, for the assertion that undesirable behavior is symptomatic of spiritual problems in many cases of emotional/behavior disorders. It may very well be that the child is a victim of those problems, rather than the instigator of them. But because of the Biblical explanation of the nature of man, we must not take a purely scientific approach to this area of Christian special education. We contend that the causes of most cases of emotional disturbance are among those things which are spiritually discerned (I Corinthians 2:14).

Again, concerning definitions, Hallahan & Kauffman (1988) have challenged the term "seriously emotionally

disturbed," which was used in PL 94-142, as being inappropriate. They opt for the terms "emotionally disturbed/behaviorally
disordered [or ED/BD]." They give a good argument for the
use of the simple word *disturbed*, but we prefer the term
emotionally disordered because of its implication of responsibility and because of the Biblical use of the words *order* and
orderliness as proper objectives for disciplined Christian living.
We do agree with Hallahan & Kauffman, however, in their
explanation of the problems in defining emotional disorders.
They list and discuss five factors that hinder a consensus on the
definition of this problem:

1. Lack of an adequate definition of mental health and
   normal behavior;
2. Differences among conceptual models;
3. Difficulties in measuring emotions and behavior;
4. Relationships between ED/BD and other handicapping conditions; and
5. Differences in the functions of socialization agents
   who categorize and serve children. (Hallahan &
   Kauffman, p. 162)

To have an emotional disturbance is to be out of harmony
with true mental health and normal behavior, and much that is
going on in public school classrooms today may be responsible
for "mental illness." If this sounds like a bold accusation,
remember that there are public educators today who believe
that any child that comes to school believing in God is "mentally ill" and needs to be delivered from his debilitating malad-
justment. Schlafly (1984) edited a volume entitled *Child Abuse
in the Classroom*, which is a compilation of excerpts from the
official transcript of proceedings before the U. S. Department
of Education during its consideration of what has come to be
known as the Hatch Amendment. Included in those transcripts
is the testimony of Lawrence Donnegan. He relates an incident

involving "serious emotional disturbance" produced by an educational program striving to help students achieve "mental health." He reports:

> In our high school recently in what was called a health class, eleventh grade students were given a series of questions for each of which they were to choose one of two possible answers. They were then told to grade their own papers on a point system according to which answer was chosen. They were then told that this was a mental health index. They were told right there in the classroom that anybody scoring above a certain number of points had a serious mental health problem and was in need of psychiatric care. (cited in Schlafly, pp. 169-170)

Through his report of the ensuing emotional disturbance among the students in that classroom, Donnegan concludes that "there is a great need to protect our students from being presented with inappropriate questions in classroom discussions relating to their personal beliefs, feelings, and attitudes" (cited in Schlafly, 1984, p. 169). We agree. There can be no acceptable definition of mental health that totally excludes the Creator of the human mind and personality. Any definition of mental health acceptable for use by Christian educators must necessarily include the Scriptural view of man as a spiritual being.

Even Hallahan and Kauffman (1988) support the agreement among mental health specialists that a mentally healthy child is usually happy. We do not disagree, but we must clarify that happiness is not therefore the objective for the Christian child. Most nonspiritual educational programs strive for happiness as an objective, since unhappiness is seen as a problem; but Christians should strive for happiness as a by-product of obedience to God, since the root problem is some form of disobedience.

Because the difficulties of definition give rise to difficulties in the classification and ultimate placement of emotionally disordered children in special education programs in general, it is expected that this same difficulty will obtain in Christian education. Several factors complicate the grouping of emotionally disordered students into subgroups based on the identification of their inappropriate behavior:

1. Lack of reliability and validity of the classification system;
2. Significance of etiology;
3. Specific legal considerations; and
4. Differences between classification systems for adults and children. (Hallahan & Kauffman, 1988, p. 167)

Not only is the reliability and validity of current classification systems very poor, but psychiatry has, in the vast majority of cases, only been able to guess at why a child is disturbed; thus the etiology, or cause, of a mental "disease" is difficult if not impossible to determine (Hallahan & Kauffman, 1988). Legal considerations come into play in the classification of emotional disorders, since some behaviors are obviously criminal and the names of the criminal behavior are easily attached to the individual demonstrating that behavior. This tendency is also seen in Christian education since behavior problems are usually related to the will and therefore can be classified as sin. It is all too easy to simplistically identify an emotionally disordered student as a "little sinner" and think that the "rod of reproof" is all he needs, when it may well be that unwise and unspiritual use of the rod of reproof may have caused his problem in the first place. Additionally, since children pass through development stages in which behavior is appropriate at one age and yet inappropriate at another, it is extremely difficult to classify behavior in children by comparing it to similar behavior in adults.

Definition and Classification

Although there is no universally accepted definition for emotional disorders, a review of the definition of "seriously emotionally disturbed" as contained in PL 94-142 would be helpful. The definition reads as follows:

(i) The term means a condition exhibiting one or more of the following characteristics over a long period of time and to a marked extent which adversely affects educational performance

(A). An inability to learn which cannot be explained by intellectual, sensory, or health factors;

(B). An inability to build or maintain satisfactory relationships with peers and teachers;

(C). Inappropriate types of behavior or feelings under normal circumstances;

(D). A general pervasive mood of unhappiness or depression; or

(E). A tendency to develop physical symptoms or fears associated with personal or school problems.

(ii) The term includes children who are schizophrenic or autistic. The term does not include children who are emotionally maladjusted unless it is determined that they are seriously emotionally disturbed. (*Federal Register,* Vol. 42, No. 163, Tuesday, August 23, 1977, p. 42478)

We agree with Hallahan & Kauffman (1988) that the federal definition "though based on one that is frequently cited by professionals as helpful and reasonable, is flawed" (p. 166). A careful analysis of the federal definition allows one to conclude at least three problems. First, it is strangely redundant to state in (ii) that "the term includes children who are schizophrenic or autistic" when the same children are so aptly described in points A through E in (i). Second, the five characteristics delineated in (i) necessitate inclusion of socially maladjusted children, yet the statement in (ii) clearly excludes them. Finally, the phrase "which adversely affects educational performance" suggests that students who exhibit any combination of the five characteristics in (i) and who have satisfactory academic performance will not be included (Hallahan & Kauffman, 1988).

Even though there is little, if any, definitional unanimity among professionals, there is general consensus that an emotional/behavior disorder will include:

- Behavior that goes to an extreme—behavior that is not just slightly different from the usual.
- A problem that is chronic—one that does not quickly disappear.
- Behavior that is unacceptable because of social or cultural expectations. (Hallahan & Kauffman, 1988, p. 165)

Our concern, however, goes far beyond the educational difficulty or scientific validity of the definition. We maintain that a scientifically valid definition may never emerge because of its un-Biblical conceptual model of man. Proponents of a psychiatric/scientific approach to mental health seek to address problems but have available to them only those resources which can be observed or perceived through the senses. We can never hope to help an emotionally disordered human being until we have first determined whether we are dealing with a "natural man" or a "spiritual man" (see I Corinthians 2:9-14).

In a very real sense, every natural man, unregenerate and spiritually dead, is behaviorally disordered. There can be no hope of lasting change in the life of an unsaved person without regeneration. The new birth is prerequisite to any progress in his proper adjustment. But Christian education must not be allowed to hide behind the platitudes of offering salvation to people with serious problems and expecting them automatically to work out their problems for themselves. Sanctification is a process that begins at salvation. Although in its eternal consequence its fulfillment is guaranteed (Romans 8:28-29), the process of sanctification continues throughout the Christian life, and we shall see that it can be fostered by Christian education.

We also find it useful to consider the generally accepted but very broad dimensions of emotional disorders described by Achenbach and his colleagues (e.g., Achenbach, 1985). They hold that students with emotional disorders have externalizing (aggressive, acting out) behaviors or internalizing (immature, withdrawn) behaviors. Mild or moderate disorders of this type have "most often been referred to as neurosis, or psychoneurosis . . . [whereas] children with severe or profound disorders are usually said to have psychosis, schizophrenia, or autism" (Hallahan & Kauffman, 1988, p. 169).

Classifying students with emotional disorders as having externalizing or internalizing behaviors is not inconsistent with Christian education. The Christian special education program will undoubtedly need to address these disorders in the very near future. An understanding of them and a Biblical approach to them is mandated by the reality of their existence, as well as the Scriptural support for intervening to whatever degree possible. Adam's first response to God after the fall was "withdrawal" (Genesis 3:8-10), followed by "aggression" (Genesis 3:12).

Prevalence

Because of the definition problems, we are also unable to accept any of the current statistics offered for the prevalence of emotional disorders in American society. Since we reject the common definitions of emotional disorders because of their exclusion of the spiritual nature of such problems, and since comprehensive research has been impossible within Christian education without working definitions, we are unable to provide alternative statistics. Whether we accept the federal government's estimation that 1% of the school-age population is seriously emotionally disturbed (U.S. Department of Education, 1986), there is a need for dependable data compiled by professional Christian education researchers to help determine the prevalence of emotional disturbance in the community most often seeking Christian education.

By no means do we assume that all students in Christian schools are Christians, nor do we assume that those who are Christians cannot have emotional disorders. Although we are unable to suggest a statistical appearance of emotional disorders in Christian education, those involved in Christian special education should expect to receive applications at some point from students classified by professional evaluators as emotionally disordered. A wise application of the saving and sanctifying influences of Christian education should be offered as the alternative to the inconsistent and often ineffective secular approach. Emotional disorders are a very real problem. Unfortunately, there are no simple answers. The complexity of the situation is drastically reduced for Christians, however, when we recognize that one of the major causes is a spiritual problem.

Identifiable Causes

We cannot argue that emotional disorders are solely due to sin or willfulness in all children. Although sin and spiritual blindness are a primary root cause in many cases, we should not automatically rule out all causes identified by secular educators. Emotional disorders "have been attributed to four major factors: biological disorders and diseases, pathological family relationships, negative cultural influences, and undesirable experiences at school" (Hallahan and Kauffman, 1988, p. 171). These causes, or combinations thereof, can also be influenced by contributing factors. These causes are approached differently depending upon the conceptual model that the educator uses to seek to understand the problem. Hallahan & Kauffman (1989) discuss six such conceptual models that have been generally recognized, and we will offer a seventh.

1. *Biological approach:* the view that genetic, neurological, and biochemical factors may cause disturbed behavior

2. *Psychoanalytic approach:* the view that traditional psychoanalytic concepts can be used to probe mental processes of the brain to find the underlying causes of disturbance

3. *Psycho-educational approach:* the view that discovering why children behave as they do is important, but so is the acquisition of academic and daily living skills

4. *Humanistic approach:* the view that behavioral disorders are symptomatic of a child's being out of touch with self and feelings

5. *Ecological approach:* the view that ED/BD (emotional disorder/behavioral disorder) results from poor interaction of the child with elements of the social environment

6. *Behavioral approach:* the view that all behavior is learned; therefore, ED/BD represents inappropriate learning (Hallahan & Kauffman, pp. 163-164)

7. *Spiritual approach:* the view that behavior is a reflection of choices made in the will, which is fed by the knowledge in the mind; therefore, emotional disorders can be remediated through the "renewing of the mind" (Ephesians 4:23) and right choices of the will

Again, we believe that the spiritual approach cannot deny whatever validity there is in these other approaches; we do well to consider these perspectives to help us understand the problems that we have so far been unsuccessful in correcting. Biological factors have not been determined to be at the root of the problems for mildly and moderately emotionally disordered children (Hallahan & Kauffman, 1988), but there are obvious biological considerations for those who are severely or profoundly disturbed. Many qualified Christian counselors recognize the value of understanding distinctions in temperament, which are built into a child before his birth. Even secular educators recognize a possible connection between an unharnessed, unmanaged temperament and behavior disorders. For example, Kauffman (1989) notes that some researchers have found that "children with any kind of temperament might develop behavior disorders, depending on child-rearing practices of their parents and other adults" (p. 155).

In recent years, a number of tools have been developed that are useful to the Christian educator in determining specific temperament problems or personality types, information that will better enable the Christian educator to develop an individual education plan for a specific student. We recommend the Taylor-Johnson Temperament Analysis (Geier, 1990) test. This test provides an analysis of nine different temperament tendencies and their opposites graphed in a variety of ways. The graphs are shaded for easy interpretation within specific norms, and behavioral tendencies are characterized as "excellent, acceptable, improvement desirable, or improvement needed." The respondent answers a series of 180 questions about himself in a specific context. His responses are then compared with the responses given by his socioeconomic, educational, and age group, and they are graphed for easy interpretation. Specific training is required for one to be able to use the Taylor-Johnson Temperament Analysis [see Taylor & Morrison (1984)], but its use can greatly aid the evaluation of the child's emotional disorder and the development of his IEP.

An increasingly popular instrument that we have used successfully is the Personality Profile (Carbonell and Rohm, 1990b) and its various adaptations. The authors have adapted the measurement instruments produced by Performax Systems for use in Christian schools and churches. The child's profile is available for use by teachers who have not received the formal training provided by Performax System in a package called *Personality Wise* (Carbonell & Rohm, 1990a). All of these materials use the "DISC" model, in common use in the business world, to measure basic personality types. In the "DISC" model, the D represents a dominant personality, the I represents an influential personality, the S represents a steadfast personality, and the C represents a cautious or compliant personality. We believe it is superior to the earlier and more simplistic approach of the four basic temperament types popularized by Tim LaHaye (1966), although there are some similarities. The Personality Profile is much more scientific in its measurement of personality types. An understanding of the dominant characteristics of personality predetermined by biological factors—or, as we understand it, divine design—will give the Christian teacher or parent a tremendous advantage in helping to overcome the difficulties in this area of special education.

Too often, Christian schools have certain clearly defined rules based on Bible principles and a series of behaviors defined thereby which are expected of and imposed upon all students without regard to their different personalities or temperaments. Some children are more talkative, perfectionistic, dominant, or submissive than others. These are personality characteristics which can be stifled, producing emotional difficulties for children in a legalistic environment which does not recognize the Scriptural fact that we are all "fearfully and wonderfully made" as individuals worthy of respect by others.

The relationship between family factors and emotional disorders is an area in which many Christian educators inappropriately assume themselves to be experts. Because we see education as the primary responsibility of the family, and the Christian school as an extension of the family's efforts to train up their child in the way he should go, it is easy for us to blame the family or to relinquish those areas in which we are ineffective to the realm of "the family's responsibility." We would do well to consider the results of empirical research on family relationships conducted by secular educators. They have found that "the influence of parents on their children is no simple matter and that deviant children may influence their parents as much as the parents influence them" (Hallahan & Kauffman, p. 173). We have observed this to be true in our work in special education. Problem children do not simply reflect problems in the home; they also cause problems in the home.

Christian education has the added advantage of being able to offer a ministry of reconciliation, not only to the student enrolled in its special education program, but to the family that will agree to be submissive to the counsel of the supporting church or school administration. Unquestionably, dysfunctional families contribute to the emotional disorders of students in them. A number of helpful counseling ministries are available in local churches and metropolitan areas around the country. Family intervention is properly conducted as a ministry of the local church. If parents find themselves in an environment where competent counsel is unavailable within the local church, they should seriously consider relocation, so that they can place their family within a ministry which takes the counseling ministry to families seriously and does not simply delegate it to professionals outside the church. Those parents who face the difficult task of placing their emotionally disordered child in a special education program should be encouraged to consider the possibility of family counseling to whatever degree it is determined necessary by those who are sincerely seeking to help their child.

Cultural factors that determine values will have a definite effect on the emotional stability of the children within a given society. We have the compounded influence in American society, however, of an alternative reality presented on television to that in which we live our daily lives. In our view, many emotionally disordered children today struggle with an inability to distinguish true reality from the television "reality." Postman (1985) has discussed this difficulty and its impact on education in his book *Amusing Ourselves to Death: Public Discourse in the Age of Show Business.*

He explains the development of electronic media in the late nineteenth century and their impact on human thinking. He concludes:

> This ensemble of electronic techniques called into being a new world—a peek-a-boo world, where now this event, now that, pops into view for a moment, then vanishes again. It is a world without much coherence or sense, a world that does not ask us, indeed does not permit us to do anything. A world that is, like the child's game of peek-a-boo, entirely self-contained, but like peek-a-boo, it is also endlessly entertaining . . . as some psychiatrist

once put it, "we all build castles in the air." The problems come when we try to live in them. The communications media of the late 19th and early 20th centuries, with telegraphy and photography at their center, called the peek-a-boo world into existence, but we did not come to live there until television. Television gave the epistemological bases of the telegraph and the photograph their most potent expression, raising the interplay of image and instancy to an exquisite and dangerous perfection; and it brought them into the home. (Postman, pp. 77-78)

Of course, the debate continues about whether hostile behavior is fostered by violence on television. Interestingly, Kauffman (1989), after reviewing a number of research studies investigating the effect of television violence on behavior, concluded that "a large body of evidence indicates that viewing TV violence tends to increase antisocial behavior, particularly in children and youth who are already at risk for social and academic problems" (p. 215). Yet there is a contradiction among some of those who do not agree with us that television violence unquestionably fosters violent behavior. Some may say there is no connection between violent entertainment and violent behavior but also insist that physical discipline of a child produces physical aggression in that child. We see this as a patent contradiction.

Others have argued for the use of television as an effective tool in education, and the "highly successful" example of Sesame Street is frequently used to illustrate. Again, Postman (1985) responds:

We now know that Sesame Street encourages children to love school only if school is like Sesame Street, which is to say, we now know that Sesame

Street undermines what the traditional idea of schooling represents. Whereas a classroom is a place of social interaction, the space in front of a television set is a private preserve. Whereas in a classroom, one may ask a teacher questions, one can ask nothing of a television screen. Whereas school is centered on the development of language, television demands attention to images. Whereas attending school is a legal requirement, watching television is a act of choice. Whereas in school one fails to attend to the teacher at the risk of punishment, no penalties exist for failing to attend to the television screen. Whereas to behave oneself in school means to observe rules of public decorum, television watching requires no such observances, has no concept of public decorum. Whereas in a classroom, fun is never more than a means to an end, on television it is the end in itself. (p. 143)

Although our recommendation may seem archaic, unscientific, and prejudiced, we suggest that in the Christian special education program any attempt at intervention in emotional disorders must necessarily include a limiting of the exposure of the student to the false reality of television. While we deplore immoral or vulgar behavior, we agree with Postman (1985) that, in addition to sex and violence, perhaps the chief disadvantage of television is the absolute unreality of everything on it. It is a make-believe world. Emotional disorders are, if anything, an inability of the child to function appropriately in true reality. We submit that true reality is not merely the scientifically observable world, but eternity. The time/space continuum in which we live is only a shadow of that reality. Television is simply a contrived and artificial reflection of that which is subjectively chosen for our entertainment from that shadow. There are students in our Christian schools today who are thoroughly familiar with, and acting out in their daily behavior, behaviors that they have observed the night before on television—or worse, from R-rated videotapes which their parents have brought into the home. These influences reflect cultural factors which run contrary to the purposes of true sanctification of an emotionally disordered child.

School factors which produce emotional or behavioral disorders are recognized even by secular educators. Inappropriate behavior is often learned from classmates. The strict discipline of Christian schools and their rigid requirements, which can easily result in suspension or expulsion, are necessary in order for Christian schools to be what they are. But for those with true emotional disorders who find themselves expelled from Christian schools, there should be alternatives. When a rebellious child is given adequate opportunity and encouragement from his teachers and parents to change his behavior and yet chooses not to change, he may find himself excluded from Christian education, even its special education programs. But if an emotionally disordered child wants to change his behavior and his parents are supportive of his efforts in that direction, he should have Christian education alternatives available to him. Expulsion may solve the immediate problem for the school. But in the long run, if litigation follows, such a decision may prove to be unwise; and it could eventually jeopardize the school's right to exist. (Readers are referred to an article published in *Exceptional Children* by Bartlett [1989] on expulsion of children with disabilities.)

Administrators and pastors should be constantly vigilant to determine whether expectations are reasonable, whether behavioral standards encourage movement in the right direction, or whether they expect perfection to be in place in the child's behavior on the day he enrolls. It must be remembered that disciplinary methods can correct, but they may contribute to emotional disorders. If we are to approach this problem as a spiritual need, we must have spiritual wisdom in doing so. If these programs are to be successful in our schools, there will be no substitute for the leadership of the Holy Spirit in the lives of those in charge.

Scriptural Remediation

Believing that emotional disorders are symptomatic of root problems that may not be readily identifiable or easily corrected, we offer the following guidelines for Scriptural remediation. We argue that the cause of the emotional disorder is the true disorder and that the cause is what should be remediated and corrected. Emotions are seldom impaired in those who are having "emotional problems." They do not need to have their emotions healed, but the behavior corrected that is causing the emotional pain. Adams (1973) asserts that "words like 'emotional problems' are euphemisms. Nobody has emotional problems; there is no such thing as an emotional problem" (p. 109). Emotional difficulties are the unpleasant result of wrong choices in the will, as a general rule.

Wrong Approaches

Freud, the originator of psychoanalysis, held that the nature of man could be explained in terms of the id, the ego, and the superego. The ego was said to be the conscious, volitional self; the superego was the learned system of values which controlled the ego and often suppressed or imposed "false guilt" on the person who received contrary impulses from the subconscious drives of his id. The obvious remediation for this false guilt was to reprogram the superego to bring it into line with the more natural drives of the id. In other words, when a person felt guilt for violating his own rules or values, he only needed to redefine the rules so he would not feel guilty (Adams, 1970). This un-

Biblical view has fallen into disrepute even among non-Christian counselors in recent years. Noted authors in psychology including Glasser and Mowrer have written extensively on the essential factor of personal responsibility in human behavior (Adams, 1970).

Reports frequently come to us from counselees in "therapy" with secular counselors and mental health professionals that they are held responsible to live consistently within the boundaries of their own faith or ethical system. Of course, little or no effort is made to assist the counselee in the clarification or strengthening of this "ethical system." The possibility of a revealed standard of behavior for all men is outside the comprehension of the secular system with the single exception of "social norms," sometimes synonymous with "public policy."

There is little encouragement in the secular defection from Freudian psychoanalysis, since a true defection cannot occur as long as most modern psychology grows from that root. Pastors have been bombarded with the insistence that they lack the training to counsel "serious psychological problems." No minister would be allowed to testify in court as an expert on human behavior regardless of the changed lives he has to his credit through the Lord's help. The American education and government structure has accepted wholesale the "medical model" of mental illness. This medical model remains basically unchallenged in the minds of many secular and Christian educators alike. We contend, however, that the pastor, in conjunction with the school administrator and the special education teacher, has an important and pivotal role in addressing the needs of emotionally disordered students in Christian school special education programs.

Just as the Freudian psychoanalytic theory of man has left a seemingly indelible influence on so-called Christian psychology, other theories are vigorous in their persistence. A notable view that greatly affects the thinking of numerous Christian leaders and educators is transactional analysis. Transactional analysis theory is similar to the Freudian trinity of man but uses the terms "parent, adult, and child" to refer to the superego, ego, and id, respectively. Minirth (1977) states that "in transactions with others, we are always acting and feeling like one of these entities" (p. 59). Whether we respond from our feelings (our "child") or from our judgments and biases (our "parent"), we are driven or controlled by one of these components of our personality. This view has given rise to great error in recent years, and it has been adopted into the church and Christian school. Christians hold to the trichotomist view that man is best described as spirit, soul, and body (I Thessalonians 5:23, Hebrews 4:12). Any conceptual model of man used in counseling or remediation of emotional disorders that excludes his spirit is incomplete and unacceptable.

The Need for a Biblical Approach

Man's spirit is the realm of God-consciousness (I Corinthians 2:11-12), just as the soul is the realm of self-consciousness and the body is the realm of consciousness of the world around us. We are all aware of the five gates into the body—the senses through which we receive information and input. Smelling, tasting, feeling (the tactile sense), hearing, and seeing are the only avenues through which information from the environment can penetrate the outer man, the body, to enter the seat of intelligence. There are also five gates into the soul that are identified in Scripture (Larkin, 1918). These are the faculties of reasoning, imagination, memory, affections, and conscience. Scripture is rich in its description of these aspects of the soul and uses each of them frequently in various ways. There is only one gate to the spirit of man, however—the will (John 7:17). Any explanation of the nature of man that does not acknowledge the function of the will in addressing the emotions and behavior of man is inadequate and ineffective. We know that behavior is determined by the will, but we are sometimes reluctant to acknowledge that emotions are produced by behavior and will. "Sinful behavior leads to unpleasant emotional experiences . . . the way to get relief from these is not by attacking the emotions, but by changing (repenting of) the behavior" (Adams, 1973, p. 110).

Of course, we recognize there are some emotional disorders that are organic or chemical in nature. In our view these biophysical problems are in a minority and can usually be ruled out with a comprehensive physical examination (which we suggest as a part of the initial evaluation before placement in the special education program). Adams (1973) sheds light on this subject:

> The source of one's problems, in the instances of non-organic difficulties . . . is not an emotional impairment or malfunction but lies *behind* the unpleasant visceral (etc.) responses that the [student] wishes to expel. These emotions are organic bodily responses that are largely involuntary and are triggered by behavior, thoughts, and attitudes. The problem is not emotional, but *pre-emotional.* The emotion is triggered by (1) immediate conscious thought and/or action, or (2) unconscious habit patterns that automatically release emotional responses. The solution lies not in direct attacks upon the emotions (drugs, alcohol, frontal lobotomies, etc.), but in rooting out the *cause* of the emotional response. If there is specific behavior or thought that is directly associated with the undesirable emotion, then it may be dealt with concretely. If the emotional response resulted from a well-developed sinful response pattern no longer requiring conscious thought to set it in motion, then the solution lies in

discovering the pattern and dehabituating the counselee through the sanctifying work of the Spirit by means of His Word. The pattern must be broken and replaced by a Biblical one. (pp. 110-111)

It is encouraging that a number of excellent resources have been prepared in recent years in response to the myths of psychiatry. The work of Adams (1973) is well known and essential reading for any pastor who desires to free himself from the bondage of secular limitations on his ministry of counseling. In addition, M. Bobgan and D. Bobgan (1985) have written several helpful books that should also be read carefully and frequently. Just as pastors can overcome the resistance within our society to their Biblical counseling of their flock, so can Christian educators overcome the restrictions that have been placed on their ministries by training themselves to be Biblical counselors. A key to success in this endeavor is to remember that a "Christian counselor" is not necessarily a Biblical counselor. Special education teachers who strive to assist the student in the remediation of his emotional disorders must not simply be Christian counselors—they must be Biblical counselors.

Marty Von (personal communication to author) of Northland Baptist Bible College has said, "Counseling is listening until a Biblical parallel comes to mind, then sharing that parallel in the power of the Spirit." This is a good simple guideline for the Christian teacher who finds a need to counsel his students. Admittedly, special education for the emotionally disordered child includes more than "regular teaching" plus counseling. But far greater progress is made in the Christian school than in the secular program when Biblical principles are made clear both in the academic subjects and in classroom interaction.

The Role of Christian Teachers

Christian school teachers should not sell themselves short because their secular counterparts claim superior credentials. Christian special education teachers with sufficient ability and education in their field have the added advantage of spiritual wisdom and discernment. The track record of secular special education is not very impressive in the area of emotional disorders. In fact, we suspect that some special education techniques (e.g., reality therapy, life space interviewing) felt to be panaceas for disabled students have inflicted damage in classrooms for some time. Thomas H. Gallaudet, whose work with deaf persons is renowned even today, introduced the sight-reading method for the deaf as early as 1830. His influence on Horace Mann through their Unitarian connections led Mann to embrace the sight-reading method in the emerging school system as early as 1838 (Blumenfeld, 1981). Thus phonics training was on the way out because a "special educator" had discovered a pragmatic method that looked good to another self-proclaimed educational expert. Interestingly, the first line of Gallaudet's primer was "Frank had a dog; his name was Spot." Look familiar?

Although the fact is an embarrassment to those who know it, it should be pointed out that another innovative "science" was adopted by the Normal School at Lexington, Massachusetts—where Mann was Secretary of the Board of Education—that same year. The science was phrenology. Granted, this event is not recent, and Christian school teachers should not assume that secular errors guarantee the correctness of Christian methods. But, with proper preparation, the Christian special education teacher will be able to define and address the emotional disorders that are not biophysical in nature. Of course,

> A Christian school should be concerned about the
> professional as well as the spiritual preparation of

its teachers. Knowledge of the student and mastery of the subject to be taught as well as of the methodology of its presentation are necessary for effective teaching. Jesus Christ knew His students (John 2:25) and His subject matter and was competent in every conceivable legitimate technique of imaginative, resourceful teaching. He, therefore, taught with a commanding assurance and vigor that amazed the multitudes (Matthew 7:29). No amount of carefully prepared educational materials, however important they may be as tools, can compensate for the lack of a carefully prepared teacher: one who has followed the spiritual and professional example of the Master. (Bell, Frederick, Fremont, Horton, Rumminger, Salter, & Smith, 1978, pp. 10-11)

The public school system should have nothing to fear from the healthy competition of a nearby Christian special education program that is successfully teaching emotionally disordered students. As Dobson and Bauer (1990) have said,

> The beauty of the free enterprise system is that it pits the wisdom, ingenuity, hard work, and dedication of one entrepreneur against his competitor across town . . . It is time for the educational consumer—the parent—to be served by an enthusiastic, entrepreneurial school district that desperately wants to please him or her. (p. 266)

Nowhere is the Christian school more able to provide the necessary pressure that the public system needs to improve its record than in the area of emotional disorders. It is no doubt naively optimistic to hope that it would recognize the need to foster the spiritual nurture which can most effectively correct these disorders.

Adolescent Instabilities

It needs to be understood that emotional instabilities are present to some degree as a natural part of adolescence. Strict Christian parents sometimes expect their children to be able to bypass these struggles. A spiritually minded adolescent who has loving, supportive parents should be able to grow into adulthood with a minimum of turmoil, with normal "ups and downs" accepted. But some students in Christian schools have a difficult time, and some Christian homes are not very supportive during this period of growth, even though they desire a Christian education for their child. Reaves and Austin (1990), in their recent guidebook for parents, offer this encouragement:

> It is not always easy to tell the difference between normal adolescent behavior and serious trouble. The smoothest adolescence is rough. Physical changes occur faster than kids can adjust to them, and as a result young people often feel abnormal, even monstrous. They don't feel in control. Their feet are too big. They outgrow their clothes overnight. For boys and girls alike, sexual desire becomes part of their lives at a time when they are likely to feel undesirable or at least insecure about their looks. New hormones are coursing through their veins, and the mix changes daily. Hormones affect behavior; mood changes may occur every few minutes. Your daughter was squealing with delight a moment ago, but now she's in her bedroom sobbing, and she doesn't know herself what brought on the change . . . A physical, emotional, and social upheaval of this magnitude is going to cause pain, and the pain is almost certain to surface somewhere. Often it results in behavior that adults find baffling or appalling. (p. 4)

Although the description of adolescence above was written by secular authors, it is helpful to consider. Young parents are sometimes young Christians, and they may need patient help from the pastor and school administrator in coming to a balanced view of adolescence. It is not uncommon for parents of adolescents to have unreasonable expectations that produce frustration when the inconsistency of their young people has them baffled. These same authors have written, although omitting the fact of sin, that "exasperating as normal adolescent behavior can be, it's basically harmless. Serious trouble is not. It may be life-threatening. At the very least, the adolescent's capacity for developing into a responsible adult may be at stake" (Reaves & Austin, 1990, p. 5). But, whether offering a program of remediation for emotional disorders that merely impair educational progress, or perhaps offering more intensive intervention to correct or control deviant behavior that has put the child's life in danger, the non-Biblical approach consistently fails to address the root problem.

Genuine Hope

Christian education alone offers genuine hope for these children. Those who become "well-adjusted" according to acceptable secular standards cannot be shown to have improved because of these programs of remediation, and many are pressured further into wrong choices in behavior. Christian schools must reach out to those with emotional disorders, giving them Christ's message of God's love and man's responsibility, offering hope and help for effective and useful living.

Just as children with physical or mental limitations can learn to glorify God through their difficulties, so can children who have suffered debilitating emotional pain. Some well-meaning Christian authors (Bobgan & Bobgan, 1985) have told us that we must experience the depth of our emotional pain in order to be "healed." They have us probing the depth of our pain instead of the height of God's love. We do not have to encourage a student to search for the deepest experience of his emotional suffering in order to help him accept his circumstances and glorify God. What is true for a physically handicapped child is true for an emotionally disordered child. He can cope—he must—and God will help him. It is absurd that some adult Christians spend so much time and energy focusing on "emotional problems" when there are others with physical and mental problems that will limit them throughout life who are happy and well-adjusted. Those with healthy bodies and sound minds cannot be allowed to waste those assets on self- pity because their feelings have been hurt.

Berg (personal communication to the author, 1990) has pointed out the Christian response to suffering:

> We cannot expect God to make us an exception to the suffering and disappointment that comes from being a part of a creation that groaneth and travaileth. He expects us rather to be examples of how men can live honorably before God in spite of what we are going through. Our courage to go on doesn't come from the hope that all the pain will go away (it will always hurt when a girl recalls the abuse of her father; it will always hurt when a boy remembers that he grew up without a father). Our courage must come from the fact that we have Immanuel (God with us) in the hurt and pain. We, like Paul, can even learn to "glory in our infirmities" especially as the "outward man" perishes and the "inward man is renewed day by day."

The fiery trial is not alien to the Christian life; it is basic to it (I Peter 4:12-13). It is no less appropriate to say to an angry and bitter person that he should accept his circumstances in the grace of God than it is to say the same to a person with no legs.

The Use of Scripture: Four Steps

Intervention in the Christian school milieu for emotionally disordered students must include consistent use of Scripture, not psychological "therapy." The Scripture is sufficient:

> All scripture is given by inspiration of God, and is profitable for doctrine, for reproof, for correction, for instruction in righteousness: that the man of God may be perfect, thoroughly furnished unto all good works. (II Timothy 3:16-17)

These verses teach the nature, purpose, and use of the Scriptures: the nature of Scripture—inspired by God; the purpose of Scripture—to mature and prepare the man of God for every good work; the use of Scripture—to teach, reprove, correct, and instruct in righteousness. To prepare the special education teacher for work with emotionally disordered students, we must look in detail at this fourfold use of Scripture.

The Scriptures are profitable for doctrine. To understand that the Scripture is sufficient to correct emotional disorders that are not biophysical, the teacher must have a conviction that the Scriptures are profitable for teaching, or doctrine, as the only source of revealed truth. The two main truths that the Christian teacher must be thoroughly familiar with are man's need of salvation and man's need of sanctification. Man's condition is clearly stated in Romans 3:10-12, 23; 6:23. God's solution to this condition is found in Romans 5:8; John 3:16a. Man's responsibility to God's solution is in Romans 10:9-10, 13; John 3:16b. God's response to man's responsible acceptance of God's solution is I John 5:11-13; John 5:24. These few verses should be readily available to any Christian teacher—most effectively through memorization. They simply and succinctly present the Bible doctrine of salvation. The educator who dismisses the primacy of this truth is not involved in Christian education regardless of the position held or the title claimed.

Similarly, the doctrine of sanctification must be clearly understood and effectively taught to emotionally disordered students. Often, those teachers who are proficient at a simple presentation of the plan of salvation are unprepared or unaware of the need to lead their students into God's plan of sanctification. I Thessalonians 4:3a and 5:23 state the Biblical mandate for us to pray and prepare to help students in this area of growth. God's goal for us in sanctification is change and growth in love for God and others (Matthew 22:37-40; I Timothy 1:5). The means through which He accomplishes this goal in us are the Word of God and the Spirit of God (John 17:15-17; II Peter 1:3; 3:18; II Corinthians 3:18). The method with which we cooperate is the putting off of the old man, renewing our minds, and putting on the new man (Ephesians 4:22-24). Other major passages of Scripture which must be understood by the emotionally disordered child include Romans 6-8, 12; Galatians 5; Ephesians 4-6, Philippians 3-4; Colossians 3; I Thessalonians 4; James 1, 4; I Peter 1-2; II Peter 1. "The themes found in these passages must dominate the believer's thoughts and actions if Biblical change is to take place" (Berg, personal communication to the author). The emotionally disordered student needs, above all, sanctification. What he needs is to be "perfect[ed] in love" (I John 4:18).

Of course, these are not the only doctrines that we should include in the IEP of an emotionally disordered student, but they are of primary importance in the remediation of his disorder. Christ is the answer to his root problem; Christlikeness is the answer to his surface problems. Having based the response to the disorder on the Biblical doctrines of salvation and sanctification, the Christian teacher or parent can proceed to the reproofs of Scripture to help the student understand the function of the human conscience and assist him in strengthening it through obedience to the Word of God.

The Scriptures are profitable for reproof. The reproofs of Scripture are the most effective tool available to the Christian educator to bring the student to a realization of behavior that is causing guilt and/or other emotional difficulties. *Reprove* means "to make a charge of guilt and prove it is true; to prove guilty." Through reproof, God uses His Word to work in the conscience of man so that he can understand his responsibility for unacceptable behavior. Those who deny God's work in man's conscience will not be able to understand the normal function of emotions—especially those emotions that are considered by educators and psychologists to be disordered.

An understanding of the function of the conscience is essential for proper use of the conscience. Far from being the result of a conflict between the "id and the ego," the conscience is in a very real sense the "alarm system" placed within man by his Creator to alert man to behavior that is unacceptable to God. This internal alarm system works in two ways: by judging our actions and by making us uncomfortable or miserable. Scriptural support for the fact of these functions is strong. Hebrews 5:13-14 tells us that the conscience "bears witness" to sin. Psalm 51:3 demonstrates that it puts sin "before" us. I John 3:21 reveals that it condemns or confirms our actions, II Corinthians 1:12 that it "testifies" of our behavior. Not only does the human conscience judge our actions; it also produces an emotional response within us.

As an afflicter of human emotions, the conscience produces the symptoms of emotional disorders. Proverbs 28:1 speaks of the fear of consequences that is necessary to correct behavior. John 8:9 tells us of the shame that the Pharisees experienced. David writes in Psalm 32:3-4 and 38:10, 17 of the literal, physical pain produced by afflictions in the conscience. An incomplete work of the conscience is referred to in II Corinthians 7:9-10 as the "sorrow of the world" which "worketh death," but a sensitive and mature work of the conscience is a "godly sorrow" which leads "to repentance." It is a serious error to succumb to the psychological insistence that the pangs of conscience are the problem rather than the symptom and that they must be relieved immediately at all costs.

The human conscience can, of course, be "adjusted." Unfortunately, it can be corrupted by repeated sinning as surely as it can be fine-tuned to effective use by repeated obedience to the Word of God. Instead of exercising the senses (conscience) in accordance with Hebrews 5:13-14, it is possible to sear the conscience—to cauterize it so that it does not feel pain at all. The conscience can become defiled (Titus 1:15), and it can be "past feeling" (Ephesians 4:19). The condition of too many students in our schools is that "their foolish hearts are darkened" (Romans 1:21). With Biblical reproof, they can be helped as their own consciences "accuse or excuse" them (Romans 2:14-15). Rather than denying the pain of conscience as a mere emotional disorder, students can learn the healthy benefit of "taking heed" to it "according to thy word" (Psalm 119:9).

The Scriptures are profitable for correction. Not only do we have in the Bible the doctrine that tells us what is right and the reproof for our consciences that tells us what is wrong; we have the corrective truths that tell us how to make it right. The word that appears as "correction" in our Bibles means "making something stand up again; righting something." The term deals with the Biblical response to guilt that has been proved by the Word of God. Although there are numerous approaches offered within education to remedy emotional disorders, the only truly effective method of correction is the Bible method—confessing and forsaking sin. Confession and repentance are the only two actions available to man that truly remove the emotional pain that unacceptable behavior produces.

Confession of sin includes repentance. To confess sin means agreement with the charges made against us. Confession is agreement with God that we have been proved guilty by the Word of God, or agreement with our human accusers that we have been proved guilty by the evidence. True confession is far different from the "apologies" many have been taught to offer. An "apology" can easily turn into a defense. Those who would Biblically confess must be taught to avoid statements like "I apologize" or "I'm sorry." They must not be allowed to offer statements like "If I wronged you I'm sorry" or "I'm sorry if I hurt you." Instead, the student with emotional pain due to guilt must Biblically confess by declaring, "God has shown me I was wrong when I . . . Will you forgive me?" Biblical evidence for the demand that we confess our guilt is found in Psalm 32:5; 38:18; 51:1-4; Luke 15:18; I John 1:7-10; and similar passages.

To complete the process, the repentance of confession must be followed by the reconciliation of forgiveness. Isaiah 43:25 and 55:7 and I John 2:1-2 demonstrate the essential principle of forgiveness and reconciliation. The goal of confession/repentance is the reconciliation of the estranged relationship. When we ask forgiveness, we require the offended party to respond but then not to raise the issue again. In fact, God places reconciliation above worship in Matthew 5:23-24. Our belief is that many who suffer from emotional disorders actually suffer the conviction of sin or the frustration of incomplete "apologies." They have tried to accept responsibility for an offense but have phrased their "apology" in terms that accused the offended party or made it impossible for the offended party to know that they were truly accepting responsibility. To the pain of conscience for the offense is added the anger over not being forgiven and the resulting guilt that anger produces.

After confessing comes forsaking—an essential part of Biblical correction. If a person does not forsake wrong behavior, his relief from painful emotions will be only temporary. As with confessing, forsaking is understood best in the light of Proverbs 28:13. Ephesians 4:17-32 instructs us in "putting off the old man." Forsaking sinful behavior is the essence of "putting off the old man." Since correcting involves putting things back (as far as possible) to where they were before the sinful pattern developed, forsaking sin will include any or all of the following actions: restitution (Luke 19:8), restriction, and removal of the physical things that are connected with the temptation. The student must come to understand that repaying those offended is necessary to correction. Restriction of the liberties that led the student into sinful behavior is often essential to protect him from failure in the future. Voluntary removal of those sources of temptation that support the sin habit is required for lasting victory. If these restrictions or the removal of supporting things or circumstances is imposed on the student against his will, it will not correct the behavior but will instead create a new area of failure in the student's life. An unwillingness to correct wrong behavior or be corrected by others is an indicator of incomplete reproof, inadequate teaching about the wrongness of the behavior, or the student's incomplete repentance.

The Scriptures are profitable for instruction. Herein lies the key to emotional disorders—dealing with the root problem that produced the emotional difficulty in the first place. Not only must we become aware of the immediate problem and correct it, we must also lead the student into the proper behavior that will prevent failure in the future. We replace the wrong patterns of behavior with correct ones through instruction. The goal of the Christian teacher who would help a student with an emotional disorder is not to make him feel better, but to help him live better, to be better, to learn the ways of God that bring true joy into human life.

The Bible itself makes it quite clear that there is a specific method we are to employ in order to have the full benefit of the changes that Scripture works within us. We must fully incorporate the words of Scripture into our hearts and minds (meditation), and then we are to discipline ourselves in daily obedience to its principles and precepts (habituation). Unless both of these elements of instruction are properly incorporated into the life of the individual who needs help, behavioral change and the resulting emotional improvement will be incomplete. A failure in this critical area of "instruction" is the reason so many Christians fail to see lasting improvement in their lives and why others do not believe that such change is even possible. It is the Word of God that tells us what is right, where we are wrong by that right standard, and how to get right again. The Word of God is also the only true source of permanent change. The instruction that follows the decision to change behavior is the means to this permanent change. The Christian school is uniquely equipped to provide this instruction as a normal part of its curriculum, and it is especially capable of fine-tuning the needed instruction within the parameters of an IEP for special education application. In order to help the administrator or teacher make this application, we must look more closely at the meditation and habituation processes.

Meditation

We have suggested that emotional disorders (those that are not the result of biophysical causes) are the spiritual "pain" resulting from behavior that must be changed. We should also be able to agree that behavior is the result of the thinking process. Wrong behavior grows out of wrong thinking. Right thinking does not guarantee that right choices will follow, but it makes them much more likely. Thus, the root problem is in the concepts or ideas from which the person reasons to conclusions. These conclusions contribute to the decisions that control behavior and produce emotions. Bringing the mental processes under the influence and eventual control of the truth of Scripture involves the mind and will. Right thinking is not just a mental process, but a volitional process as well. The student must be encouraged to apply himself in every area of responsibility. He needs to understand that any point of unwillingness in submission or any undiscipline in duty will contribute to failure and discouragement, repeating the emotional pattern from which he seeks relief.

The truth here is found stated succinctly in James 1:21-25:

> Wherefore lay apart all filthiness and superfluity of naughtiness [put off the old man], and receive with meekness the engrafted word [be renewed in the spirit of your mind], which is able to save your souls. But be ye doers of the word [put on the new man], and not hearers only, deceiving your own selves. For if any be a hearer of the word, and not a doer, he is like unto a man beholding his natural face in a glass: For he beholdeth himself, and goeth his way, and straightway forgetteth what manner of man he was. But whoso looketh into the perfect law of liberty, and continueth therein, he being not a forgetful hearer, but a doer of the work, this man shall be blessed in his deed.

These same elements are stated in Ephesians 4:17-32 regarding the responsibility to put off the old man and put on the new. Biblical instruction is the means whereby we "put on the new man."

The first responsibility is meditation. This activity corresponds to "hearing" in the verses above. Of course, mere hearing in the normal sense will not produce memorization. But since the inappropriate behavior has become habitual, the hearing of correcting truth must also become habitual. This will not be possible unless the truths of the Word of God are in the mind and available for the Holy Spirit to call up instantly. Memorization is the only means through which this can be done everywhere and at any time. Otherwise, meditation will be a temporary activity practiced only when it is possible to have an open Bible in hand. Memorization seems painfully like busywork to the average student and even more so to emotionally disordered children. It may be necessary to incorporate some sort of reward system for positive reinforcement until the actual benefits of the meditation process become recognizable to the student.

By no means do we intend the concept of meditation to be understood in the sense that it is used in Transcendental Meditation or encouraged by Eastern mystic religions or the New Age human potential and creativity movements. These false teachings hold to the view that the one meditating is either to focus on nothing (empty his mind) or to focus on himself to discover his own "potential." These ideas are contrary to Scripture and have nothing in common with Biblical meditation. They are practices in which no believer should ever participate. Much television watching is similar to this kind of meditation in that the viewer is not generally required to think, but simply to allow his emotions to experience the material presented. Biblical meditation is the opposite: a process of concentration that is to be continued until change occurs.

In James 1:21-25 we find the basis for concentration and continuation in meditation. The activity of concentration (v. 25) is *parakupto* "looketh," meaning to lean over and peer intently within. The object of our concentration is the "perfect law of liberty" or the Word of God. The goal of concentration is to become a "doer of the work" or to have a changed life. As Berg (personal communication to the author) has stated, "Christian meditation is concentration (rational, intensive thought) on a specific content (the Word of God) that leads to reflective inner conversation with myself and positive Biblical change in action." For further study and application of this principle, the teacher should focus on the student's understanding of Joshua 1:8; Psalm 1; 19:14; 49:3; 119:9-11; and Proverbs 15:28.

Mere concentration will be helpful, but continuation is essential for the full benefit to be realized. Concentration must be continued until what we study is permanent ("not a forgetful hearer"). We must continue in concentration until what we study is productive ("doer of the work"). The young person we seek to help with his emotional disorder must be taught the truth of I Timothy 4:15-16: "Meditate upon these things [concentration]; give thyself wholly to them; that thy profiting may appear to all [productive]. Take heed unto thyself, and unto the doctrine; continue in them [continuation]: for in doing this thou shalt both save [spare] thyself, and them that hear thee." The most effective method for Biblical meditation of which we are aware was developed by Berg (in preparation). The method he uses, and with which he has seen lasting results in the lives of hundreds of students, is called the Memorize, Analyze, and Personalize (MAP) Method; it appears in Appendix 2 at the end of this book. We recommend that the MAP method be incorporated directly into the IEP of the emotionally disordered student, with specific passages of Scripture assigned as a normal part of the student's curriculum.

Lasting Change

In addition to "hearing," the student has a responsibility for "doing." Whereas hearing is the process of being renewed in the spirit of the mind, doing is the process of putting on the new man. Painful emotions will not be replaced with pleasant and appropriate emotions until inappropriate behavior (the old man) is replaced with proper behavior (the new man). A Biblical view of human nature includes a number of factors involved in lasting change. There are **debilitating factors** which include our sinful nature and sinful habits. There are **facilitating factors** which include truths we must know and decisions we must make. It is essential for the teacher and parent to understand these factors, and it may be appropriate to include instruction about them in the schedule of verses the student is to memorize.

If the child is very young, he may be able to be helped by a simple application of the Biblical principles that govern these factors of lasting change without a thorough understanding of the factors themselves. In such cases a simple reward/punishment plan is helpful so long as it is not taken to the extreme of "behavior modification" psychology. It will be essential for the child's parents to understand the factors for change, however, and to be helped to change their own methods of dealing with the emotionally disordered child. They must understand that continued conflict between their methods and God's methods will most likely add to their child's emotional disorder. If the student is an adolescent, it will be helpful to instruct the child in the elements involved in lasting change, since his behavior is primarily under his own control rather than under the control of others. To decide what specifically to teach a student about how this process actually works, first determine the child's ability to take responsibility for his own behavior: the greater the child's ability to be responsible for himself, the greater the amount of information he needs. As with every other academic discipline in special education, the less ability the child has to make rational choices about his behavior, the more he will need to be taught through direct instruction and repetition rather than reason.

We turn now to the **debilitating factors** of our sinful nature and our sinful habits. A review of the Biblical teaching on these subjects will help the teacher properly evaluate the student's specific needs. The Bible clearly teaches that men have the capacity to leave God out of their lives and concentrate on pleasing self (Romans 6-8). This capacity is sometimes called "the old man" (Romans 6:6; Colossians 3:9) to emphasize its source, Adam. It is sometimes called "the flesh" (Romans 7:18; Ephesians 2:3). This capacity within man is in constant conflict with the new nature within believers (Galatians 5:17; Romans 7:15-25; 8:6). Thus, our sinful nature produces conflict and struggle within us as a normal state of existence. The parent or teacher of an emotionally disordered child should not expect unpleasant emotions to disappear entirely, any more than a doctor would expect his patient never to experience pain. The goal is to help the student first understand the behavior-to-emotion link and then use the emotional signal to alert him to correct his behavior. Of course some emotions are not the result of wrong behavior. Sadness, loneliness, frustration, and many other emotions are the normal response to life's circumstances. But these are not emotional disorders; they need to be endured rather than remedied.

Not only must the teacher consider the factor of the student's sinful nature, but he must also focus on specific sinful habits with which the student needs help. Our sinful nature manifests itself in habit patterns that further contribute to emotional pain. Man has the capacity to learn to respond automatically and comfortably instead of deliberately and awkwardly. As the student has "exercised" himself in a particular manner of life, so he will tend to behave in similar situations. The following passages address this capacity within us.

1. Jeremiah 13:23—"accustomed [trained] to do evil"
2. Jeremiah 22:21—"manner [course of life] from thy youth"
3. I Corinthians 5:33—"evil communications [companions] corrupt good manners [moral habits]"
4. I Timothy 4:7—"exercise [train] thyself . . . unto godliness"
5. II Peter 2:14—"an heart exercised with covetous practices [trained in greed]"
6. Hebrews 5:13-14—"senses exercised [trained] to discern good and evil"

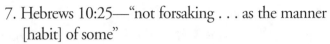

7. Hebrews 10:25—"not forsaking . . . as the manner [habit] of some"

8. Hebrews 12:11—"unto them which are exercised [trained] thereby"

When sin has become habitual, it is often extremely difficult to impress the person with the "need to know" that alone will motivate him from within. The most damaging thing we could do to a student without this "need to know" about his sin habit, is to remove the God-given alarm which was designed to produce this need within him. It is our conviction that methods of helping students with emotional disorders that do not consider a relationship between emotional pain and sin habits are not only educationally unsound and ineffective, but in fact wicked.

Fortunately, there are encouraging elements involved in lasting change. The **facilitating factors** mentioned above include truths we must know and decisions we must make. The fundamental truth to be mastered is that we are no longer under the obligation to sin when we have been born again. Romans 6:6-12 explains that our union with Christ removes our obligation to sin. In this passage we are said to be "dead to sin." This does not mean that we cannot sin. Teachers and preachers sometimes err in insisting that "dead men do not do this" when correcting people about sinful behavior. True, but they are not physically dead; they still have the capacity to sin because they have a human will. Death always means separation of some kind. Here the death of our "old man" means that we have been separated from the obligation to obey its lusts. The old nature is now like a deposed dictator who has been overthrown by a new leader. We may choose to take orders from him if we desire to do so, but we are under no obligation to obey him; we have a new ruler who will give us new orders and protect us from him whenever necessary.

A parallel truth to the fact of our deliverance from the obligation to sin is that this deliverance does not automatically empower us to obey God. Many who know that they are no longer under the bondage of sin mistakenly assume that doing right will therefore come automatically. Often emotional disorders are nothing more than an excessive load of guilt and despair because of the failures that grow out of this assumption. Although we are not obligated to obey our old nature, we are not empowered to obey God until we consciously choose to please God and yield control to Him. The Bible calls this "walking in the Spirit" or "being filled with [controlled by] the Spirit." Just as a willful choice to receive Christ begins the process we call sanctification, so do daily choices to submit and yield control to the Holy Spirit contribute to the process of sanctification.

There are three essential decisions that must be made as we act on the knowledge above. First, we must choose to please God by saying "no" to self (the flesh). We must choose to "put off the old man"; "deny self"; "take up the cross"; and so on. Second, we must choose to do the right thing regardless of how we feel (Romans 6:12-13, 19). Finally, we must choose to practice these two decisions with a conscious acknowledgment of the reality of the sinful nature and sinful habits. These three decisions will enable the student to develop new habit patterns. New habits coupled with the enablement of the Holy Spirit to respond to new difficulties will produce emotional stability. New habits take time to develop, however, especially when we are simultaneously trying to break old habits. The choice to practice the first two decisions of putting off the old man and putting on the new will require sustained, daily effort (Luke 9:23). The practice will be likely to fail without an understanding on the student's part of the need for endurance and on the parents' and teacher's part of the need for assistance.

Motivation and Endurance

Disciplined training will discourage the student unless he is meditating on the benefits of the practice and continuing in his desire to please God. The parents and teacher must use this desire as a motivator to the emotionally disordered child since his emotional responses in the past have been inappropriate. This desire is itself a "new habit" with which to replace the old emotional habits. Legalistic demands to discipline himself will discourage the emotionally immature or disordered child much more quickly than the average student. The family must be taught the truth of Hebrews 12:11-13—"Now no chastening [structured training] for the present seemeth to be joyous, but grievous: nevertheless afterward it yieldeth the peaceable fruit of righteousness [the goal] unto them which are exercised [trained] thereby. Wherefore lift up the hands which hang down, and the feeble knees; and make straight paths for your feet, lest that which is lame be turned out of the way; but let it rather be healed."

Endurance is one of the great needs in all Christian school students today. Hebrews 10:35-36 tells us to "cast not away therefore your confidence, which hath great recompense of reward. For ye have need of patience [endurance], that, after ye have done the will of God, ye might receive the promise." But endurance can be fostered in a student with the right kind of assistance from parents and teachers. Hebrews 10:24 reminds us to "consider one another to provoke unto love and to good works." Hebrews 3:13 admonishes us to "exhort one another daily, while it is called Today; lest any of you be hardened through the deceitfulness of sin."

As the sanctifying benefits of meditation and a renewed mind replace the old ways of thinking with correct thinking, the student will be helped significantly. The truths of the Word of God will yield within him a different way of looking at life

Figure 7.1

Carnal Response to Life's Problems

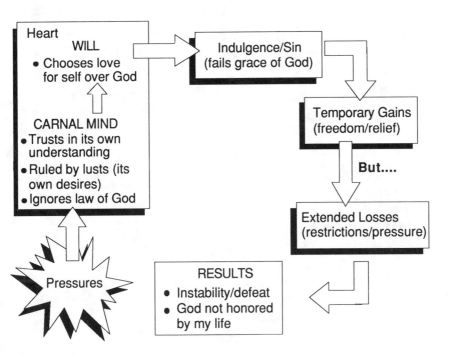

Figure 7.2

Spiritual Response to Life's Problems

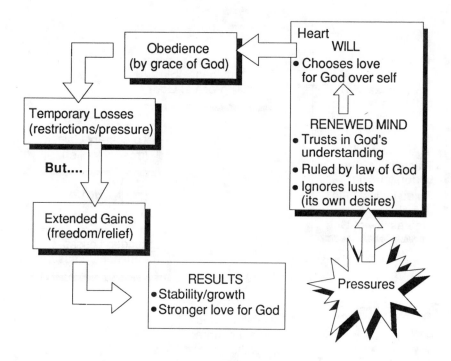

and its pressures. Rather than the habitual inappropriate emotional responses, the student will begin to experience proper emotions that he will understand are the God-given response mechanisms to circumstances and behavioral choices. Through meditation (concentration and continuation) he will begin to experience the blessings of a "renewed mind." Armed with this powerful spiritual weapon, he will be able to trust in God's understanding about the nature of and the solution to his problems (James 1:2-3; I Peter 1:6-7; II Corinthians 4:16-18). With a renewed mind, he will be very much aware of what the Law of God has to say about his trouble and will be able to be committed to handling it God's way. He will be able to say "No" to the lusts of his flesh and will choose to handle life's problems in a way that will produce growth and stability.

A Spiritual Choice

Emotional disorders are usually spiritual problems. A spiritual response to life's problems will produce spiritual growth. An emotional, un-Scriptural response that is based on a desire for relief in the emotions alone is a carnal response to life's problems; it will only produce additional emotional pain. In a very real sense, an emotional disorder is simply the result of a carnal response to pressure permitted by God—pressure intended to lead us to Himself in salvation or to further our progress in sanctification. We have found the accompanying diagrams, Figures 7.1-7.2, to be extremely helpful in explaining how the choices that we make contribute to the instruction phase of the four-step process of Scriptural modification of human behavior.

Biblical change is not a mysterious process, but it comes only through a commitment to do things God's way. He reminds us, "For my thoughts are not your thoughts, neither are your ways my ways, saith the Lord. For as the heavens are higher than the earth, so are my ways higher than your ways, and my thoughts than your thoughts" (Isaiah 55:8-9). The process of change and growth described in the last several pages grows out of the Scriptures themselves, where God tells us His ways. He has provided no alternative. Therefore, there is no reason for us to think that He will bless any competing methods that man can engineer, whether they be the simplistic efforts of emotionally disordered children or the complex psychological methodology of professional educators. Human emotions are God-given; when our sinful natures or the consequences of sin in general have produced disorders in emotions, they must be God-ordered.

References

Achenbach, T. M. (1985). *Assessment and taxonomy of child and adolescent psychopathology.* Beverly Hills, CA: Sage Publications.

Adams, J. E. (1973). *The Christian counselor's manual.* Grand Rapids, MI: Baker Book House.

Adams, J. E. (1970). *Competent to counsel.* Phillipsburg, NJ: Presbyterian & Reformed Publishing Co.

Bartlett, L. (1989). Disciplining handicapped students: Legal issues in light of Honing v. Doe. *Exceptional Children, 55,* 357-366.

Bell, R., Frederick, K., Fremont, W., Horton, R., Rumminger, E., Salter, G., & Smith, P. (1978). *The Christian philosophy of education.* Greenville, SC: Bob Jones University Press.

Berg, J. (Speaker). (in preparation). *Biblical counseling for Christian workers: A counseling training series.* (Videocassette Recording [no number]). Greenville, SC: Bob Jones University Press.

Blumenfeld, S. L. (1981). *Is public school education necessary?* Old Greenwich, CT: The Devin-Adair Co.

Bobgan, M., & Bobgan, D. (1985). *How to counsel from Scripture.* Chicago, IL: Moody Press.

Carbonell, M., & Rohm, R. (1990a). *How to be personality wise.* Atlanta, GA: Institute of Leadership Technology, Inc.

Carbonell, M., & Rohm, R. (1990b). *Personality Profile.* Minneapolis, MN: Carlson Learning Company/ Performax Systems International.

Dobson, J., & Bauer, G. L. (1990). *Children at risk: The battle for the hearts and minds of our kids.* Dallas, TX: Word Publishing.

Federal Register. (1977). *Implementation of part B of the Education of the Handicapped Act.* Washington, DC: Department of Health, Education, and Welfare, August 23.

Geier, J. (1990). *Taylor-Johnson Temperament Analysis.* Minneapolis, MN: Carlson Learning Company.

Hallahan, D. P., & Kauffman, J. M. (1988). *Exceptional children: Introduction to exceptional children* (4th ed.). Englewood Cliffs, NJ: Prentice Hall.

Howard, J. G. (1979). *The trauma of transparency: A Biblical approach to inter-personal communications.* Portland, OR: Multonomah Press.

Kauffman, J. M. (1989). *Characteristics of behavior disorders of children and youth* (4th ed.). Columbus, OH: Merrill.

Kirk, S., & Gallagher, J. J. (1983). *Educating exceptional children.* Boston, MA: Houghton Mifflin Co.

Krathwohl, D. R., Bloom, B. S., & Masia, B. B. (1964). *Taxonomy of educational objectives: The classification of educational goals—Handbook II: Affective Domain.* New York, NY: David McKay Company, Inc.

LaHaye, T. (1966). *Spirit-controlled temperament.* Wheaton, IL: Tyndale House Publishers.

Larkin, C. (1918). *Dispensational truth or God's plan and purpose in the ages.* Philadelphia, PA: Rev. Clarence Larkin.

Minirth, F. B. (1977). *Christian psychiatry.* Old Tappan, NJ: Fleming H. Revell Co.

Postman, N. (1985). *Amusing ourselves to death.* New York, NY: Penguin Books

Reaves, J., & Austin, J. B. (1990). *How to find help for a troubled kid: A parent's guide to programs and services for adolescents.* New York, NY: Henry Holt & Co.

Schlafly, P. (Ed.). (1984). *Child abuse in the classroom: Excerpts from Official Transcripts of Proceedings before the U. S. Department of Education.* Westchester, IL: Crossway Books.

Taylor, R. M., & Morrison, W. L. (1984). *Handbook for the Taylor-Johnson Temperament Analysis test.* Los Angeles, CA: Psychological Publications, Inc.

U.S. Department of Education. (1986). *To Assure Free Appropriate Public Education for all Handicapped Children. Eighth Annual Report to Congress on Implementation of the Education of the Handicapped Act,* Volume 1. Washington, DC: Government Printing Office.

CHAPTER EIGHT

Learning Disabilities

Ross Fichter

Introduction

*T*he classroom door bursts open. Philip, an eight-year-old bundle of energy, loudly stumbles to his desk. As he lays his books down, he explains, "I'm sorry I'm late, teacher; I couldn't find my other sneaker." After shoving his books into the desk and missing the coat hook with his jacket, he flings himself into his chair. Bible class is first. Philip's turn comes to recite his verse; he mumbles a few of the key words and dejectedly returns to his seat. He searches haphazardly through his desk for his pencil and comments loudly, "Someone has taken my pencil again." During reading class, he misses his turn to read because he lost his place while trying to tie his sneaker. Miss Anderson determines that today Philip will finish his workbook page, but she becomes discouraged after helping him with six words in the first sentence. She is sure he is just doing this for attention. After all, in math, Philip is one of only five children so far *who knows all his addition and subtraction facts. He just doesn't want to read.*

Does this sound familiar? Is Philip a rebellious child? How many teachers and parents in Christian schools are convinced their children are just lazy, or rebellious, or simply looking for attention, when the root problem is really a learning disability—a "hidden disability" as Wallace & McLoughlin (1979) call it? What is a learning disability? How do we know the difference between it and willful disobedience?

According to statistics from the U.S. Department of Education (1986), approximately 11% of the school-age population in public schools is disabled in some way. And almost half of all disabled students are learning disabled. Because of the preponderance of this special education category, Christian parents and educators should become more familiar with it. Therefore, this chapter focuses on definition, causes, characteristics, interventions, and diagnosis of learning disabilities.

Definition of Learning Disabilities

Educators, parents, and legislators have had a difficult time developing a definition that they can all agree upon. Many definitions have been proposed. We will consider the two used most frequently by educators today. In 1975, the Education for All Handicapped Children Act (Public Law 94-142) provided the following definition for a learning disability, which is the definition most frequently used by schools and service agencies today (Hallahan and Kauffman, 1988):

> "Specific learning disability" means a disorder in one or more of the basic psychological processes involved in understanding or in using language, spoken or written, which may manifest itself in an imperfect ability to listen, think, speak, read, write,

spell, or to do mathematical calculations. The term includes such conditions as perceptual handicaps, brain injury, minimal brain dysfunction, dyslexia, and developmental aphasia. The term does not include children who have learning problems which are primarily the result of visual, hearing, or motor handicaps, of mental retardation, of emotional disturbance, or of environmental, cultural, or economic disadvantage . . . [There must be] a severe discrepancy between achievement and intellectual ability in one or more of the following areas: oral expression, listening comprehension, written expression, basic reading skill, reading comprehension, mathematics calculation or mathematics reasoning. (Federal Register, December 29, 1977, p. 65083)

In 1981, the National Joint Committee for Learning Disabilities provided an alternative definition which is not as ambiguous as the federal definition. This definition reads:

Learning Disabilities is a generic term that refers to a heterogeneous group of disorders manifested by significant difficulties in the acquisition and use of listening, speaking, reading, writing, reasoning, or mathematical abilities. These disorders are intrinsic to the individual and presumed to be due to central nervous system dysfunction. Even though a learning disability may occur concomitantly with other handicapping conditions (e.g., sensory impairment, mental retardation, social and emotional disturbance) or environmental influences (e.g., cultural differences, insufficient/inappropriate instruction, psychogenic factors), it is not the direct result of those conditions or influences. (Hammill, Leigh, McNutt, & Larsen, 1981, p. 336)

Among the many definitions of learning disabilities, at least four elements or descriptors of learning disabled children have been more widely included and discussed than others: (a) psychological processing problems; (b) discrepancy between intelligence and achievement; (c) manifestation in academic areas; and (d) the intrinsic nature of a learning disability.

Psychological Processing Problems

Children who have a learning disability have problems in processing information presented to them. There is difficulty somewhere in the receiving, sorting or organizing, storing, or retrieving of information. Problems are present in one or more of these psychological processes. Presumably, this difficulty is due to a breakdown in one or more functions of the central nervous system. These disabilities are specific problems of an organic nature which are just as real as blindness or deafness. One young lady referred to her problem as having a "short circuit" in her electrical system.

Discrepancy Between Intelligence and Achievement

A discrepancy·is present between the learning potential and the achievement of learning disabled students. The intellectual ability of these children is often equal to that of an average or above-average student. A gap is present between the learning potential and the academic performance, especially in the areas affected by their learning disability. According to Sutton (1991), the minimum number of difference points between a child's IQ score and achievement scores that will qualify him for special education services in learning disabilities programs varies from one state to another. This discrepancy factor often causes considerable frustration to teachers and parents. They can recognize the learning potential of the child, but because of the inadequate performance shown by the child, teachers and parents become convinced that the student is rebellious or lazy. Sometimes these children will in fact become lazy or rebellious because of the frustration with failure. Much determination is required for them to try consistently when they experience constant failure. A former sixth-grade student would study for two or three hours for tests and work extra hours on homework assignments in hopes that a perfect score would surely be achieved this time! This student displayed confidence when entering the classroom, only to be disillusioned once again by failure. However, God enabled this unusually determined student to succeed in graduating from high school and college. Left to their own inventions, most children with learning disabilities give up after a few years of daily frustration. They would rather view themselves as lazy than "stupid," which is very often the underlying concept they have formed of themselves. The learning potential is present; help, however, is needed to develop this potential and achieve success.

Manifestation in Academic Areas

The definition of learning disabilities contained in PL 94-142 makes it clear that a learning disability will manifest itself in one or more specific academic areas or in the achievement of a specific academic learning task. Children with learning disabilities may experience more difficulty in one area of achievement than another. That is, there may be a problem in only reading, or math, or oral language. But their biggest area of academic difficulty is reading (Hallahan & Kauffman, 1988). Achievement in areas not affected by their learning disability may be average or above. More than one academic area can be affected by a learning disability; for example, a problem with auditory sequencing can interfere with the ability to remember the sequence of letters to correctly spell a word, the ability to follow oral directions, or the ability to remember the logical sequence of steps in a math problem. A graph of the achievement scores of these children often shows a great difference in the achievement levels for various academic areas.

Intrinsic Nature of a Learning Disability

All other factors which could contribute to the significant learning problems experienced by these children have been investigated and excluded. Physical examinations have excluded the possibility that sensory impairments or illness could be the cause of the difficulties in the learning process. The environment of the child has been evaluated for the presence of inadequate instruction, cultural or language difference, or inadequate social stimulation. Interviews with the child and his parents and teacher have discounted the possibility of emotional or family problems contributing to the learning problems. A full investigation of the child's environment and physical condition is completed for the purpose of excluding all other possible causes of the child's problems.

These four common elements bring us to the understanding that a problem exists which causes these children to live with frustration and failure every day from their first exposure to a formal learning situation. They do not understand why they cannot achieve and are confused about themselves. They are crying out for help in a world that they do not understand.

Specific Learning Disabilities

Hallahan and Kauffman (1988) state that "by definition, if there is no academic problem, a learning disability does not exist" (p. 126). Public Law 94-142 specifies seven specific academic areas in which a learning disability may occur. Five of these areas reflect language arts skills, and two have to do with mathematics skills. A description of each of these follows.

1. *Listening comprehension*—processing and remembering oral language
2. *Oral expression*—ability to express oneself orally, with the proper syntax, semantics, and pragmatics of oral language

3. ***Basic reading skills***—decoding skills, word attack and recognition skills from simple alphabetic recognition to structural analysis of complex sentences

4. ***Reading comprehension***—interpretation and meaning of words, phrases, and sentences of written language

5. ***Written expression***—handwriting skills, spelling, and beginning writing skills that convey simple thoughts as well as abstract ideas

6. ***Mathematics calculation***—basic facts and computation skills including problems using basic mathematical operations (addition, subtraction, multiplication, division) as well as other lower-order math skills

7. ***Mathematics reasoning***—ability to solve word problems in math and understanding the logic behind them

Causes of Learning Disabilities

Although professionals do not know all the causes of learning disabilities, there is evidence to support the fact that certain influences can put a child at high risk for the development of a learning disability. These include environmental influences, heredity, and damage to the central nervous system.

Environment

We do not know exactly how much or in what ways the environment of a child can cause him to develop a learning disability. Research has proved that malnutrition and insufficient stimulation in infancy and early childhood can interfere with normal development in a child. In 1973, Cruickshank and Hallahan summarized the available research on the effects of environmental deprivation and malnutrition. On studies conducted on animals and children, a definite relationship between malnutrition and learning disabilities could not be established. However, the majority of evidence suggests that severe malnutrition at an early age can affect the central nervous system, thereby affecting the learning and development of the child. In *Early Intervention for Handicapped and At-Risk Children*, Peterson (1987) states, "Children reared in unnurturing, depriving, and substandard environments are more likely to develop poorly and to show depressed intellectual, language, and academic performance" (p. 139). It follows that sufficient nurturing and stimulation in infancy and early childhood may reduce the potential for a child to develop a learning disability.

Allergies to substances in the child's environment have been cited by some as a possible cause of learning disabilities, but more extensive research is needed to determine the influence of allergies in this area. It has been our experience that some children have performed considerably better when allergenic substances have been removed from the environment. However, it is unknown whether these have been the cause of their problems or an intensifying factor. Treating the allergies will at least cause the child to feel better and therefore perform better in school. This is also true of children who have sensitivities to certain substances such as sugar and artificial food colorings and additives. For example, one student ingested artificial food additives and became almost unteachable. His attention was very limited, hyperactivity increased, and learning declined drastically. His statement that he felt as though there were "worms crawling under his skin" was believable to all who observed him. Obviously, this boy's learning disability was affected by his environment though not necessarily caused by it.

Heredity/Genetics

Some types of learning disabilities may be inherited. Although the research in this area is not conclusive at this time, certain types of disabilities in reading, writing, and spelling have been found to run in families. Some types of learning disabilities have occurred throughout several generations of a family, especially in males. In a genetic study conducted in 1950, Hallgren reported that out of the 276 children and their families studied, 116 demonstrated significant reading, spelling, and writing problems (labeled as dyslexia). Of these 116, 88% reported other family members with learning disabilities.

Hermann (1969) conducted a study of identical twins. This study included 12 sets of identical twins in which both were classified as dyslexic. Out of 33 sets of fraternal twins, Hermann found that in 11 sets both twins had reading disabilities. Finally, we are aware of one couple in our community who adopted seven children, all natural children of the same mother and father. The adoptive mother told us that each of the seven children has been evaluated and classified as learning disabled in the public schools. This example, along with the studies cited above, suggests that some types of learning disabilities may be inherited.

Central Nervous System Damage

Damage to the central nervous system can be a result of trauma or disease before, during, or after birth. Certain circumstances during the prenatal period can result in injury to the central nervous system of the child. Some of these examples include nutritional deficiencies in the mother, presence of infectious diseases (e.g., from rubella, certain viruses, influenza, and chronic diseases), difference in Rh blood factor, mother's use of some types of medication, and tobacco, drug, or alcohol abuse by the mother. During birth the infant's central nervous system can be affected by long and hard labor, lack of oxygen to the brain, or injuries from medical instruments. Premature, breech, or dry birth can also result in trauma. During infancy or early childhood, damage can occur from brain concussions that result from accidents. Brain damage can also occur from oxygen deprivation (e.g., from encephalitis, meningitis, measles, scarlet fever, or accidental poisoning).

Research is continuing the search for possible causes of learning disabilities for the purpose of prevention more than cure. We discuss these possible causes in order to alert parents and teachers to certain conditions which, if present, may indicate the possibility of a learning disability.

Contributing Factors

Some conditions, which are not necessarily causes of a learning disability, can contribute to the severity of the disability or compound the effects of it. However, the presence of these conditions does not always result in the development of a disability. These predisposing or contributing factors generally emanate from the physical or psychological condition of the child. Unlike the causes of a disability, these factors can some-times be remediated to reduce their effect on the child.

Many physical conditions can influence the ability of a child to learn. The presence of such conditions as visual and auditory defects (including blindness and deafness), confused spatial orientation, mixed laterality, hyperactivity or hypoactivity, poor body image, and poor motor coordination can contribute greatly to the learning problems of a child with a learning disability. Other physical conditions which can be included in this list are poor health, physical disabilities, or developmental disabilities (e.g., cerebral palsy). Very often at-tention deficit disorders and emotional problems or disorders can accompany a learning disability.

The child's environment also can contribute greatly to the problems being experienced at school. Some of these factors include poor nutrition, lack of proper rest, poor teaching, and social deprivation.

It is not always necessary for the teacher to know the exact cause of a child's disability in order to help him learn. However, the teacher needs to be aware of any predisposing or contributing factors present. These factors often need to be remediated so that acceptable progress can occur. Teachers need to know the areas in which disabilities exist and how to remediate and teach to compensate for these disabilities. Our goal is to help the student accept himself as God created him and to aid him in becoming all that God has planned for him to become.

Characteristics of Learning Disabled Students

How can we recognize a child who has the potential for a learning disability? At the elementary school level there are some common characteristics that should alert us to the possibility of a problem, especially when we observe a combination of several on a regular basis or over a long period of time. Common characteristics of learning disabled children appear in Appendix 3.

Learning disabled students in secondary grades share some of the same characteristics as elementary-age learning disabled students, yet the learning disabled adolescent probably has more difficulty in learning than do younger learning disabled students. Not only does he have to deal with the problems associated with his disability, but he also has to face the pressure and the problems of growing up. Adolescence is a transition period between childhood and adulthood during which many changes take place physically, cognitively, emotionally, socially, and spiritually. Growth rate increases and physical appearance changes; abstract thinking abilities develop; sexual maturity takes place; peer pressure increases and social acceptance becomes more important; self-consciousness increases and a new self-image develops; and attitudes are established toward God and authority. These changes just add to the pressure and the problems that an already frustrated learning disabled student has to face, and they make it even harder for him to concentrate on the already difficult task of learning.

In her book, *Learning Disabilities: Theories, Diagnosis, and Teaching Strategies*, Lerner (1985) characterizes students with learning disabilities as "passive learners" (p. 244). Other professionals have stated that because of their lack of ability to come up with valid solutions when presented with problems, many learning disabled students have developed an attitude of "learned helplessness" (Torgesen, 1982; Wiens, 1983). When faced with a problem, they wait for someone to give them the solution or work it out for them instead of trying to figure it out for themselves. In so doing, not only do they continue to struggle with many unsolved problems, but they also suppress the development of their creative thinking abilities. Some common responses of learning disabled students, when asked a question or posed with a problem, might be "I don't know," or "I can't do it," or "I can't figure it out"; and then they give up. For the most part, they are telling the truth. They have not learned how to figure things out or to solve problems because they have stopped trying to think. In the past, failure has been the most common outcome of their efforts. Consequently, to avoid further failure and embarrassment, they do all they can to avoid tasks in which they will be required to think.

As a result of their past failures, many learning disabled students exhibit poor self-concept and poor self-esteem (Lerner, 1985). They become discouraged and frustrated very easily when they cannot do something, and they develop the attitude that they are not good at anything. Often, because parents and teachers do not understand the problems that learning disabled students have or why they exist, these students have the feeling of being constantly nagged about their behavior and lack of achievement. They feel that they cannot do anything right. The foundation of this attitude lies not in their disability or in their lack of achievement, or even in the way other people treat them. Rather, it is their lack of understanding of God and His working in their lives. These students are the way they are because God wanted them to be that way in order to fulfill some special purpose in His plan. A self-centered outlook on life is what creates feelings of worthlessness in these students because they cannot be and do what they wish they could. Actually, the problem is not a poor "self-concept"; it could be better termed a poor "God concept." God does not make mistakes. Only when they accept themselves as God made them and accept His will for their lives will they get over this poor self-concept and be able to accomplish what God has for them to do. Learning disabled students can claim as well as anyone, "I *can* do all things *through Christ* which strengtheneth me" (Philippians 4:13).

Another problem that many learning disabled students face is lack of social acceptance resulting from poor social skills. They have difficulty understanding the feelings and reactions of others. Therefore, they cannot respond correctly to either positive or negative feedback from their peers. These students overreact in many situations, causing others to avoid them. As a result, they do not make friends easily and they cannot maintain the few friendships that they do manage to establish. Not all learning disabled students have trouble in this area, however. A person's inadequate social behavior depends on the interaction of many different variables—his personality, the type and degree of his disability, and his social environment and background, as well as many unknown variables. All of these factors must be taken into account when determining the cause of social ineptitude. Whatever the cause, deficiencies in social skills play a big part in the achievement of a learning disabled student.

A great many learning disabled students have attentional problems. The problem is not that they cannot pay attention; it is that they cannot pay attention to the right things, to the relevant stimuli. Their attention is easily distracted by any little thing—an insect flying around the classroom, someone outside walking past the window, a string hanging from the teacher's clothing, or an interesting picture in the textbook. Distractors are not always tangible, however. They can also come in the form of problems in some area of the students' lives, problems that they cannot get out of their minds. Any extra "noise" (anything that distracts attention from the relevant stimuli) can keep a student from paying attention and further reduce his chances of learning. Since high school requires extended periods of concentration and attention while studying and listening to lectures in class, attention problems can seriously retard the academic progress of learning disabled students (Lerner, 1985).

Two of the most serious and debilitating characteristics of learning disabled students, especially in adolescence, are a lack of motivation and a lack of organization. These not only are caused by a learning disability; they also magnify the adverse effects of a learning disability on the learning process.

One complaint that is heard from many teachers about their learning disabled students is that they are lazy. Although this is not the problem itself, it is a symptom. The real problem is a lack of motivation—the absence of a *cause* for activity or exertion. In many cases students will not try because they have no reason to try. There is nothing to motivate them to put forth the effort needed in order to accomplish something. If past effort has yielded nothing but failure and criticism, is it any wonder that a student will eventually give up and stop trying? Professionals agree that when a student is not motivated, he will not accomplish nearly as much as he is capable of, if anything at all (Mercer, 1987). Thus, lack of motivation can be a big contributor to the discrepancy between a student's ability and his achievement.

Poor organizational skills is another characteristic associated with learning disabilities (Lerner, 1985). Organization here does not refer just to keeping one's desk neat or writing out a schedule of the day's activities, even though these are important aspects of it. It also includes the ability to systematically classify and process ideas and concepts in the mind in order to understand how they all relate to one another. A further aspect of organization is being able to differentiate between and respond correctly to several different stimuli simultaneously. A deficiency in any of these areas could contribute to problems in selective attention, poor management and use of time, and unacceptable response in social situations. A lack of organization is not just a problem by itself; it is a major factor contributing to many other characteristics that are associated with learning disabilities. Without both external and internal organizational skills, a learning disabled student lacks the necessary foundation for overcoming his disability, and intervention will not attain its maximum level of effectiveness.

Diagnosis of Learning Disabilities

A doctor cannot prescribe medication to enable a sick person to get well until he knows exactly what is wrong with his patient. Likewise, a teacher or parent will not know how to help a child with a learning disability until there is evidence that the disability is present. Just as there are indicators of a physical illness, there are certain outward symptoms which testify to the possible presence of a learning disability (e.g., reading decoding problems, writing numbers inappropriately, inability to comprehend what is read, or lack of organization). If the parent or teacher is alert to the fact that a particular child is not performing up to his ability level, he or she will begin to look for certain symptoms. Although many children will manifest some of these symptoms at different times in their lives, children with learning disabilities display more of these symptoms with more regularity and intensity. Teachers and parents should carefully monitor children who display these symptoms frequently and over an extended period of time to see if there is sufficient cause for a professional evaluation. Once a child's disability has been identified and confirmed, steps can be taken to remediate the problem through a number of special education options.

Teachers need to be aware of some of the characteristics of learning disabilities in order to be able to identify the child who needs further investigation. Often the child's parents will notice the problems first. Teachers also need to be listening to what the parents are telling them. Parents will furnish information which can often lead teachers to the solutions to their students' problems. Many times, annual achievement tests given by teachers will show general academic problems the child is experiencing. Interviews with the child can provide important information. The teacher or parent then can request further professional testing through their local school district or through private testing agencies. After a battery of tests has been administered, the student's disability will be defined and rec- ommendations for placement will be made by a multidisciplinary team. An individual education plan (IEP) meeting is held, and the IEP is developed for the child.

Professional Testing

The most frequently used tests for a psychological evalua- tion are discussed in Chapter 5 of this book. Some tests, however, are used specifically in diagnosing a learning disability. The tests to be included in the test battery will be determined by the age of the child and the types of problems suspected. Often included are tests of general intelligence and achieve- ment in reading, written expression, spelling, and math. De- pending on the child, tests designed to measure his/her developmental level, academic readiness, and social and emo- tional adjustment may be included. In order to pinpoint a particular problem area, tests of oral language, auditory or visual perception, sensory-motor integration, and motor development may be administered.

One commonly-used achievement test is the Peabody Individual Achievement Test—Revised (PIAT-R) (Markwardt, 1981). This is a general individualized achievement test that covers reading recognition, reading comprehension, mathematics, spelling (the correct spelling is picked from four choices), and general knowledge.

The Slingerland Screening Tests for Identifying Children with Specific Language Disability (Slingerland, 1970) is a screening test sometimes used to assess the possible presence of a learning disability in reading, writing, spelling, speaking, and listening for children from preschool through junior high school level. This test is a written test that also includes visual and auditory memory, sequencing, and discrimination processes.

The Bender Visual-Motor Gestalt Test for Children (Bender, 1938) assesses the child's performance in copying designs in order to measure his visual-motor integration. This test may also be used to give an indication of problems of general organization and emotional adjustment.

The Illinois Test of Psycholinguistic Abilities (Kirk, McCarthy & Kirk, 1968) is an individual diagnostic test which assesses a child's communication skills from the ages of 2-4 (2 years, 4 months) to 10-3. There are 12 subtests, which include visual and auditory reception, association, closure, and memory. Also included is evaluation of verbal and motor expression. This test has resulted in the development of remedial language programs such as the Peabody Language Development Kits (Dunn, L. M., Horton, D. B., & Smith, D. D., 1981) and the GOAL Language Development Kits (Karnes, 1972). Other diagnostic tests may be found in Appendix 5.

We must emphasize that although the results of these tests may provide assessment of a child's problem areas, they should not be used alone to determine the child's instructional goals. Many things can influence the scores on professional tests, such as (a) the emotional or physical condition of the child on the day of the testing; (b) fear of strange people or strange places; (c) the rapport with the person conducting the test; and (d) the ability of the person conducting the test to adapt the test to the personality and individual needs of the child.

The results of a professional battery of tests should be used to determine the types of further assessment measures needed for developing the instructional goals to be included in the child's educational plan.

Diagnostic Assessment of the Child

The teacher may need to give diagnostic tests to determine the child's specific strengths and weaknesses in several academic or developmental areas. For example, the Brigance Diagnostic Inventory of Basic Skills (Brigance, 1983) is a criterion-referenced test of readiness, reading, language arts, and math skills from kindergarten through sixth grade. This is a diagnostic test that assists the teacher in determining instructional objectives, and the class record provides a way to record the child's progress.

The *Stanford Diagnostic Mathematics Test* (Beatty, Madden, Gardner & Karlsen, 1976) and the *Stanford Diagnostic Reading Test* (Karlsen, Madden & Gardner, 1977) may be administered individually or in a group in Grades 1-12. For testing a child with a reading disability, certain test modifications may be needed. A child with a writing disability would need to give answers orally to the tester or on a tape recorder. Also, time limits may need to be adjusted for some children. These tests provide instructional objectives and suggestions for teaching.

In order to determine the child's strengths and weaknesses in particular areas, a tester administers specific diagnostic tests to aid the teacher in developing the instructional goals and teaching strategies to be included in the IEP. Tests such as the *Durell Analysis of Reading Difficulty* (Durrell & Catterson, 1980), the *Wepman Auditory Discrimination Test* (Wepman, 1973), the *Test of Written Language-2* (Hammill & Larsen, 1988), and the *KeyMath–Revised* (Connolly, 1988) math diagnostic test can be very useful in diagnosing specific problem areas. Publication information for some of the commercially available diagnostic tests is listed in Appendix 5. Both survey and inventory tests are included according to subject areas.

Teachers can develop their own informal inventories, error analysis procedures, skill diagnostic checklists, survey tests, or probes to assess and identify specific problem areas. For instruction on how to make these, please refer to books on remedial teaching methods and books covering the diagnosing and instruction of learning disabled children (e.g., *Teaching Students with Learning and Behavior Problems* [Hammill and Bartell, 1986] and *Teaching Students With Learning Problems* [Mercer and Mercer, 1988]). Chapter 5 also provides more information on testing and assessment.

Programs for Learning Disabled Students

God has created and placed each one of us in His body as it has pleased Him (I Corinthians 12:18). We all have certain strengths which we can use to help build the body, and we all have certain weaknesses which God uses to build us. As we parents and teachers acknowledge our strengths as God-given abilities that we possess through no merit of our own, and as we accept our limitations as God-given opportunities through which Christ's power can be seen, we can encourage our children and our students to accept their strengths and weaknesses as from the Lord and use them for His glory. All young people, special education students or not, need to realize that

God loves them completely and righteously. He has an individual purpose and plan for their lives, and He has equipped them with exactly what they need to accomplish this purpose and fulfill His plan. There is nothing they cannot do that God wants them to do. They can do "all things through Christ which strengtheneth" them (Philippians 4:13).

Can we expect a child, however, who does not know how to sit in a classroom, organize his materials, or even begin an assigned task to be able to function in a regular classroom without some direct intervention from us? We first need to teach these children how to learn. In her book, *No Easy Answers: The Learning Disabled Child,* Smith (1980) states that "teaching the learning disabled child how to learn may be more important than the task itself" (p. 44). We know that not all children learn in exactly the same manner. This is especially true of children with learning disabilities. We therefore need to find alternative methods and materials to supplement or replace the traditional instruction they would receive in a regular classroom. Our goals for these children should be to provide remediation, to teach compensation strategies in dealing with their disabilities, and to build up their strengths and gifts. All of these require a systematically planned special program for each child (an IEP). There are several types of special education settings available to students with learning disabilities. What follows is a brief description of these and of the children that are typically served in each.

Self-Contained Classrooms

Severe learning disabilities may prevent a child from learning with normal classroom procedures and teaching techniques. Normal techniques may confuse him and intensify his problems, rather than help him. If so, this child needs to be in a special classroom where he can be given specialized learning instruction and help for his disability. This type of classroom is referred to as a self-contained classroom.

Self-contained classrooms are not as prevalent as other types of special education classrooms (e.g., resource rooms). One large-scale study by Pyecha (1981) found that only about 5% of the learning disabled students receiving special services were rated as having severe disabilities. Most learning disabled students have moderate or mild conditions that can be sufficiently served in other, less intense types of programs.

Some residential and day schools limited to special and remedial education services provide self-contained classrooms (e.g., Hidden Treasure Christian School). Some students have a problem at first adjusting to a special school, but we have found that most adjust well to their new environment when they begin to see that for the first time they are experiencing success and are discovering that they can learn. This environment becomes "least restrictive" to them because they have finally been set free from the restriction of constant failure.

This type of specialized classroom could also be set up in a regular Christian school with a teacher trained to diagnose and ameliorate learning disabilities. The class should be limited to five or six students normally and no more than eight students even if the teacher has an aide. We already know that a smaller class size results in more direct teaching time for each student. Since learning disabled students do not learn independently or incidentally, we need to provide more active learning time for each of these students in smaller classes.

Typically, a student is in a self-contained special education class for more than 50% of the day. The special education teacher would be responsible for most of the student's academic instruction (reading, math, etc.). Some children, depending on the severity of their learning disability, would be able to participate in physical education, music, art, home economics, and vocational classes with nondisabled students in a regular classroom for part of the day. It may be necessary to provide some special supplemental services for students who have special needs (e.g., speech, physical therapy, or occupational therapy).

The program for each student in a self-contained classroom is highly structured and is tailored to the student's individual needs. Primary and elementary teachers need to remediate disabilities, teach and strengthen basic skills, provide instruction in academic subject areas, and explore careers. Secondary teachers need to add to these areas instruction in learning strategies, organizational skills, compensation techniques, and vocational skills. Each student's program must be closely monitored, both by the teacher and by the student himself. If the student reaches the point where he demonstrates that he can survive academically in a traditional classroom, the school or parents need to provide all of the services the child will need (e.g., tutoring, special materials and equipment, and counseling) to be successful in the new learning environment. We must remember that learning disabilities do not just disappear, as some people think. And for the most part, children do not grow out of these learning disabilities. We need to encourage and support a learning disabled student as much as possible. The Scripture tells us to "bear the infirmities of the weak" (Romans 15:1).

Resource Rooms

For students with mild to moderate learning disabilities, the resource room can provide opportunities to acquire the basic skills necessary for success in a regular classroom. In this type of program students leave the classroom during scheduled periods of time for individual or small-group instruction in the resource room. They spend up to 50% of their instructional time in a specialized remedial program and return to their regular classroom for instruction in areas where special help is not required.

The resource teacher and the regular classroom teacher work together to develop and implement each child's specialized program. The regular classroom teacher communicates the specific problems that the child is having in the classroom. The resource teacher then observes the child in his class and assesses suspected problems through analysis of his classwork and through diagnostic testing. The teachers work together to produce an IEP for the child that incorporates remedial activities and compensation techniques for the resource and regular classroom programs. One important responsibility of the resource teacher is to recommend to the regular teacher materials and methods best suited to the child's unique needs. At times it may even be necessary for the resource teacher to assist the child's teacher in modifying regular classroom instruction through the use of specialized techniques and methods. The child's complete program is closely monitored by the resource teacher to determine if and when the child no longer requires direct special education services. Once the child returns full time to his regular class, the resource room teacher observes him and recommends adjustments necessary for his continued success. At times the resource teacher may be called upon to conduct workshops for the other teachers in how to modify instruction for the LD students in regular classrooms.

A special education teacher can serve a total of 20-30 children in a resource room program. Depending on whether an aide assists, between 6 and 8 children would be present in the room in a given hour. This type of program is more affordable to most Christian schools than a self-contained classroom. However, it must be noted that not all learning disabled children can profit from instruction in a regular classroom; some may need full-time special instruction. Many children with moderate disabilities will progress well in a resource program that is set up properly. Many helpful ideas for setting up a resource program can be found in the book, *The Resource Teacher: A Guide to Effective Practices*, by Weiderholt, Hammill, and Brown (1983).

Other Service Delivery Programs

Some children with mild learning disabilities may be able to stay in the traditional classroom. At times only the help of a tutor in difficult areas may be needed. The student would remain in the regular classroom for most of the day and leave only for tutoring. Tutoring may be done either at school during the day by older students, volunteers, and/or special tutors, or at home by parents or a special tutor. The regular classroom teacher would make suggestions for the tutor and would receive written feedback from the tutor in return. Some students find peer study partners helpful for drill and review.

A special education teacher would consult with the regular classroom teacher and provide advice on how to meet the individual needs of specific children who have mild learning disabilities. The special education teacher would also recommend and/or provide special materials, methods, and equipment.

Some schools have an itinerant special education teacher available to them. This teacher serves different schools on specific days of the week. Children who do not require direct special education services every day can benefit from the services offered by an itinerant teacher one or two days per week. In this way, two or three Christian schools can make use of one teacher who is trained in remedial teaching procedures and techniques.

Teaching Methods

Special education is based on the principle of individualizing education—teaching each student according to his own needs and abilities. Smith (1980) states a basic principle: "It is our job to find out how [a student] learns, and then teach him how he learns" (p. 114). This principle should direct every remediation technique or teaching strategy that we use in working with learning disabled students. We know that every person the Lord creates is unique, different from others He has created. When it comes to teaching learning disabled students, we could also say that every student learns in his own way. The teacher has the responsibility of determining what techniques and methods work best for an individual student and then using those particular methods in a way that will best meet that student's needs.

Teaching methodologies for students with mild disabilities in general and for learning disabled students in particular are varied and numerous. They include direct instruction, multisensory approaches, cooperative learning, metacognitive training, peer tutoring, computer-aided instruction, task analysis, programmed instruction, and learning strategy acquisition and usage, to name just a few. We believe it is particularly important that parents and teachers become familiar with two of these methods.

Task Analysis

Many tasks that a student must learn are actually made up of a series of small steps. Learning disabled students frequently display deficiencies in memory and sequencing ability (Kirk & Chalfant, 1984; Lerner, 1985). Therefore, the teacher should not expect the student to be able to learn all the steps of a certain skill all at once. The student needs to have the skill broken down into its most basic components with each part being taught separately and in order (Kirk & Chalfant, 1984; Lerner, 1985; Smith, 1980). Once the first subskill is learned adequately, the next one may be taught, then each one thereafter when mastery of the previous one has been attained. As each subskill is mastered, the student should practice performing the previous subskills in order until the entire task can be performed to completion without error. This method of teaching can be applied to virtually all academic skills, especially in the areas of mathematics, reading, and language arts; it also applies to specific sports and motor skills taught in physical education class.

Multisensory Approach

Not all learning disabled students learn best through the same learning modalities. Lerner (1985) believes that "some learn best by listening (auditory modality), some by looking (visual modality), and some by touching (tactile modality) or by performing an action (kinesthetic modality)" (p. 281). For many students, but not for all, using a combination of modalities and employing multiple senses will help them to learn better and more efficiently. With more senses actively involved in the learning process, there is a greater likelihood that the student will receive and process more information about the subject being taught. Some students can understand a concept more fully if they can hear it being explained, see it being demonstrated, and experience it for themselves with some form of physical movement. However, this approach may not be successful with all students. Fernald (1943), one of the earlier special educators of this century, is known for pioneering the multisensory approach to teaching. This approach is also known as the VAKT (visual-auditory-kinesthetic-tactile) approach. Although it is still used widely by special education teachers nationwide, research on its effectiveness is inconclusive and findings are mixed at best (Kavale & Forness, 1987).

Interventions for Learning Disabled Students

Building Motivation

One of the first tasks in designing intervention for learning disabled students, before any academic remediation can be successful, is building motivation in the student. If a student is not motivated to learn, he will not learn, no matter how much remediation is employed. A student will learn only when he wants to learn; this principle is especially true for learning disabled students. Motivation is the spark that will ignite the flame of learning.

There are two main factors involved in building motivation in a learning disabled student. First, the student must believe that the subject matter is worth learning, that it will somehow be meaningful and applicable in his life. Simply put, the student has to understand why it is important for him to learn the material being taught to him—or, for that matter, why it is important for him to learn at all. This is the first job of the teacher or parent working with a learning disabled student: to establish with the student the importance of learning and the meaningfulness of the material. Without this foundation, any attempts at building motivation in the student will be less successful.

Second, the student needs to have an active role in the learning process. Providing opportunities for active involvement can include letting the student participate in selecting subject matter, performing experiments, conducting simple research, forming goals and expectations for classroom behavior and academic achievement, and even teaching a short lesson to his classmates or his teacher. A learning disabled student will be more motivated to achieve goals that he helped to set, in subject areas that he helped to select, with rules that he helped to establish. Of course, the teacher should be the final authority in the activities the student is involved in, but there is much benefit in letting a student have a voice in deciding some of the variables that make up his own learning environment. Involving the student in the learning process will help the student begin to enjoy learning. When a student enjoys learning, he will learn for the sake of learning rather than for some kind of reward.

These two factors, making learning meaningful and involving the student, work together to build the foundation for motivation in a learning disabled student. In fact, meaningfulness is dependent on the student's active involvement. The key to making the material worthwhile to the student is to involve the student as much as possible in the learning process.

There are two basic types of motivation: extrinsic (external) and intrinsic (internal). Extrinsic motivation is reinforcement of desired behavior from sources outside of the student himself. On the other hand, intrinsic motivation has its source within the person. Here it may involve the student's reinforcement of his own behavior with positive feelings of accomplishment and self-worth. Ideally, the goal of building motivation is for the student to get to the point of being completely intrinsically motivated, needing no outside influences to prompt him to work. Although it would be unrealistic to expect full success, this is the point at which the teacher's efforts should be aimed. Although a student may always need some amount of extrinsic motivation, the teacher should encourage the student to become as self-motivated as possible.

Extrinsic motivation Extrinsic motivational techniques should be used initially when working with a learning disabled student, especially one who has experienced much failure in the classroom and has stopped trying. Some of these techniques fall under a related set of teaching skills called behavior management. Probably the most popular technique of extrinsic motivation is a **token economy** in which tokens are given for desired behavior. Students then trade tokens for back-up reinforcers, which may include edible, tangible, or activity reinforcers. Examples of back-up reinforcers would be candy, drawing paper, free time during class, special privileges, or exemption from certain assignments. In some cases, awarding points that can be used to make purchases in the school store is very effective in motivating students. When employing a reward system or a token economy with learning disabled students, there are a few rules that should be followed:

1. Rewards should be proportional to the goals for which they are given.
2. Rewards should be given only when the specific objective of the goal is met. One should not reward performance and ignore quality (Biehler and Snowman, 1990).
3. The goals should be realistic and consistent with the student's ability.
4. The basis for rewards should be individual achievement, not competition.
5. One should not rely exclusively on a reward system or a token economy; other motivational techniques should also be used.

A second technique used in extrinsic motivation is **contingency contracting**. A contract can be worked out between the student and the teacher; the contract is written up, stating expected goals for the student, conditions for the achievement of the goals, and rewards that will be given when the goals have been achieved. Both the student and the teacher then sign the contract, promising to carry out their parts of it. If the conditions of the contract are realistic and are adhered to by student and teacher, this technique is usually very successful in building the student's motivation and sense of responsibility. When this technique is first used with a student, the goals that are established should be short-term and very simple so that the student will experience success quickly with minimal effort. But the teacher should also make sure the goals are not so easy that the student gets bored with them. Gradually increasing the difficulty and the time range of the goals will help prevent the student from initially feeling overwhelmed by the amount of progress that is expected and from procrastinating on long-term goals.

Verbal feedback is a very common technique used in extrinsic reinforcement. Many people respond to the success of another with a spontaneous expression of praise. Praise can be a great motivating factor to someone striving to accomplish something, especially if that person is learning disabled. Many learning disabled students have had a "praise deficient" past because they have not accomplished much that other people consider to be worthy of their praise. For these students, a little praise can go a long way. Teachers who work with learning disabled students need to realize this. Sometimes, small tasks that seem menial to the average student become major projects for learning disabled students. Accomplishment of these tasks by learning disabled students merits the teacher's attention and praise. In working with these students, the teacher should incorporate as much praise as possible into the learning process. But praise should not be the only form of verbal feedback given. Correction and instruction are also necessary in order for the student to learn. The key, though, is for the teacher to combine praise with correction and instruction, maintaining a delicate balance and accentuating the positive. A student who is corrected in a positive manner will generally be more willing to work than a student who is corrected in a negative manner. Also, plenty of verbal feedback on the teacher's part will convey to the student that the teacher has a genuine interest in helping the student learn. No matter what other motivational techniques a teacher employs, verbal feedback is a necessity.

Intrinsic motivation The second type of motivation is intrinsic motivation. This deals with the internal motivation of a student—the drive from inside him that causes him to put forth the effort to learn. Intrinsic motivation is the ideal that teachers try to produce in students, and often this is what is lacking in learning disabled students. Because they have failed so often in the past, they have no reason to continue to try. For a learning disabled student to be able reach his maximum potential academically, there must be a certain amount of intrinsic motivation present. He cannot always depend on being rewarded tangibly for his efforts. Therefore, developing intrinsic motivation in a learning disabled student is the goal that his teacher must accomplish. The student has to want to learn in order to be successful.

The basis for intrinsic motivation is self-control skills (Mercer, 1987). The learning disabled student needs to learn how to discipline himself in order to focus his energies on the task at hand. One of the primary jobs of the teacher in helping the student to do this is to help the student get organized. Organization will help the student to see where he is going and what he needs to do to get there. Showing the relevancy of the material to the student's life is another job of the teacher in building intrinsic motivation. As stated before, the student needs to be involved. Developing self-discipline, learning organizational skills, and understanding the relevance of the material being studied will boost the confidence of the student and will make his learning experience enjoyable so that he will want to continue learning.

Finally, one very easy yet very important way to build motivation in a student is for the teacher to show that he genuinely cares about the student and wants to help him. A student can generally tell whether the teacher is really concerned about him or if he is just part of the teacher's job that must be done. A Christian teacher, especially, must demonstrate genuine caring and love toward a student. All Christians have the responsibility before God to "love one another" (Romans 13:8), and that love is demonstrated not just through words but through actions. Extra effort and patience on the part of the teacher will demonstrate to the student that he is important to the teacher and worth the time and effort expended on him. When a student sees that this extra effort and patience from the teacher are to benefit him and that the teacher genuinely loves him, he will be more willing and motivated to put forth more effort himself—if for no other reason than to please this one who really cares about what he does and what he is. Genuine love and concern for a student, with actions that show that love and concern, may do more to produce motivation in a student than any other technique that has ever been used. Just as a Christian is motivated to serve God because of His great love demonstrated to us through the sacrifice of His Son, so a student will be motivated to work because of the love shown to him by the teacher.

Teaching Organizational Skills

As stated before, a lack of organizational skills is not just an isolated characteristic of a learning disability—it contributes to and magnifies other problems that are a part of being learning disabled. For this reason, organizational skills should be one of the first things taught to a learning disabled student to help him overcome his disability. These skills include developing schedules and routines, finding a place for things and learning to put things where they belong, and establishing some priorities that will help the student make decisions concerning work that has to be done and about use of time. Organization must be prerequisite to any remediation or learning strategy in order to achieve maximum potential and success.

The first step in teaching organizational skills to a learning disabled student is to help him to organize his physical environment. Neatness and orderliness are the key words here, and the teacher needs to remember that "actions speak louder than words." What the teacher requires of a student, he should also require of himself. This is called "modeling"; it is one of the best teaching methods known to man. In His ministry on earth, Jesus himself used modeling to teach us how we should live as Christians. Paul also used modeling when he said, "Be ye followers of me, even as I also am of Christ" (I Corinthians 11:1).

To start out in teaching physical organization, designate specific places in which to put all materials and equipment that the student will be using, and then make sure that everything is put back into its proper place as soon as the student has finished using it. The teacher might even want to drill the student by quizzing him on the proper location and use of certain items, or by taking several items out and having the student put them back in their proper place within a set time limit. This procedure will help the student get into the habit of using his time wisely. A neat, clean desk is a necessity for both student and teacher. When working on classwork, the student should have out only the materials that he will need for that particular assignment or activity. Any extra "clutter" will only serve as additional distractions which will keep the student's attention away from the work at hand. Also, work stations could be set up so that the student will have a designated area to do a specific task without being distracted by other things.

Time management makes up a very important aspect of organizing the physical environment of a student. A student needs to learn to budget his time and use it wisely. It is helpful to establish time limits for the student to complete certain activities or assignments. Time limits will help a student to realize that he does not have forever to do things and that he cannot afford to waste time. Prioritizing assignments and activities through the use of color coding on assignment sheets or some other method will teach the student to recognize an approach needed to accomplish a particular task.

Another aspect in organizing the physical environment is developing schedules and routines. The student and the teacher can work together to come up with schedules so that the student will not have to wonder what is going to happen each day and how long will be spent on each activity. Weekly schedules can be written out for the student and then broken down into daily schedules so that the student will know what to expect each day. If necessary, a schedule of each class period can be written out to give an advance organizer of the activities in certain classes. Logs and charts "provide students with a visual representation of content that must be learned, the tasks that need to be accomplished, or the time frame within which the tasks must be accomplished" (Shields & Heron, 1989, p. 8). Two examples of logs and charts that could be used are assignment logs and flow charts that break projects or assignments down into subtasks.

Routines are also very important for a learning disabled student. They should be established for activities in which the completion of several steps or subtasks is required for the completion of the activity. These activities include going to the restrooms, getting ready to take a test, preparing to start school in the morning, preparing to go home in the afternoon, changing clothes for a physical education class, getting ready for lunch, and even sharpening a pencil or throwing trash away. Such activities are made up of a sequence of small tasks, any one of which could provide enough interest to a learning disabled student to distract his attention from the more important task of learning. Once routines have been established and practiced several times in these kinds of activities, they become more or less habitual for the student, and the likelihood of the student being distracted in these activities is diminished. Without routines, a learning disabled student might spend a significant amount of time in trivial activities, decreasing the amount of time available for actual teaching and learning.

A final but important part of creating an organized physical environment is establishment of a set of clear, reasonable rules. These can be worked out between the teacher and the student, following a set of guidelines, so that each knows the expected behavior and the consequences of not practicing that behavior. Just having a set of rules is not enough, however. The rules must be consistently and strictly enforced by the teacher and followed by the student in order for them to be of any value. When the rules are enforced and followed, misbehavior becomes less of a distracting factor, and teaching time can be spent more efficiently and effectively.

The second step in teaching organizational skills to a learning disabled student is to help him organize his thoughts. This is probably the more difficult aspect of organization to teach and learn, yet it is also more important. Learning is based on the ability to process information in order to understand how different bits of information relate to each other. Without being able to process information in an organized way, a student will not be able to learn as effectively or as efficiently. The process of "chunking," as described by Biehler and Snowman (1982), allows students to process and organize information more efficiently:

> **Chunking** is a technique for holding separate items of information in short-term memory by grouping them in some fashion. For some tasks, the basis of a grouping may be a rhythm or a cadence. . . . [M]any children are taught to recite the alphabet with the following rhythm: abcd-efg-hijk-lmnop-qrs-tuv-wxyz. . . . [C]hunking may be based on relationships between items. The lock combination 4-14-36 can be chunked into two digits, 99, by summing the first three numbers and the last two numbers. A further reduction can be made by grouping the two nines as 18. . . . The main purpose of chunking is to enhance learning by breaking tasks into small, easy-to-manage pieces. (p. 233)

What a learning disabled student lacks many times is this ability to relate chunks of information.

There are many activities that will help a student learn to organize thoughts and ideas into meaningful relationships. One of the most popular and useful activities is outlining. This is one of the best ways to show how different chunks of information are related through a hierarchical breakdown of the information. Another activity to improve organizational ability is classifying objects or words into groups according to similar characteristics. Practice with comparing and contrasting is also helpful in improving a student's organizational ability. Other helpful activities include those that deal with part-to-whole relationships and sequencing.

Families of Learning Disabled Students

As Smith (1980) states, there are "no easy answers" for parents and families of learning disabled children. Everyone in the family must make adjustments and learn how to accept this child as he really is and not as they wish him to be. Parents first have to accept the fact that their child indeed has a limitation that is going to require extra understanding, work, and time, and sometimes extra money (such as for special schools, classes, tutors, and/or equipment). Brothers and sisters have to accept the fact their parents are going to give more of their time and patience to their learning disabled sibling because it is needed, not because they love him more. The whole family needs encouragement, prayer, and support from everyone around them in dealing with all of the adjustments facing them.

Teachers can help the family in a number of ways. First, teachers need to explain, in terms a parent can understand, the types of problems their child is experiencing and then suggest concrete ways in which the parents can help. Their child will have to be taught some things that other children pick up incidentally or with very little instruction. They may have to help their child in certain tasks, explaining as they work—perhaps ten times after they have already shown him how to do it several times before. Many household tasks may take much longer for this child to learn than they will for their brothers and sisters.

Second, teachers can help the parents in the important area of structure and organization at home. Some parents may find this difficult to provide, because they are not used to structure and organization in their own lives. Help will be needed to assist them in organizing the child's physical surroundings and structuring his schedule. For example, a few items left on open shelves are much simpler for a child to put away than many in unorganized drawers or toy boxes. Some parents may request help in planning a schedule for the child, or helping him plan one, and assisting him in the keeping of that schedule.

A third area is support of any tutoring the parent may do. The time spent by parents in tutoring or helping their child with academic work depends on the personality of the parents, the amount of time available in their schedule, and the availability of a quiet place to work. If the parents do become involved, the teacher should work closely with them in the decisions of how much time should be spent each day in tutoring sessions, types of learning tasks to be attempted, methods for achieving success, types of reinforcement activities to be incorporated into the lesson, and ways in which the parents can record their observations while working with the child. Most important, the parent should determine that each session will be a pleasant one and that a session should be modified when it becomes unpleasant. It will be helpful for parents to know about some organizations and agencies that can give them information and help with their learning disabled child. Some of these are listed in Appendix 4.

Parents and teachers working together, guided by the Holy Spirit, can bring up these children "in the nurture and admonition of the Lord" (Ephesians 6:4) and help them to become adults who confidently serve their Lord in the unique ministry that He has planned for their lives. This is the goal for which we strive. If we educate their minds and bodies only and neglect the spiritual needs of these children, we accomplish nothing. Let us work together to bring these children into a personal relationship with their Savior so they may walk with Him and become like Him.

References

Beatty, L. S., Madden, R., Gardner, E. G., & Karlsen, B. (1976). *Stanford Diagnostic Mathematics Test.* Cleveland, OH: The Psychological Corporation.

Bender, L. (1938). *A visual motor Gestalt test and its clinical use* (Research Monograph, No. 3). New York: American Orthopsychiatric Association.

Biehler, R. F., & Snowman, J. (1982). *Psychology applied to teaching* (4th ed.). Boston, MA: Houghton Mifflin Co.

Brigance, A. H. (1983). *Brigance Diagnostic Comprehensive Inventory of Basic Skills.* North Billerica, MA: Curriculum Associates, Inc.

Connolly, A. J. (1988). *Keymath—Revised: A Diagnostic Inventory of Essential Mathematics.* Circle Pines, MN: American Guidance Service.

Cruickshank, W., & Hallahan, D. (1973). *Psychoeducational foundations of learning disabilities.* Englewood Cliffs, NJ: Prentice-Hall.

Dunn, L. M., Smith, J. O., Dunn, L. M., Horton, D. B., & Smith, D. D. (1981). *Peabody Language Development Kits* (Rev. ed.). Circle Pines, MN: American Guidance Service.

Durrell, D., & Catterson, J. (1980). *Durrell Analysis of Reading Difficulty.* Cleveland, OH: The Psychological Corporation.

Federal Register. (1977). *Procedures for evaluating specific learning disabilities.* Washington, DC: Department of Health, Education, and Welfare, December 29.

Fernald, G. M. (1943). *Remedial techniques in basic school subjects.* New York, NY: McGraw-Hill.

Hallgren, B. (1950). Specific dyslexia (congenital word-blindness): A clinical genetic study. *Acta Psychiatrica et Neurologica, 65,* 1-287.

Hallahan, D. P., & Kauffman, J. M. (1988). *Exceptional children: Introduction to special education* (4th ed.). Englewood Cliffs, NJ: Prentice Hall.

Hammill, D., & Bartel, N. L. (1986). *Teaching students with learning and behavior problems.* Boston, MA: Allyn & Bacon.

Hammill, D. D., & Larsen, S. C. (1988). *Test of Written Language—2.* Austin, TX: Pro-Ed.

Hammill, D. D., Leigh, J. E., McNutt, G., & Larsen, S. C. (1981). A new definition of learning disabilities. *Learning Disability Quarterly, 4,* 336-342.

Hermann, K. (1959). *Reading disability: A medical study of word blindness and related handicaps.* Springfield, IL: Charles C. Thomas.

Karlsen, B., Madden, R., & Gardner, E. F. (1977). *Stanford Diagnostic Reading Test.* Cleveland, OH: The Psychological Corporation.

Karnes, M. (1972). *GOAL: Language Development.* Springfield, MA: Milton Bradley.

Kavale, K. A., & Forness, S. R. (1987). Substance over style: Assessing the efficacy modality testing and teaching. *Exceptional Children, 54,* 228-239.

Kirk, S. A., & Chalfant, J. C. (1984). *Academic and developmental learning disabilities.* Denver, CO: Love Publishing Co.

Kirk, S., McCarthy, J., & Kirk, W. (1968). *Illinois Test of Psycholinguistic Abilities.* Champaign, IL: University of Illinois Press.

Lerner, J. W. (1985). *Learning disabilities: Theories, diagnosis, and teaching techniques.* Boston, MA: Houghton Mifflin Co.

Markwardt, F. C. (1981). *Peabody Individual Achievement Test–Revised.* Circle Pines, MN: American Guidance Service.

Mercer, C. D. (1987). *Students with learning disabilities* (3rd ed.). Columbus, OH: Merrill Publishing Co.

Mercer, C. D., & Mercer, A. R. (1989). *Teaching students with learning problems* (3rd ed.). Columbus, OH: Merrill Publishing Co.

Peterson, N. L. (1987). *Early intervention for the handicapped and at-risk children.* Denver, CO: Love Publishing.

Pyecha, J. (1981). A national survey of individual educational programs for handicapped children. In U. S. General Accounting Office (Ed.), *Disparities still exist in who gets special education* (p. 80). Washington, DC: U. S. General Accounting Office.

Schumaker, J. B., & Hazel, J. S. (1984). Social skills assessment and training for the learning disabled: Who's on first and what's on second? Part I. *Journal of Learning Disabilities, 17*, 422-431.

Shields, J. M, & Heron, T. E. (1989). Teaching organizational skills to students with learning disablities. *Teaching Exceptional Children, 21*, 8-13.

Slingerland, B. H. (1974). *Slingerland Screening Tests for Identifying Children with Specific Language Disability for Grade V and Grade VI.* Cambridge, MA: Educators Publishing Service, Inc.

Smith, S. L. (1980). *No easy answers: The learning disabled child at home and at school.* New York, NY: Bantam Books.

Sutton, J. P. (1991). Understanding mildly disabled students in Christian schools. *Balance, 12* (3), 1-2, 4.

Torgesen, J. (1982). The learning disabled child as an active learner: Educational implications. *Topics in Learning and Learning Disabilities, 2*, 45-52.

U. S. Department of Education. (1986). *To Assure the Free Appropriate Public Education of All Handicapped Children. Eighth Annual Report to Congress on Implementation of the Education of the Handicapped Act.* Volume 1. Washington, DC: Government Printing Office.

Wallace, G., & McLoughlin, J. A. (1979). *Learning disabilities: Concepts and characteristics* (2nd ed.). Columbus, OH: Merrill.

Wepman, J. M. (1973). *Auditory Discrimination Test* (rev. ed.). Chicago, IL: Language Research Associates.

Wiederholt, J. L., Hammill, D. D., & Brown, V. L. (1983). *The resource teacher: A guide to effective practices* (2nd ed.). Boston, MA: Allyn & Bacon, Inc.

Wiens, J. (1983). Metacognition and the adolescent passive learner. *Journal of Learning Disabilities, 16,* 144-149.

Educable
Mentally Retarded and
Slow Learning Students

John J. McCormick
Katherine S. Young

Introduction

*T*his chapter addresses the characteristics and educational needs of the slow learning and educable mentally retarded (EMR) students. Information discussed in this chapter includes (a) the rationale and criteria for classifying these students; (b) procedures for academic instruction during the preschool, elementary, and secondary school years; and (c) realistic goals for the recreational, prevocational, social-emotional, and life skill areas.

Rationale and Criteria for Classification
Educable Mentally Retarded Students

Classification and labeling provide some order in our attempts to provide services for children in need. Labels are used to determine eligibility for services in special education (Luftig, 1987), and they give us general direction in our efforts to help these children. The definitions of the different disability labels include criteria for classifying children. Tremendous change occurred over the span of about twelve years in the definition of mentally retarded students, as Kirk (1979) shows:

> In 1961 the American Association on Mental Deficiency (AAMD) defined mental retardation as (1) including subaverage general intellectual functioning (an IQ of 84 or below on an individual intelligence test), (2) existing before the age of 16, and (3) showing impairment in adaptive behavior .... In 1973 it read, "Mental retardation refers to significantly subaverage general intellectual functioning, existing concurrently with deficits in adaptive behavior and manifested during the developmental period." It defined "significantly" as having a two standard deviation deficit or an IQ of 68 or below. (p. 104)

From these two definitions one can see that some children who would have been considered EMR twenty years ago would not be classified as such now. MacMillan (1988) notes that between the years 1976 and 1981 there was a decrease of approximately 13% in students labeled mentally retarded, while at the same time there was an increase of 104% in those labeled learning disabled. The decrease in the labeling of mentally retarded students was within the EMR category. It may be that some of the children labeled today as learning disabled

257

*Educable
Mentally
Retarded and
Slow Learing
Students*

would have been labeled as higher functioning EMR children in previous years.

Nonetheless, children are typically classified as EMR today if their measured IQ falls between 55 and 70 (Hallahan & Kauffman, 1988). Subaverage intellectual functioning is not the only criterion mentioned for classifying a child as mentally retarded, however. These children must also demonstrate "deficits in adaptive behavior skills existing concurrently" with their low IQ level. Ysseldyke and Algozzine (1984) state:

> There is no formal definition of adaptive behavior, but it can be said generally that it refers to the way in which an individual functions in his or her social environment. The requirement that individuals demonstrate a deficit in adaptive behavior is included in the definition of mental retardation so that individuals who perform poorly on intelligence tests yet manage to adapt or adjust to their environment, thus functioning adequately outside of school, will not be considered mentally retarded. The decision that an individual is deficient in adaptive behavior is subjective. You might view the behavior of a given individual as adaptive, whereas several of your classmates might view the same behavior as maladaptive. Trying to define adaptive behavior is like trying to define normal behavior. (p. 19)

There are instruments to measure adaptive behavior on the basis of the information obtained from a third person, such as a parent or teacher, regarding the student's self-help, communication, and social skills. No truly accurate measure of adaptive behavior skills can be obtained, because these measures simply involve the opinions of third parties who are related somehow to the student in question. We should not underestimate the importance of careful and accurate evaluation in the areas of intelligence and adaptive behavior. The reliability and validity of intelligence tests are still a major concern today (Salvia & Ysseldyke, 1988). The standards for acceptable adaptive behavior may also differ from person to person and particularly from one environment or system of values to another (e.g., Christian versus secular environments). These considerations would lead some Christian parents to pursue further testing to verify results of which they are doubtful. This, of course, would be their right and privilege and would be appropriate.

Slow Learners

The term *slow learner* has its roots in the fields of learning disabilities and mental retardation. For example, Hallahan and Kauffman (1988) indicate that *slow learner* and several other terms (e.g., *minimally brained injured, perceptually disabled*) were used to describe learning disabled students back in the early 1960s. In fact, the slow learner children that Newell Kephart wrote about in his 1960 book, *The Slow Learner in the Classroom,* came to be known as learning disabled students some years later (Hallahan, Kauffman, & Lloyd, 1985).

Lovitt (1989), however, indicates that we should make a clear distinction between slow learners and learning disabled children. Schrag, Kirsch, and Dailey (cited in Lovitt, 1989) state:

> The learning disabled student requires instructional techniques available in special education. The slow learning student who does not have a specific [disability] is the responsibility of regular education and should not be placed in programs designed to help those with specific learning disabilities. (p. 75)

Furthermore, Lovitt (1989) reports that the board of trustees of the Council for Learning Disabilities believes that pooling

259

*Educable
Mentally
Retarded and
Slow Learing
Students*

slow-learning, low achieving, and underachieving children with learning disabled students would present several problems:

1. Incidence rates (i.e., number of students) enrolled in learning disability programs would be spurious.

2. Some learning disabled students may be denied needed special education services because of lack of room.

3. Combining these two different types of students together would dilute the quality of special education services in learning disability programs.

4. Placing students such as slow learners in special education classrooms is a direct violation of PL 94-142.

5. Placing slow learners with learning disabled students would incorrectly suggest that a learning disability is only a mild problem that can be treated through enrichment and remedial programs (e.g., ECIA Chapter I Reading and Math Labs).

Slow learners also have a close tie with mental retardation. Kirk and Johnson (cited in Kolstoe, 1976), in a 1951 book entitled *Educating the Retarded Child*, noted that slow learners were previously considered to have the highest level of mental retardation (IQ = 70/75 to 90/95), followed by educable mental retardation (IQ = 50 to 75/80), trainable mental retardation (IQ = 25/30 to 50), and dependent students (IQ = 0 to 25/30). A number of changes have occurred since the publication of Kirk and Johnson's book, however. For example, Hallahan and Kauffman (1988) note that the highest level of mental retardation today is educable mental retardation, which means the student's IQ may not go beyond 70. In an effort to characterize slow learners, Kolstoe (1976) notes:

Slow learners were described by Kirk [in a 1962 book entitled *Educating Exceptional Children*] as children who could be expected to achieve a moderate degree of academic success, although at a slower rate than average children. These children can be educated in regular grades, do not need special class placement, and can be expected to become self-supporting, independent, and socially adjusted adults. (p. 9)

Christian parents and teachers must realize that although slow learners and educable mentally retarded students may demonstrate common learning and behavioral problems in school, they are two distinct groups of children. Furthermore, educable mentally retarded children are eligible for special education services, whereas slow learners are not. Of course, since Christian schools are not bound by the mandates of federal law, some flexibility may be exercised in including slow learners in special education programs if there is available space and if classified disabled students have received first priority for service. However, school administrators should be careful to recognize the potential problems of such a practice, as delineated above.

Instruction During the Preschool Years

Joan and Bernard McNamara (1977) state that parents

are often the first to know if their child has a disability whether they fully recognize it or not [and] whether they accept it or not . . . [but] early detection is important if a child is to avoid some of the emotional scars that children with special needs must often endure when their particular needs are unrecognized, misunderstood, or unmet. (p. 6)

Currently there is considerable discussion and research regarding the early identification of developmental problems (e.g.,

261

*Educable
Mentally
Retarded and
Slow Learing
Students*

Kochanek, Kabacoff, & Lipsitt, 1990). Many parents and professionals long for the day when there will be complete and definitive procedures for identifying developmental problems early. Unfortunately, identification is often difficult, especially for slow learners and EMR children. One must remember that hasty decisions in labeling may be harmful. Yet we must acknowledge that the field of early childhood special education is one of the foremost in education today. New laws (e.g., PL 99-457) have been enacted recently concerning the rights and privileges of disabled preschool children.

Laws Governing Preschool Disabled Children

Section 672 of PL 99-457 (The Handicapped Children's Early Education Program) now mandates that there be educational provisions for children from three to five years of age who have been identified as disabled. Because of this law, the early identification of these children has become a major concern in most states. Each state is setting up its own screening procedures. These procedures undoubtedly will vary from state to state. The task of identifying these children will be enormous. Those with low-frequency disabilities (hearing or visually impaired and physically disabled, etc.) will be easily recognized. Parents of these children will more likely seek out the services that will be provided. However, the children at risk for emotional disorders, learning disabilities, or mental disabilities are less easily identified. Consequently, screening procedures and follow-up tests are being established by states to meet the requirements of this law. The law mandates that these services be aimed at meeting the needs of those identified as disabled— and of their families (Jordan, Gallagher, Hutlinger, Karnes, 1988).

An entirely new concept is seen here because it reaches into the home to help parents and other family members in meeting the requirements of the law. If a child under age 6 is classified as disabled, an individual family service plan (IFSP) must be written for him. This document will be a detailed plan prepared by professionals and parents in a special planning session, followed by regular updates and services; it is similar to the individual education plan (IEP) mandated by PL 94-142. However, as mentioned above, it will involve not only the child but other members of the family as well. Once the child is labeled, the IFSP must be developed and put into action (Jordan, Gallagher, Hutlinger, & Karnes, 1988). We must remember that these requirements apply not only to children with severe physical and mental disabilities, but also to educable mentally retarded children.

As time goes on, Christian educators and parents will have to decide whether to seek out such state-established agencies to screen and classify children. We want to have our students in an environment that will enable us to train them in the Christian faith. We want to preserve that right. So while these services are in the planning stages and are not well established, we need to continue to do everything we can to serve the needs of disabled young people. Realizing that there may be some developmental needs, let us set ourselves to the task at hand. Ecclesiastes 9:10 admonishes, "Whatsoever thy hand findeth to do, do it with thy might."

Parental Awareness of Early Developmental Problems

Through regular checkups with their child's pediatrician, along with available informative literature on child development, many parents are aware of how their child compares with a representative sample of children across the country. They are eager to see them reach each level and often point with pride to their achievements. But there are some parents who may worry if their children do not exhibit expected skills at a given age.

Some parents are concerned that their children might have some problem because of known irregularities or problems that

263

*Educable
Mentally
Retarded and
Slow Learing
Students*

occurred during the prenatal, perinatal, or postnatal periods of development. For example, there may have been a serious accident like a head injury when a child was very young. Yet there are other parents who overlook conditions that may possibly point to a serious problem. They simply do not acknowledge that anything is wrong. They love their child and expect that everything will be all right and that he will behave age-appropriately when he is ready. Friends or relatives may be aware of irregularities before the parents are. They may even suggest that the parents seek out professional help to investigate the problem. Parents need to be willing to accept such suggestions in a gracious spirit, realizing that the information was probably offered in response to their lack of objectivity and denial of the potential problems.

Professional testing can be done if one wishes. A child's doctor can recommend services available in the local area. However, these may prove expensive. J. McNamara and B. McNamara (1977) point out that there are also aids that can be used at home, such as the *Denver Developmental Screening Scale* (Frankenburg, Dodds, Fandal, Kazuk, & Cohrs, 1975) or the *Gesell Scale* (Ilg & Ames, 1965).

Early identification of developmental delays makes it possible to use early intervention. Such early training could prevent unnecessary and harmful classification or labeling, which often fosters new problems. The parent who recognizes developmental delays should also accept the child as he is and find ways to help him in a loving and understanding atmosphere, develop his skills, help him overcome disabling conditions, and help him find the place God has for him. Parents should remember that God does have a plan for their child. Parents can help their child fulfill that plan as he realizes God wants to work in his life. God wants to use each person, disabled or not, with the abilities that He has given him.

Parents must exercise caution, however. Because each child is unique in his development, they must be careful not to overreact. To unnecessarily label one at this early age could be harmful—our labeling may reduce our expectations for the child, and consequently the child may expect less of himself. Often, when we believe in a child, he believes in himself and succeeds because of it. A balance is needed, however. If we set goals too high for him, he will be frustrated and resistant because our expectations are beyond his ability. In addition, we will need to plan instruction that is commensurate with the child's abilities. As we set goals and plan instruction, we must remember to "train up [the] child in the way he should go" and help him develop to his potential.

Teaching the Child in the Early Years

Concerned parents, especially Christian parents, should make the commitment to train their child before the child is conceived. The Scripture clearly reveals that parents are the primary persons responsible for their child's training, whether the child is disabled or not. Because God has placed the child in the parents' care, the parents' concern and love for the child should be greater than that of anyone else. In Proverbs 22:6 God has commanded that they train him, and He has promised to bless that training. Proverbs 1:7-8 tells where this training should begin and commands children to heed the teaching of their parents: "The fear of the Lord is the beginning of knowledge: but fools despise wisdom and instruction. My son, hear the instruction of thy father and forsake not the law of thy mother." What an awesome responsibility parents have, and what a privilege for parents to have a part in God's plan for their child. He does not leave them alone to flounder but has promised in Psalm 32:8, "I will instruct thee and teach thee in the way which thou shalt go: I will guide thee with mine eye." Parents need to seek God's guidance each day in Bible reading

265

*Educable
Mentally
Retarded and
Slow Learing
Students*

and prayer. They can also consider the following suggestions in working with EMR children and slow learners:

1. Even before your child is born, you must set yourself to the task of proper diet and physical health that will affect the child that is to be in your care. There are excellent books on nutrition that are on the market. Your doctor will also give you guidance in this area. Do not reject or minimize the importance of good nutrition for you and later for your child. There is much to be learned about diet that can help your child to perform better in the early years and later in school.

2. Your newborn needs a lot of love. Spend some time cuddling and rocking him. Sing to him. Talk to him. Smile! Perhaps this will mean you need to wake him up sometimes just to play with him so he can become aware of the world around him. This is how he learns.

3. Enrich his life. Let him be where he can see you or younger brothers and sisters at work or play. Let him lie on a mat on the floor so he can move his arms and legs freely and see around to get the "feel" of his world. But remember he needs to learn obedience too. It may mean you will have to let him cry sometimes. Yes, he needs a lot of love; but remember that loving discipline goes hand in hand with cuddling and times of play. When he has been properly burped, is dry, and it is time for a nap, then to bed he should go. A brief time of crying will not hurt him.

4. As he grows, there are simple everyday learning activities that you can incorporate into your daily routine. Some examples of goals for these children might be these: (a) to follow and obey clearly stated directions and commands; (b) to look and listen as a

picture book is shown; and (c) to answer clearly stated questions, such as these: Which one is bigger (smaller)? What truck do you like? Is that kind? Where is your ball?

5. Develop some simple goals and objectives that meet the needs and capabilities of the child. Writing them down would help you review them from time to time. Keep them simple and realistic, and work toward them in love and gentle firmness. Insist on obedience, but do not set goals that your child cannot reach. Sometimes you may need to break down broader goals into simpler tasks. At other times you may need to make them more challenging.

6. Review and repeat as often as necessary, using variety and adding new objectives as the child is ready. Make the training of your child a challenging, interesting, and exciting opportunity given you by God. Goals and objectives should be implemented informally within the daily routine, without undue pressure, in a loving atmosphere. As you are doing this, be careful not to compare one child with another but encourage each child step by step. In II Corinthians 10:12, we are instructed that "they measuring themselves, and comparing themselves among themselves, are not wise."

7. Use everyday life situations as opportunities to teach and/or reinforce skills. Remember how you wanted to do dishes before you could do them in a really efficient manner? Children want to be a part of your world of work. You can give the small child simple tasks such as picking up toys, listening for the mailman, and bringing a big or small spoon or a wet cloth. Find ways to use the channels of sight, hearing, and touch.

267

*Educable
Mentally
Retarded and
Slow Learing
Students*

As you do this, develop such concepts as before and after, first and last, and over and under while the children play with toys or help you. You can count as they build towers of blocks, as you go up steps, or as you walk to the corner. To develop pre-reading skills, point out differences in the things around you. Let the child tell you some things he sees.

8. As the child grows, increase the complexity of the tasks. He could bring in the mail, dry dishes, empty the trash, or sweep the kitchen. He will gain a sense of responsibility, experience togetherness with the family, develop a feeling of worth, and learn to follow directions.

9. Family times such as devotions present excellent opportunities for closeness. These times can also be used to teach what educators call adaptive behavior skills. The first step is to lead the child to accept Christ as Savior, followed by day-to-day training in the way he should go. This will not be different from the way we have devotions with any child, but if the child does have learning problems his abilities must be considered. Consider these suggestions:

   • Memorize verses. Begin with simple ones that are meaningful to the child. Refer to them throughout the days and weeks as they apply to the child's life and yours.

   • Pray with your child and let him hear you pray for him.

   • Praise your child and sing with him.

   • Tell and read stories to your child. Ask questions during and after the story time such as these: Why did he do that? What do you think will happen? Where did he go? Do you think that was wise? Could this really happen? How do you know?

10. Travel time, especially on long trips, can be used to good advantage also. Car games can be made up: count all the trucks you see; count until you have ten 8s from license plates. You can also make up simple problems, such as this: "You have four blue cars and you buy two red ones. How many cars would you have then?" For reading readiness, have the child find certain letters of the alphabet. For example, "Find 11 *B*s."

These are only a few of the everyday things you can do. You will think of many more that fit your own environment and that are suitable for your child.

Ruth Beechick (1982), in *A Biblical Psychology of Learning*, concludes that "learning begins with loving discipline, first from the parents and later, when necessary, from teachers" (p. 57). As parents continue working with their children, they must remember that learning begins with the heart. Until the child's heart is right with the Lord, learning cannot be at its best.

Armed with our beliefs in the teaching of the Bible and its life-changing effects on the heart, we have a model of learning that is superior to that of the world as our children move on to the school years.

Instruction During the School Years

It may well be that a child has reached the kindergarten age and no one has seriously suspected that he has a learning problem. Many private schools require testing to determine the child's readiness for school. This testing may be done prior to kindergarten or first grade. If they feel the child is not ready, they may advise the parents to wait a year. In this event the family will need encouragement and some solid suggestions for ways they can work with their child. Suggestions in the previous section may prove helpful.

269

*Educable
Mentally
Retarded and
Slow Learing
Students*

Even given extra time and opportunities to improve their readiness skills, some children are still not ready for first grade. Some schools provide pre-kindergarten or pre-first-grade classes (sometimes called transitional first grade) which may be recommended to the parent. These classes may work on readiness and developmental skills which are necessary in order for the child to succeed in early reading and math.

In the previous section we pointed out that hasty labeling should be avoided because of individual differences in the development of children and because of the potentially harmful effects of labeling. This holds true for school children also. Nevertheless, teachers may have children in their classrooms whose performance and/or class achievement is notably low, children who may need additional help. Thus, understanding identification is important.

Indicators for Identifying At-Risk Children

Bowman (1987) discusses a number of basic characteristics of at-risk children:

- Academic problems such as basic skills deficiencies in reading and math
- Low achievement and/or motivation
- Poor self-concept
- Slow rate of learning when compared with peers
- Inattention during classroom activities
- Acting out or attention-getting behaviors
- Poor attention patterns
- Poor work habits and/or organizational skills
- Social and cultural differences which differ from community norms (p. 5)

If the teacher recognizes a problem in a child's performance, it is her responsibility to notify her supervisor or principal of her concern. The parents too need to be informed and advised about ways they can help to improve their child's performance.

However, we must realize that teachers vary in their tolerance of behaviors. What one teacher may tolerate, another teacher may not. Because of this difference, when a teacher reports a problem it should not be concluded immediately that professional testing is necessary. Other steps (e.g., pre-referral interventions) should be taken first. (See Chapter 5 for more information.)

Developing a Curriculum for Slow Learners and EMR Children

Barnes and Barnes (1989) provide guidelines for building a curriculum to meet the requirements of slow learners and EMR children. These guidelines were developed to identify more specifically what needs to be taught. The major goal and objective of continually moving them toward the most normal setting has been kept in mind not only for the school years but on into adulthood. Barnes and Barnes (1989) state, "Too often these children continue in an academically oriented program for too long a period of time, leaving much too short a period of time to work on life skills necessary to function as an adult in the community" (p. 125). They stress the need for sincere communication between the school and parents, the benefits of group parent meetings, volunteer programs, and the participation of parents in "establishing what the goals and objectives of their children's programs should be" (p. 125). The following areas were the basis for establishing the goals and objectives that they developed:

- Academic goals and objectives
- Recreational goals and objectives
- Prevocational and vocational goals and objectives
- Social and emotional goals and objectives
- Life skills goals and objectives (p. 126)

Curricula at all levels should address these areas. In the sections that follow, we will take each of these areas and describe curricula at different grade levels for EMR students. However,

271

*Educable
Mentally
Retarded and
Slow Learing
Students*

each Christian school could well profit from the process of developing its own Christ-centered curriculum, though it may be similar in part to what public schools may offer. It is also important that teachers and administrators consult with parents in curriculum development. As we involve parents and as they understand the goals and objectives, they will more readily support the program and help make it successful.

Academic Goals and Objectives

Young children in pre-kindergarten through third grade may have developmental lags. But with the proper evaluation and training, many can eventually be integrated into a regular class. Integration should be the goal whenever possible.

Teachers should give special attention to the child's rate and style of learning as they plan a program for his optimal learning. At Hidden Treasure Christian School, different educational approaches are used. For the visual learner the Dolch Sight Word List (Dolch, 1948) has been valuable. Salt cards (made by teachers and parent volunteers) have helped tactile and kinesthetic learners. These salt cards are made by printing words on cards, outlining them with glue, and sprinkling salt on them. The children trace the words with their fingers as they read them. This allows them to receive the information not only visually but also through a sense of touch and movement. Auditory learners have profited from an intensive phonics program. However, many students need a combination of these. The Language Master (see Audiotronics in Appendix 6) and Tok-Bac (see Incentives for Learning in Appendix 6), along with the tape recorder, are of benefit to the auditory learner, and the sight learner will benefit from them also. Earphones might be supplied for the students to use at learning stations where these devices are located. To develop the communication skills of reading, writing, speaking, and listening, teachers must keep trying a variety of methods.

In reading there needs to be at least some knowledge of phonics. But whether using a rigid phonics program, a so-called linguistics program, a sight program, a reading experience program, or a combination of these, the teacher will need to have patience, encourage the student, and show enthusiasm for even small successes; and the student will need persistence.

Writing and spelling activities can be correlated with the reading program. Educators' Publishing Service (EPS; see Appendix 6) has developed many workbooks that are excellent for correlating these skills for both the visual and the auditory learner. EPS has provided needed practice for the student and saved much valuable time for the teacher. Developmental Learning Materials (DLM; see Appendix 6) has an excellent series for spelling.

As the child continues to develop, he may use EPS's language program, which is excellent for teaching capitalization and punctuation skills at the elementary level. As soon as the child is able, the teacher can dictate simple sentences for practical use of these skills.

"Show and tell" is an excellent technique for encouraging speaking skills. It also can be used for listening skills by asking appropriate questions like "What did she say her pet's name was?" or "Who told us about a trip?" Reading to students and asking questions (why, who, when, where, or "what do you think will happen next") will help develop comprehension skills for those who cannot read; and they will give the teacher some insight into the students' strengths and weaknesses in these areas. For those who can read, the *Specific Skills Series* (see Barnell-Loft in Appendix 6 for address) covers many comprehension skills; levels A-C are suitable for kindergarten through Grade 3. The child can work on these exercises independently, but checking the work daily and making corrections is vital to his success.

273

Educable
Mentally
Retarded and
Slow Learing
Students

Development of mathematics skills should move from the concrete to pictures and then to the abstract (Mercer & Mercer, 1989). The teacher must have readily available plenty of manipulatives (popsicle sticks, counters, Cuisenaire rods (see Cuisenaire in Appendix 6 for address) and worksheets (more than would be used with nondisabled students) with pictured illustrations and exercises to strengthen the skills. *Touch Math,* helpful to students who have poor memory for math facts, can be utilized for the four major operations. Some may contend that these techniques are "crutches." They may be perceived this way, but in some cases they are needed. One home school parent told of the frustration he had in teaching his child to memorize the multiplication facts. Finally he made the decision to allow her to use the multiplication chart so that he could go on with teaching multiplication with multiple digits. The child was challenged by the new work and eventually learned the facts by using the chart. A modification of the math facts chart has been used at Hidden Treasure Christian School to help students memorize the facts. The procedure consists of taping different math facts on each desk corner with the answers taped inside the desk at corresponding corners. Other facts could be taped at one corner of the chalkboard with the answer on the opposite corner. Other spots in the room can be used for more facts. The exercise of locating the fact and looking for its answer elsewhere aids in memorizing them. When they are removed, the child can be seen going through the motions of looking at the spots to help him to recall the facts.

The practical use of math must also be presented. Often, because a child lacks the skill to read written story problems, he is not exposed to them. Furthermore, there is a lack of good material in this area. Slow learners and EMR children need this skill, and they need the challenge of making mathematical decisions of whether to add, subtract, multiply, or divide. They will need many varied materials to aid in gaining skill in solving problems. Finally, continual review is needed as new skills are taught.

In the upper elementary years, that is, Grades 4-8, slow learners and higher-functioning EMR children may be able to continue on in their regular class. Barnes and Barnes (1989) hold that "for many students who are able to fit into the regular classroom in academic areas, this should be their last opportunity to really push for skill improvement" (p. 142). They will need much encouragement and help. As they continue to develop specific skills, they will profit from such things as the use of a calculator in math or the use of a tape recorder to record a history or science lesson that can be replayed for later study. Because these students will need to spend more time and to work harder to succeed, they will need much encouragement. At the same time, they will learn valuable lessons in perseverance.

Barnes and Barnes (1989) point out that some of the students, on the other hand, "seem to be falling further behind, regardless of the amount of time spent" (p. 142). These students need to continue to work on skills, but they and their parents need to be aware of future programs that will offer training suitable for them in the high school years. In a sense "this can be a time in which academics are de-emphasized" (p. 142). Their application to practical life skills will be important. These skills include such things as letter writing, telling time, money skills, safety and health awareness, knowledge of community organizations and projects, newspaper use, and telephone directory skills.

During the high school years (Grades 9-12) the academic skills that the student worked so hard to develop in the previous years must now be applied to life situations. He must gain practice in reading the newspaper to find information concerning sales or job opportunities or actually writing letters to thank someone—for example, a speaker who has presented helpful

275

*Educable
Mentally
Retarded and
Slow Learing
Students*

information on job opportunities. A continuation of in-school opportunities for work, where the student learns to follow directions and do a thorough job, presents excellent training. Math skills must be used in such things as planning budgets, balancing a checkbook, and buying needed items of food or clothing. Wise use of time, practical use of measuring skills, and an introduction to the costs of living (rent, food, clothing, car, and utilities) are essential. In social studies the newspaper can be used to foster everyday awareness of what is going on in the world. Group discussions of current issues, as well as some teaching on voting and the importance of participating in elections, will be beneficial. This does not mean that there cannot be meaningful units of history, government, and geography incorporated into the program. Science is often of real interest to EMR students, and they should be encouraged to have an interest in as many fields as possible.

Recreational Goals and Objectives

Some people may consider recreational goals to be unnecessary, but this is an area where children in pre-kindergarten through Grade 3 who have academic and developmental weaknesses can find enjoyment, success, and a "feeling of belonging" (Barnes & Barnes, 1989).

Barnes and Barnes (1989) list three goals in this area: (a) promoting recreational skill development; (b) developing leisure-time pursuits that are age-appropriate; and (c) encouraging physical fitness. Parents and teachers should encourage such activities as swimming, bowling, roller skating, bicycle riding, or hiking when these activities are appropriate and available. Some of these could be school activities and later become leisure-time pursuits. At all times the activities should be pursued in a wholesome atmosphere. Some of these activities can be included in youth activities at church, Awana clubs, camps, Boy Scouts, or Girl Scouts. In some areas there are special camps for disabled students which fill a need for interacting with others. Subjects such as art, music, and physical education can influence a child to pursue appropriate leisure-time activities such as crafts, singing, or sports.

For EMR students in Grades 4-6, recreational goals should continue those stressed in the earlier years but be more advanced. It may be that a student will show greater skill in one specific area, and he can teach a younger child and gain a sense of accomplishment. This skill could be in the realm of sports, arts and crafts, or music. As mentioned before, because of his struggles academically, he often feels inferior, and successes in this area are important to him.

EMR students at the high school level, as well as other levels, should plan their activities according to Bible principles and center them around church functions. They should be encouraged to plan activities to keep physically fit, and they should engage in leisure-time activities such as arts and crafts, gardening, woodworking, and music.

Prevocational Skills

Even at a very young age, through studying units on community helpers children can become aware of different occupations. Barnes and Barnes (1989) state, "It is also important for the teacher, parents and other adults dealing with the children to keep a positive approach regarding the dignity of work in all jobs and occupations" (p. 140). At Hidden Treasure Christian School, students can develop respect for a variety of employment opportunities, as their teachers conduct field trips to businesses that might present possibilities of future employment, as they invite people from different occupations to speak to the children, and as they give students opportunity to help with classroom chores. Developing proper attitudes about authority, finishing work on time, following directions, and working with others are skills that young EMR children can

277

*Educable
Mentally
Retarded and
Slow Learing
Students*

learn. Academic skills needed for different occupations can also be learned.

In the upper elementary and junior high years, EMR students will need guidance as they study different occupations and the abilities that will be required for each. It is important for them to have an awareness of their abilities in pursuing a particular kind of work, as well as the willingness and ability to be trained in new skills that are essential for that occupation. Vocational training in high school will often be the next step, but while students are still in the upper elementary and junior high years, they must continue to work on money skills, social skills, and occupation-related skills such as punctuality, following directions, and proper attitudes toward authority. When possible, in-school tasks can be incorporated into their training as well as assigned home tasks with a system of self-evaluation to teach them responsibility.

High school EMR students should be aware of their strengths and weaknesses as they look toward possibilities for future employment. The parents' and teacher's part in guiding them to have realistic expectations of future work possibilities is important to their success. Some students will be able to participate in on-the-job training that will provide feedback as to their strengths and weaknesses. Other students may go on to vocational training. They must understand that their ability to do a job will not necessarily ensure that they keep it, but their ability to work with others is a skill to be developed also.

Social-Emotional Goals and Objectives

Barnes and Barnes (1989) indicate that the following social-emotional goals and objectives are important:

1. Assisting children in learning how to interpret social cues and develop appropriate responding behaviors;
2. Providing socializing opportunities;

3. Educating significant others; and

4. Providing direct instruction in these areas. (p. 140)

In working with EMR children in pre-kindergarten through Grade 3, Christian educators have the best opportunity to help them develop the Christian alternative to what secular educators call self-concept and self-esteem. As has been before mentioned in discussion of adaptive behavior skills, the Christian educator teaches a child his relationship to God and man and leads him to accept Christ as the only way to salvation. The worth is not in himself but in Christ, our wonderful Savior. And Christ promises to be with His own to the end. There is no greater reason to seek to live a pleasing life unto Him. He promises to give wisdom to those that "fear" (respect) Him. This includes wisdom on how to interpret social cues and develop appropriate responding behaviors. Parents and teachers armed with God's Word can teach these children with confidence.

In the upper elementary years, as in the earlier years, the EMR student's reliance on God through Jesus Christ will be the answer to the many changes in his life that will take place as he meets more people, is expected to take more responsibility for his own behavior, and makes adjustments to the physical changes in his body. Throughout these years Christian teachers and parents can help a child establish standards that will follow him through life. They can also help him realize the importance of Christian fellowship as a means of social, emotional, and spiritual support.

For EMR students at the high school level, it is important that students continue to rely on Scriptural teaching in dealing with their emotions and those of others. The Christian school has the greatest opportunity to help EMR students develop acceptable behavior when the students themselves rely on God for salvation and guidance. Opportunities for Christian fellowship in and outside the school are of great importance in helping them learn to respect the feelings and ideas of others.

Life Skills and Goals

Life skills include "age appropriate self-help skills [such as] (a) personal hygiene and grooming, (b) health and nutrition habits, (c) safety and survival skills, and (d) domestic skills" (Barnes & Barnes, 1989, p. 141).

During the pre-kindergarten through Grade 3 years, slow learners and EMR children are often behind in developmental and academic areas. The teacher may need to work closely with the parents to develop the student's habits of personal cleanliness and other general life skills. The teacher can develop units on health, nutrition, and safety; and some domestic skills (dusting, running a sweeper, washing desks, or straightening a bookshelf) can even be practiced at school.

Life skills and goals are part of the overall curriculum as EMR children grow into the upper elementary years, because the goals and objectives in each area are directed toward preparing these students for life. However, Barnes and Barnes (1989) point out some areas that should be given special attention for children in the upper elementary years:

- Improvement of the basic hygiene skills of all students.
- Promotion of self-help skills such as cleaning, laundry, understanding of purchasing power, proper eating habits and weight control, independence and mobility around the community, safety around the home, contributions to family life, including cleaning, cooking and assisting other members of the family with household chores.
- An understanding and appreciation of the variety of [community] services that are available. (p. 146)

As previously stated, life skills are part of the total education for all EMR students. At the high school level, some suggestions to strengthen these skills for EMR students are as follows:

1. If possible, a group of students can handle planning of trips. This can include planning for expenses, arranging for lodging (if any) and transportation, setting up an itinerary, and establishing standards for behavior.
2. Boys might plan a bachelor weekend and take responsibility for the shopping, cooking, and cleaning that will be necessary.
3. Girls could engage in a similar activity that could include child-care responsibilities.
4. Volunteers who would be willing to "apprentice" one of these students for a week in the home, on a farm, or in a small business could be of considerable help in meeting the need for practical experiences that could lead to later gainful employment.
5. And finally there could be group homes established to give a further training period for these students to develop skills for productive and normal lives in the community.

Their education must prepare them for life. Teachers should let EMR students "grow up," encouraging them to assume more responsibility as they are able. Some will be eager to do so. Others will need a little push. As they go on, their teachers should pray that they might glorify God in the place He has for them.

Summary

There are many things to be learned about slow learners and EMR children, new methods to be tried, educational materials to be provided, and job opportunities to be made available. Classifying, labeling, placing, assessing, and teaching slow learners and EMR students can be either a discouraging

281

*Educable
Mentally
Retarded and
Slow Learing
Students*

and defeating experience or a challenging and rewarding area of service to the Lord.

Hidden Treasure Christian School provides an education in an environment for EMR and slow learner children that is as normal as possible, where each student has an opportunity to mingle with those who have similar limitations and also with those who have a variety of physical and/or mental disabilities. It is refreshing and rewarding to see the acceptance these students have for each other. The students come face to face with their individual needs and learn to work hard to overcome them. The teacher's job is to provide the materials and instructional methods that will help each child to reach his goals. The child's progress and growing confidence reward and challenge the teacher, the student himself, and his parents.

Some who read this are home schooling parents. Some are teachers and parents from private and Christian schools. Others are in the public schools. Each has his own convictions for the domain he has chosen for his child's education. Valuable information has been drawn from these domains to help in assessing student needs, in searching out effective methods, and in presenting some ideas for developing curricula.

As we have stressed in this chapter, the child's relationship to God and man is central to his education. When a child receives Christ as his Savior, he has the advantage of a model of learning based on spiritual needs of the heart. He has in him the fear of God, which is the beginning of knowledge. Furthermore, as he memorizes and applies Scripture to his own life, he avails himself of the promise of Joshua 1:8–that he will "make [his] way prosperous and . . . have good success."

References

Barnes, D. B., & Barnes, C. K. (1989). *Special educator's survival guide: Practical techniques and materials for supervision and instruction.* West Nyack, NY: The Center for Applied Research in Education.

Beechick, R. (1982). *A Biblical psychology of learning.* Denver, CO: Accent Books.

Bowman, J. E. (1987, April). *When is intervention an ounce of prevention?* Rockville, Maryland: Montgomery County Schools, Department of Education Accountability and Department of Special and Alternative Education. Paper presented at the American Educators Research Conference, Washington, DC.

Dolch, E. W. (1948). *Graded reading difficulty worksheet.* Champaigne, IL: Garrard Press.

Frankenburg, W., Dodds, J., Fandal, A., Kazuk, E., & Cohrs, M. (1975). *Denver Developmental Screening Test Revised Reference Manual.* Denver, CO: LA-DOCA Project & Publishing Foundation.

Hallahan, D. P., & Kauffman, J. M. (1988). *Exceptional children: Introduction to exceptional children* (4th ed.). Englewood Cliffs, NJ: Prentice-Hall.

Hallahan, D. P., Kauffman, J. M., & Lloyd, J. W. (1985). *Introduction to learning disabilities* (2nd ed.). Englewood Cliffs, NJ: Prentice-Hall.

Ilg, F. L., & Ames, L. B. (1965). *School readiness: Behavior tests used at the Gesell Institute.* New York, NY: Harper & Row.

283

*Educable
Mentally
Retarded and
Slow Learing
Students*

Jordan, J. B., Gallagher, J. J., Hutlinger, P. L., & Karnes, M. B. (1988). *Early childhood special education birth to three.* Reston, VA: Council for Exceptional children.

Kephart, N. C. (1971). *The slow learner in the classroom* (2nd ed.). Columbus, OH: Charles E. Merrill Publishing Company.

Kirk, S. A. (1962). *Educating exceptional children.* Boston, MA: Houghton Mifflin Co.

Kirk, S. A., & Johnson, G. O. (1951). *Educating the retarded child.* Boston, MA: Houghton Mifflin Co.

Kochanek, T. T., Kabacoff, R. I., & Lipsitt, L. P. (1990). Early identification of developmentally disabled and at-risk preschool children. *Exceptional Children, 56,* 528-538.

Kolstoe, O. P. (1976). *Teaching educable mentally retarded children* (2nd ed.). New York, NY: Holt, Rinehart & Winston.

Lovitt, T. C. (1989). *Introduction to learning disabilities.* Boston, MA: Allyn & Bacon.

Luftig, R. L. (1987). *Teaching the mentally retarded student: Curriculum, methods, and strategies.* Boston, MA: Allyn & Bacon, Inc.

MacMillan, D. L. (1988). Issues in mild mental retardation. *Education and Training in Mental Retardation, 23,* 273-89.

McNamara, J., & McNamara, B. (1977). *The special child handbook.* New York, NY: Hawthorn Books, Inc.

Mercer, C. D., & Mercer, A. R. (1989). *Teaching students with learning problems.* Columbus, OH: Charles E. Merrill Publishing Company.

Salvia, J., & Ysseldyke, J. E. (1988). *Assessment in special education and remedial education.* Boston, MA: Houghton Mifflin Co.

Ysseldyke, J. E., & Algozzine, B. (1984). *Introduction to special education.* Boston, MA: Houghton Mifflin Company.

Trainable and Severely/Profoundly Mentally Retarded Students

Mary E. Behymer

Introduction

*E*ducation in America has undergone many changes since the days of the one-room schoolhouse. It has changed from a time and place where children of wide age ranges and abilities met together to learn the basics of reading, writing, and arithmetic. It has also changed from a time and place where, in spite of a caring teacher's best efforts, slower children were often scorned by their more academically capable peers and were humiliated to the point of leaving school altogether. In those days severely or profoundly disabled children never saw the inside of a classroom. Instead, they were kept at home, safely protected from the critical eyes of mainstream society.

Over the years there has been a drastic transformation in how the general public perceives and treats disabled persons. We have begun to accept disabled persons as individuals, thinking of their disability as just one facet of the whole person. One has only to consider various advertisements in the media to see an increase of disabled children and adults presented as actors and models. They are not being singled out as strange or unusual, but being portrayed as people who benefit from the product being sold. We frequently see disabled people at a number of public places, such as shopping centers, restaurants, and sporting events. As a society, we are no longer startled or surprised by their presence. More and more people realize the right of disabled people to enjoy the same benefits that nondisabled people take for granted. This change has been a slow and sometimes painful process as parents fought for the right to love their children openly and to provide for them a more normal life. Because an accepting attitude is more prevalent today, it is difficult to believe that, even as recently as fifteen years ago, some parents of Down's syndrome children were still being counseled by their physicians to place their newborn children in institutions and to forget that they were ever born! More important than attitudes is the fact that our society now mandates the right of every child to an appropriate education, regardless of how severe the disability.

As Christians and educators, we have two major responsibilities toward disabled students entrusted to our care. One is that we do our best to meet the educational and spiritual needs of these students. The other is that we be willing to help other Christians become aware of these needs so that Christ's example of love and acceptance toward disabled people can be followed by others. Before these responsibilities are fulfilled, however, we must understand and accept God's view of disabled persons.

289

*Trainable
and Severely/
Profoundly
Mentally
Retarded
Students*

God's View of Mentally Retarded Persons

We need to consider God's Word and then adjust our imperfect perceptions in the light of His perfect view. Because God is omniscient, we can be assured that He is never surprised when a child is born mentally retarded. Because He is perfect, we can know that He is doing what is right. In Psalm 139:14, the psalmist exclaims, "I will praise thee; for I am fearfully and wonderfully made." The surrounding verses indicate clearly that God knows all about a person even before his physical development begins. Psalm 18:30 reminds us, "As for God, his way is perfect." He never makes a mistake or a wrong decision.

Jesus always ministered to people with special needs. The Gospels are filled with instances of His meeting the physical and spiritual needs of these people. Matthew 9:35-36 tells us that Jesus preached to, taught, and healed numerous people in the cities and villages. When He saw a crowd gathered together, "he was moved with compassion on them, because they fainted, and were scattered abroad, as sheep having no shepherd." His compassion toward those in need was clearly seen in His willingness to help them. One of the most beautiful examples of this came in response to the disciples questioning why a certain man was born blind (John 9:1-41). They asked, "Master, who did sin, this man, or his parents, that he was born blind?" The Lord explained to His disciples that sin had nothing to do with the man's condition, but that he was blind in order that God would be glorified. In this example, Christ glorified the Father by miraculously giving the blind man sight. When God chooses to allow a disability to remain, He is best glorified by our acceptance of the person as God made him.

God's love for us is not contingent upon who or what we are. Rather, His love is freely given because of who He is. Certain terminology in special education today (e.g., subaverage, deficits) suggests that the child is not complete or whole and that he is somehow substandard. In direct contrast, God uses such phrases as "fearfully and wonderfully made" (Psalm 139:14).

That God places a high value on every individual He creates is unquestionably demonstrated in the priceless sacrifice of Jesus Christ. While man focuses on what the disabled person cannot do, God expects fulfillment of His preordained will for that individual (Ephesians 2:10). In God's eyes that person was born fully equipped to do the job that He has planned for him to do, regardless of the type of job and the severity of the disability. Unfortunately, earthly ideas of success still dominate our thinking. We often establish a person's value by how much he earns, owns, or contributes to society. For example, the status of a physician is generally thought of as higher than that of a street sweeper. These attitudes could not be farther from the truth shown in God's Word. Jesus admonishes us not to work for personal or material gain, but instead to work to serve God (Matthew 6:19-21). What seems to be a small responsibility to us may be deserving of great reward in God's eyes. It is not up to us to decide whether or not a disabled person's contribution in life is worth something. Rather, we need to give our preconceived notions over to God. Psalm 62:5 says, "My soul, wait thou only upon God; for my expectation is from him." As we give up our imperfect human ideas, we then allow the Holy Spirit to show us what our expectations for disabled children truly ought to be. We are to look at disabled people as God does and do our best to help each one reach the full potential that God has given him.

Man's View of Mentally Retarded Persons

To be effective in meeting the needs of mentally retarded students, we must establish a general understanding of mental

291

*Trainable
and Severely/
Profoundly
Mentally
Retarded
Students*

retardation as man defines it. The American Association of Mental Deficiency (AAMD) refers to mental retardation as "a significantly subaverage general intellectual functioning existing concurrently with deficits in adaptive behavior and manifested during the developmental period" (Grossman, 1983). The three major criteria in this definition are (a) presence of subaverage general intellectual functioning, (b) deficits in adaptive behavior, and (c) manifestation of this condition during the developmental period.

"Subaverage intellectual functioning" represents a score from an individually administered test of intelligence that falls more than two standard deviations below the mean (Hewett & Forness, 1977). This translates to an IQ score beginning at 70 or below. "Adaptive behavior" describes the way a person meets the standards of independence and social responsibility that are expected of his age and cultural group (Kirk & Gallagher, 1983). For example, this would include one's ability to walk, talk, take care of personal needs, communicate, and apply previously learned skills to everyday life (Hewett & Forness, 1977). These skills illustrate a person's ability to adapt to new situations or environments. Manifestation of the condition "during the developmental period" simply means that it must exist during the first eighteen years of life (Hewett & Forness, 1977).

Trainable Mentally Retarded (TMR) Persons

Classification Criterion

The category of mental retardation includes persons whose conditions range from mild to severe. Consequently, specific classifications of MR include educable, trainable, and severely/profoundly MR. When a trainable mentally retarded (TMR) person is mentioned, people almost exclusively think of a

Down's syndrome child. Though many children with Down's syndrome fall into the TMR classification (Kirk & Gallagher, 1983), they are far from alone. Although more than 200 causes of mental retardation are known, it is impossible in most cases to determine the exact cause (Hewett & Forness, 1977). TMR is a classification label for students whose IQ falls between approximately 25 and 50 (Davis, 1980).

Characteristics

Many trainable mentally retarded persons demonstrate similar general characteristics. There is a delay in the development of their physical and motor abilities (Kirk & Gallagher, 1983). Speech or language development is often slower than that of nonretarded peers (Hallahan & Kauffman, 1988). There is often difficulty with the metacognitive processes, or understanding how one thinks, reasons, and plans strategies (Hallahan & Kauffman, 1988). These children may also possess splinter skills. Davis (1980) defines these as "specific and isolated skills that have limited relationship or value to the . . . whole." An example of this might be a child who can manipulate snaps but cannot dress himself. Problems in motor or muscle development will often cause TMR children to "appear . . . awkward and clumsy and to walk with a stiff, robotlike gait" (Kirk & Gallagher, 1983). Because these developmental delays are so marked, TMR children will probably be recognized at an early age, perhaps even at birth (Kirk & Gallagher, 1983).

Parents' natural tendency is to compare their child's progress with that of other children within the family and outside the family. When a child lags behind in sitting, walking, crawling, or talking when compared with others the same age, parents may begin to feel uneasy. They may, at this point, share their concerns with a family physician. If the doctor concurs, developmental screening can begin. (For more information on testing procedures, see Chapter 5.)

293

*Trainable
and Severely/
Profoundly
Mentally
Retarded
Students*

Realistic Goals

Professionals generally agree that TMR students can achieve early elementary grade-level academics (especially if taught in a functional manner) and can master self-care, social competence, and simple vocational tasks (Kirk & Gallagher, 1983; Hallahan & Kauffman, 1988). TMR adults may eventually learn to function semi-independently with consistent supervision. Current practice in educating TMR students emphasizes teaching them skills that will help them to "function independently in a social and work environment" (Hallahan & Kauffman, p. 77).

Severely/Profoundly Retarded Persons

Picture a pretty nine-year-old girl with blond hair and blue-grey eyes. I'll call her Sarah. Now picture her in a wheelchair. Don't think of a typical wheelchair that you might see provided at shopping malls and amusement parks. Sarah needs one with special adaptations to keep her head from falling forward and closing off her air passage. She must be slightly reclined and have specially designed pads which help keep her body from sagging so that it can sustain the weight of her head. Her low muscle tone makes her appear floppy, like a child's rag doll, and provides little control over her body. You see, Sarah is a profoundly mentally retarded child who also has an orthopedic impairment. She will always need a wheelchair and will require complete care for her entire life.

Sarah is not a "vegetable." She is little girl who will mature into a young woman, if the Lord allows. It is not a shame that she is so pretty. Her physical beauty may be the very quality which will encourage others to befriend and interact with her. Please don't feel sorry for Sarah. She is simply who she is. Her physical and mental limitations do not prevent her from feeling the gamut of emotions that you and I feel. She experiences happiness, sadness, excitement, fear, loneliness, contentment, frustration, and joy when there is reason to feel so. Her handicap prevents her from expressing verbally what she is experiencing, but she sends a clear message through nonverbal cues like facial expressions, attitudes, the tenseness of her muscles, and the tone of her vocalizations. She likes eggs, but not when they are fried. She enjoys listening to music, but only when she is in the mood for it. She likes to look at animals, but she doesn't care much for having their fur touch her skin. In short, Sarah has definite preferences just as you and I do.

Her educational goals are drastically different from those of the traditional academic program most people envision when they think of school. Yet Sarah attends school five days a week from August to June each year. Her class includes six other students — one walks independently, two must use walkers, and three are nonambulatory. Her teacher and two assistants schedule as many group activities as are appropriate, but most of the teaching is done on a one-to-one basis. Sarah is learning to use a spoon to scoop bites of food from her plate. She is learning to activate an electronic switch with just light pressure by her elbow in order to turn on a tape player. She is also strengthening her neck muscles by holding her head upright for increasing amounts of time.

These instructional objectives may seem insignificant to some people, but for Sarah they offer freedom. Learning to scoop her own food will give her the dignity of deciding what she wants to eat at what time. Operating a tape player independently permits her to choose how to spend some of her time, rather than being shuttled from one activity to another at another person's control. Holding her own head erect will help alleviate some of the boredom she may feel by allowing her to look around at different things in her environment. These seemingly small steps are actually great milestones to Sarah.

Much has been said recently about the "quality of life" for people like Sarah. Suppose that living consisted only of sleeping, waking, being fed, being changed, and being made comfortable. Life would be incredibly dreary, would it not? Yet many severely and profoundly retarded people are expected to live this type of existence. If Sarah's care-givers assume that she is incapable of feeding herself, expressing preferences, or feeling emotions as we do, they may also conclude that her life has little or no "quality" to it. Although Sarah may never play on a soccer team, attend college, or marry, she can still enjoy the life that God has given her. If she is aided and encouraged by caring people, Sarah will learn to do many things that will facilitate her reaching the full potential that she is capable of achieving. Again, it is crucial that we give up our human, fallible, and often unreasonable expectations, giving them over to the Lord in exchange for His perfect guidance and plan for her life.

This characterization of Sarah represents a typical profile of many severely/profoundly retarded children. There are others with less severe limitations than Sarah. There are still others with even more restricting disabilities. Each child is different. These children's differences, likes and dislikes, preferences, and personalities teach us to look past the disabilities and learn to know and respect the people inside.

Teaching severely and profoundly mentally retarded children in a school setting is a relatively new concept. Before PL 94-142 mandated education for all disabled persons, it was not considered to be appropriate or beneficial for these students to be in an instructional setting. Since severely and profoundly retarded children have difficulty with even basic skills (e.g., eating, dressing, and toilet training) many people concluded that they were not able to be educated at all. This kind of reasoning, albeit narrow, is consistent with the previously held notion that education meant only mastering the basics of reading, writing, and arithmetic (i.e., academics) rather than teaching a broad range of skills that prepare students for adult life.

Classification Criterion

A child's classification as severely or profoundly retarded (as opposed to educable or trainable mentally retarded) depends primarily upon the results of an intelligence test. Severely retarded persons show an IQ score of four or five standard deviations below the norm, while the IQ scores of profoundly retarded children are more than five standard deviations below the norm (Davis, 1980). According to Hallahan and Kauffman (1988), this translates to an approximate score of 20-25 to 35-40 for severely retarded and below 20-25 for profoundly retarded individuals. Teachers of severely/profoundly retarded students often see official test results which identify the student as being untestable. This happens when the person administering the test believes that the test is not appropriate or would not establish an accurate score.

When designing a child's individual educational plan (IEP), however, the focus should not be on the IQ score. Professionals are beginning to question the usefulness of these scores and would like to see alternatives to the traditional concept of intelligence testing. Smith (1969) states that intelligence tests "serve to destroy and impede the real business of education" (pp. 30-31). Neither should the focus be on the labels *severely* or *profoundly* retarded. Instead, teachers should concentrate on the type and amount of intervention necessary to encourage as much independence as possible for that child. Because of the nature and severity of their disabilities, however, severely and profoundly retarded students will probably require complete care all their lives.

Characteristics

Though each person is created as a unique individual, severely or profoundly retarded persons may share some common characteristics. They may have multiple disabilities. The development of their motor skills will likely be far behind that

297

*Trainable
and Severely/
Profoundly
Mentally
Retarded
Students*

of their same-aged nonretarded peers. Communication skills may appear to be minimal or nonexistent. Because of these marked differences, early detection of the disability is very likely. Severe and profound retardation can be a congenital condition (present at birth), the result of an injury, or even the result of a physical illness such as spinal meningitis or Reye's syndrome. As with a trainable mentally retarded child, the exact cause of the disability may never be identified. If the condition is present at birth, the severity of the retardation and the possible presence of other disabling conditions may prompt immediate detection of the disability. Fortunately, the earlier the disability is detected, the sooner educational intervention can begin.

Multiple disabilities Many severely/profoundly retarded students have more than one disabling condition at the same time (concomitant disabilities). One particular child may be blind as well as severely retarded. Another may be orthopedically impaired, deaf, and mentally retarded. There is no specific pattern for children with severe or profound retardation. Each person is unique, and the disabilities that he has are part of what makes him who he is. We need to remember that God creates individuals, each of whom He knows before he is born. He does not approach it the same way we do when we make uniformly shaped cookies, all from the same dough. He chooses to make each person different and gives each of us one or more specific spiritual gifts to use for His glory.

Motor skills Gross motor skills (using the large muscles of the body) and fine motor skills (such as those used for eating or dressing) are very obviously delayed in severely or profoundly disabled students. Much of their education may consist of developing these skills to usefulness. Like trainable mentally retarded students, they may possess splinter skills which do not seem valuable for overall functioning. The teacher must learn to recognize these skills and find a way to make them useful to the student. For example, one child may be able to raise his arm above his head. Although this skill may not seem particularly useful in itself, the teacher could use it to teach the child to comb his own hair.

Communication skills   Communication skills of severely or profoundly retarded people must be nurtured. Unfortunately, most people tend to think that communication must occur through verbal means, either in spoken or in written form. But many of these students are nonverbal. However, this does not mean they are unable to communicate. Communication is defined as "the exchange of thoughts, messages, or information" (*American Heritage Dictionary,* 1983, p. 141). We are all born with the desire to make our needs known. Consider the newborn babe who arrives in this world with no understanding of the spoken or written language of his culture. Without a word, he effectively conveys to his parents his need for food and warmth. His communication is expressed primarily through crying, the rooting reflex, and snuggling. A nonverbal retarded child may employ similar techniques in order to communicate (Bigge, 1982). He may use eye contact, facial expressions, body movement, or vocalizations (sounds made by his voice). "Exchange of . . . information," as used in the definition provided above, implies that at least two people must be involved. This means that part of the burden of communication is on the sender and the passing of information is shared by both sender and receiver. The effectiveness of any attempted communication from a severely or profoundly retarded child will depend largely upon the perceptiveness of the intended receiver.

Realistic goals

There are a number of aspects to consider when developing an educational program that provides both beneficial and realistic goals for severely and profoundly mentally retarded children. One must consider the degree of independence the child may realistically be expected to achieve. When complete independence is not feasible, the student should be encouraged to participate as fully as his disability will allow. Related specialists (e.g., speech and language, occupational, and physical therapists) may provide support for the parents and special education teacher as they develop the student's educational objectives. Above all, those developing the program must think of the student as a person first—a person whose personality, likes, and dislikes make him who he truly is inside.

Increased levels of independence Because they will need care their entire lives, it is not realistic to expect severely or profoundly retarded children to acquire all the skills necessary for independent living. However, it is appropriate to encourage them to learn to do as much for themselves as possible. Usually in a given school all students identified as severely or profoundly retarded are educated in the same classroom because their educational goals are similar (developing an effective communication system, self-help skills, increased social competence, and simple work skills).

Ancillary therapy The most beneficial educational program for these children utilizes a team approach involving the parents, the teacher, and other specialists whenever appropriate (speech, occupational, and physical therapists). Each specialist brings to the team unique responsibilities and expertise from which the child can benefit. Working together, this multidisciplinary team can develop realistic goals for the student.

The traditional concept of speech therapy which focuses on specific speech disorders such as articulation difficulties is not stressed as much today with severely and profoundly retarded students as it has been in the past. Current interest and practice by speech therapists is more in the direction of helping the child develop and use a formal system of language and communication (Hallahan & Kauffman, 1988). There are many different ways to accomplish this goal, and the methods will vary from student to student. Some children may learn to use simple words in sign language such as *eat, go, drink, please,* or *want.* Other children may require the use of communication boards having pictures, line drawings, or simple words printed on them. With this method, a child locates the visual representation of his need and points to it. Some students may be able to manipulate a more compact version of a communication board such as a wallet or small photograph album. Students with severe physical limitations may need to develop a consistent use of body language or vocalizations. For example, a "yes" answer could be indicated by a single nod of the head or a smile. Expressing a desire for a specific item or object may be indicated by maintaining eye contact with the item. With many students, vocalizations can be shaped to consistently represent something specific. If the child consistently vocalizes a long *e* sound, he may learn to use that particular sound to mean "eat." Whether the student needs help in learning to convey his thoughts to others (expressive language) or in understanding what is said to him (receptive language), a good speech therapist will act as a communication facilitator between the child and the intended listener. If speech therapy is not available, the teacher and the parents must assume the primary responsibility for that role in developing and encouraging communication.

Depending on the disabilities involved, occupational therapy and/or physical therapy may be needed. Occupational therapy is not synonymous with vocational training. Davis (1980) defines it as "the use of creative and manual activities designed to help various types of disabled individuals achieve greater mastery of their bodies and increased ability to cope socially in their environment" (p. 113). These activities can range from pencil and paper tasks to sensory stimulation using various types of auxiliary equipment. Children who have poor oral motor skills would benefit from receiving occupational therapy. Many severely or profoundly retarded students have

301

*Trainable
and Severely/
Profoundly
Mentally
Retarded
Students*

oral motor problems, which involve difficulty using the musculature of the mouth. This can include trouble with biting, chewing, tongue lateralization, or swallowing. After evaluating the student's needs, the therapist designs specific exercise and feeding programs which will help strengthen good muscle control and inhibit improper reflexes and habits. These programs can then be followed by teachers and parents to provide consistent practice for the child.

Physical therapy is warranted when a child has an orthopedic impairment. Range-of-motion exercises[1] can be prescribed in order to increase movement ability and prevent contractures from developing or worsening. The therapist or doctor should demonstrate the appropriate techniques and watch as the parent or instructor performs the exercises with the child. Once the proper techniques are learned, it is not usually necessary for the therapist or doctor to be present each time the exercises are administered. However, great care should be taken to insure that the prescribed exercises are being followed exactly. Besides providing guidance and input to the teacher for correct positioning of the students, the physical therapist also motivates the student to develop better body management skills. Wherever appropriate, physical therapists will encourage the development of ambulation.

What has been described provides only a general indication of the various therapists' roles in the education of severely and profoundly retarded students. In any case, a therapist's training and experience can provide an invaluable resource for parents and classroom teachers as they develop the child's individualized education plan.

Partial participation Since complete independence is not a realistic goal for severely or profoundly retarded children, the

---

[1]Lay persons should be cautioned that attempts to perform these exercises without proper training can result in permanent damage to the child's physical condition. It is imperative that such exercises be done only under the supervision of a qualified therapist or doctor.

concept of partial participation is crucial to their education. Instead of completely excluding students from an activity in which they are not able to function independently, the teacher can make adaptations allowing them to participate to the fullest degree possible (Reynolds & Mann, 1987). For example, students who cannot independently enter a restaurant, order food, pay, and eat the meal can still partially participate in the activity. The teacher might provide a written order card for students to show the waitress at the appropriate time. The card would have preselected menu choices, based on the student's preferences. It might say something like this: "Hello, my name is _____. I am disabled and cannot talk. I would like to order a cheeseburger, large fries, and a medium Coke. Thank you!"

Students who cannot independently bake a cake can participate by stirring the batter or cracking the eggs. Students who are unable to walk all the way to the lunchroom can use walkers for part of the trip and finish in wheelchairs that have been placed halfway down the hall for them. A student who cannot completely feed himself may be able participate by raising the spoon to his mouth after being helped to scoop the food. A physical education class of severely and profoundly retarded students can even play a game such as kickball. Each student is assigned a helper who guides him through the game. When the ball is rolled to a student who is nonambulatory, his helper may kick the ball and push his wheelchair around the bases. The principle of partial participation not only allows students to develop increased independence, but it also permits them to be involved in a wide variety of activities from which they would otherwise be excluded.

A person first   The most important factor in educating severely or profoundly retarded students is to be aware of the person inside. Teachers must learn to recognize the students' likes, dislikes, and preferences, and then respect their personalities and choices, remembering that each student is different. A

303

*Trainable
and Severely/
Profoundly
Mentally
Retarded
Students*

student may not need to learn the same things as the others in his class. Meetings with the parents to discuss and agree upon the priorities for their child's education are essential. A team effort between the teacher, the student, parents, and any specialists involved will provide students with the most useful educational experience.

Educating Mentally Retarded Students

In order for realistic goals to be established, it is imperative that those working with mentally retarded students be aware of the characteristics and learning problems of mentally retarded persons. The teacher who is attentive to the student's needs and has a good understanding of the nature of mental retardation can achieve the appropriate balance between extreme and inadequate expectations, allowing the student to be challenged toward realistic goals without frustrating him.

Basic Techniques and Methods of Instruction

There are a number of guidelines one should follow in working with mentally retarded students in an educational environment. The teaching techniques employed should be in terms and methods suitable for the student's functioning level. For example, many experts agree that use of concrete terms, repetition, and actual hands-on practice are very effective (Luftig, 1987). Instruction and practice in a task should take place, as often as possible, in a naturally occurring environment. This gives the student, who has difficulty transferring previously learned skills, the opportunity to master the needed skill in the locale in which he will be using it. It also allows naturally occurring cues and consequences to be a motivating factor. For example, a student who is grocery shopping and leaves without paying is likely to be stopped by a store employee before exiting the premises. Care should be taken by the teacher to develop an understanding with the store management about the student's needs. Many workers in the community are very accepting and are pleased to be part of the student's education. It is appropriate, at times, to provide relevant practice in the classroom setting. Often the instruction and practice begins in the classroom and then moves to the actual site for mastery.

Task analysis Whether we realize it or not, we have all had experience to some degree with task analysis. Following directions in recipes or assembling a child's toy are both processes involving task analysis. Task analysis is a specific method of providing consistent, systematic instruction for mentally retarded students. Its purpose is to divide a complex task into its more simple component parts, thus allowing the teacher to organize instruction for concentration on areas of difficulty (Mercer & Mercer, 1989). A task analysis can be general or very detailed, depending upon the needs of the student. Usually the more severe the disability the more detailed the task analysis will need to be. This allows a severely or profoundly disabled student to work toward a target goal while taking small enough steps to prevent frustration. Small gains, by our standards, are really great victories to a disabled child and are as much cause for celebration as learning to ride a bicycle would be for a nondisabled child.

Breaking a task down into its component parts also helps the teacher recognize where adaptations could facilitate the student in accomplishing the task (Bigge, 1982). In Figure 10.1 the objective for Sarah K. is to remove her zippered jacket. Two of the steps require that she grasp the zipper and pull it down. If Sarah has difficulty maintaining a grasp on the zipper, the teacher can adapt it by placing a metal ring (found in school supplies or on key chains) through the zipper tab. Sarah would be able to maintain her grasp by hooking a finger or thumb through the ring. This simple adaptation allows her to achieve mastery of a step that might be impossible to accomplish otherwise.

Task Analysis Form

Figure 10.1

Name

   Sarah K.

Objective

   Removing zippered jacket

Cue Hierarchy
 I = Independent
 V = Verbal prompt
 P = Physical prompt
 G = Guidance (total assistance)

Component Steps	Date													
	2/7	2/8	2/9	2/10										
Grasps zipper	I	I	I	I										
Pulls zipper down	V	I	V	I										
Separates zipper at bottom	P	P	P	V										
Grasps (L) wrist cuff	V	V	I	I										
Pulls arm from sleeve	I	I	I	I										
Adjusts grasp on sleeve	P	P	P	V										
Frees (L) arm from sleeve	I	I	V	I										
Grasps (R) wrist cuff	I	I	I	I										
Pulls arm from sleeve	I	V	I	I										
Adjusts grasp on sleeve	V	V	I	V										
Frees (R) arms from sleeve	I	I	V	I										
Puts jacket down	P	V	V	V										

Figure 10.2

Task Analysis Form

Name _____

Cue Hierarchy
 I = Independent
 V = Verbal prompt
Objective _____
 P = Physical prompt
 G = Guidance (total assistance)

Date

Component Steps

DATE	NAME	1	2	3	4	5	6	7	8	9	10	%	COMMENTS
10-15	**Money Skills**												
	Rick add quarters & nickels up to $1.00	+	+	+	−	+	+	−	+	−	+	70%	problems with $.75 plus nickels
	Jamie	+	+	+	+	−	+	−	+	+	+	80%	tries to go too fast!
	Sue add quarters, dimes, & nickels up to $1.00	+	−	−	+	−	−	+	+	+	−	50%	
10-15	**Using a calculator**												
	Rick add two items	−	+	+	+	+	+	+	−	+	+	80%	
	Jamie find tax amount	−	+	+	−	+	−	−	+	+	−	50%	begin new step today
	Jeff recognize "+" and "="	+	+	+	+	−	+	+	+	+	+	90%	
10-15	**Recognizing written words from a group of words**												
	Rick field of 15	+	+	+	+	+	+	−	+	+	+	90%	problems with "gentlemen"
	Sue field of 15	+	−	+	+	+	−	+	+	+	+	80%	
	Jeff field of 6	+	+	+	−	−	+	+	+	−	+	70%	new word "exit"

Data Collection Form

Figure 10.4

DATE NAME

TRIALS

COMMENTS

1 2 3 4 5 6 7 8 9 10 %

309

*Trainable
and Severely/
Profoundly
Mentally
Retarded
Students*

Another benefit of task analysis is that it provides a means of evaluating the student's progress. The student's performance can be recorded on the task analysis form. Figure 10.2 is a sample blank form.

Monitoring progress Consistent data collection is essential to monitoring the student's progress. Once goals and objectives are outlined in the child's IEP, a means of recording performance levels for each objective should be established. Recording must be done as frequently as possible in order to represent the child's ability accurately. If an objective is practiced only once a week (such as grocery shopping), the data should be collected each time. An objective that is practiced daily or several times a day (such as washing hands or following directions), can be recorded as many times as possible. Data should be recorded by the person working with the student at that particular time. The teacher needs to establish a good habit of collecting data and should instruct any assistants or classroom volunteers to follow her example.

There are several methods of recording data, and the most appropriate method will depend upon the specific objective. Some goals are conducive to an anecdotal record, which provides a short narrative account of the student's performance. Recording can also be done while the objective is being practiced. For example, if the objective is for the student to count the sum of various coins with 90% accuracy, the student's first attempt to count the coins is recorded. If the attempt is correct, a positive response symbol is recorded. If the first attempt is incorrect, a negative response symbol is recorded. Recording is now suspended, and the student is given a chance to correct his mistake. If the second attempt is incorrect, the teacher should count with the child to demonstrate the correct answer. When a new problem is given, recording resumes. Two examples follow:

> *Example 1*
> Rick:
> Add quarters & nickels
> (range .30 - $1.00) [+ + + - + + - + + -] 70%
> *Example 2*
> Rick:
> Add quarters & nickels
> (range .30 - $1.00) [+ - + + + - + +] 75%
> In Example 1, Rick was given 10 different trials and obtained 70% accuracy. It is best to obtain at least 10 trials each time in order to easily compute the percentage correct. Example 2 shows that even with fewer trials, a percentage correct of the number of trials can still be determined by dividing the number of correct responses by the actual number of trials. (Six correct of eight trials : 6 divided by 8 equals .75 or 75%).

If several students have the same goal, practice and data collection can be done in a group situation. Each student takes a turn answering the problem while the others watch. The time they spend waiting is not wasted because they are reinforced by the working student's effort. Keeping small-group work to two or three students will help avoid the likelihood of boredom. Each day's data collection can be transferred to a single form for each student. This form displays, at a glance, where the student is in relation to the mastery criterion for each objective. (An example of one day's record keeping for a TMR class appears as Figure 10.3; and Figure 10.4 is a blank data collection form. Without actual written records, it is unlikely that the teacher will know when the student has achieved the mastery criterion for the objective.

311

*Trainable
and Severely/
Profoundly
Mentally
Retarded
Students*

Age-appropriateness Keeping activities and educational tools appropriate to the chronological age of the student is very important. For example, it would not be suitable to assign a puzzle designed for a pre-school-aged student to a 12-year-old child. Though it is not inappropriate to use a puzzle activity with a 12-year-old, the teacher should make sure that the content of the puzzle is appropriate for the child's chronological age. Planning activities that are socially acceptable for a child's actual age serves two purposes. First, age-appropriate activities help those who come in contact with mentally retarded students to see them as people rather than "babies." Second, it helps the educator to keep the curriculum content functional and meaningful for the child.

A Functional Approach

When designing an educational program, we should give attention to the physical development and life experiences that the student has had. The key is to make the curriculum functional, or useful to the student's life. For example, suppose the goal for a student is to develop better fine motor skills and eye-hand coordination. And suppose that a teacher chooses a skill like coloring a picture to accomplish this goal. Whether or not coloring a picture is meaningful to the child will depend largely upon his age. Although a younger child may benefit from the coloring activity, it would be virtually meaningless for an adolescent, since most adolescents do not participate. Perhaps a more functional objective that accomplishes the same goal for most mentally retarded students, and particularly mentally retarded adolescents, might be to practice sewing buttons on fabric or to place coins in appropriate vending-machine slots. It is imperative that we evaluate the activity on the basis of its usefulness to the student.

One aspect of adapting to our environment is the ability to take something we have previously learned and apply it in a new situation. If, for example, a nondisabled person learned how to press the button on a soap dispenser in order to get soap, and then he encountered a dispenser which required him to pull a lever instead, he would probably be able to make it function. Luftig (1987) explains that mentally retarded students have difficulty generalizing previously learned skills to new situations. A mentally retarded person may become frustrated or bewildered when he faces a soap dispenser that differs from what he is used to operating. Students need to practice skills in naturally occurring environments and be exposed to a wide variety of circumstances in which the skill can be used. If a child learns to recognize colors, rote-count by fives to one hundred, or button a doll's dress, but he can't sort his laundry, make change for purchases, or put on his own shirt, then his education is simply inappropriate and useless.

A good way for a teacher to determine the validity of a functional activity is to answer the question, "If the child does not master the particular skill now, will someone have to perform it for him when he is an adult?" There is probably little chance that someone would have to color a picture or rote-count by fives for a mentally retarded adult, since these activities are not typically required of a nondisabled adult. But it is very probable that someone would have to help a mentally retarded adult get dressed if he has not mastered this skill. Education even for nondisabled students in the regular classroom should be designed as preparation for life. Smith (1969) states that one of the major goals of educators is to "assist their students in acquiring higher and higher levels of competency" (p. 43). Thinking of education as life preparation will help the educator of mentally retarded students to accept the fact that teaching reading, writing, and arithmetic may not be appropriate unless it helps the child function more independently in life.

Developing a functional curriculum Many schools are beginning to follow the example set by a pilot community-based

313

*Trainable
and Severely/
Profoundly
Mentally
Retarded
Students*

program in Dekalb, Illinois (Freagon, Wheeler, Brankin, McDannel, Costello, & Peters, 1983). Their curricular guide divides instructional areas into four main categories. They are (a) domestic skills, (b) recreation and leisure skills, (c) vocational skills, and (d) community skills. While these four areas can encompass any goal or objective involving academic or life skills, they do not provide for the spiritual needs of the child. Believers are exhorted by Scripture to teach, train, and nurture children in the ways of the Lord (Psalm 78:4-7; Proverbs 22:6; Ephesians 6:4). It is for this reason that, in addition to the four areas enumerated by Freagon et al. (1983), a fifth area in Bible should be incorporated into a Christian school curriculum for retarded children. One should bear in mind that these five skill areas are not mutually exclusive. Instead, their interdependence contributes toward effectively accomplishing the intended goals for the student. Planning the student's long-term goals and short-term objectives within these major areas will encourage the development of useful skills without neglecting the student's spiritual needs. This approach will help the student to function as independently as possible in life.

Skill areas The **domestic area** concentrates on skills that will be necessary for functioning independently in a home environment, such as cooking, cleaning, self- help, sewing, and coordinating clothing.

The **recreation and leisure area** teaches skills that the student can use throughout his life inside and outside the school environment. It helps to develop interests and activities for the appropriate use of free time, such as sports skills, indoor games, social interaction skills, talents, and hobbies.

The **vocational area** emphasizes the development of skills that are task-oriented. It teaches work-related skills adapted for various age and functioning levels. Whenever appropriate, the vocational area concentrates on skills that will increase the employability of the student, such as following routines and directions, job duties, vocational awareness, and time management skills.

The **community area** provides the opportunity for teaching skills necessary for successful integration into community settings. This is accomplished through relevant practice in the classroom and situational performance in the actual setting (such as grocery and department stores, restaurants, gas stations, and the post office). A primary benefit of this skill area is that mentally retarded people learn and work alongside nondisabled individuals. Practice of these goals will also help to educate people in the community who may not have contact with mentally retarded persons on a regular basis. Careful management of this area will do much to help our society continue to accept and understand the needs of mentally retarded people. [Parents may find helpful information provided by local chapters of national organizations for persons with retardation. See Burek, Koek, and Novallo (1989).]

The **Bible area** provides the student with instruction in Biblical principles and gives him the opportunity to practice and internalize these Scriptural principles.

Keeping in mind that education is preparation for life, the special education teacher and the parents can begin working together to develop a useful and effective educational plan for the student. Table 10.1, covering the first four areas, is a general guide to aid teachers and parents in considering functional age-appropriate goals for trainable or severely/profoundly mentally retarded students. This list is by no means exhaustive; it should not be regarded as an inflexible curricular guide but as a reference tool.

Teaching the Bible Area The spiritual needs of mentally retarded students may be the most difficult to determine. This is because the spiritual area deals with a condition of the heart, rather than concrete or visible needs. The greatest guidance a

Table 10.1

315

*Trainable
and Severely/
Profoundly
Mentally
Retarded
Students*

Domestic

Food: Eating (A)
Basic skills: biting, chewing, swallowing, drinking, self-feeding,
          adaptations, choosing
Table manners

Food: Meal Preparation
Nutrition
- Exposure to healthful food choices (A)
- Four food groups: recognizing, classifying foods (A)
- Planning balanced meals (J, S)
- Planning balanced menus (S)
- Determining groceries needed (J, S)
  (For shopping see **Community** area)

Storing foods
- Where to store them: refrigerator or cabinet, easy access (A)
- Preventing spoilage (J, S)
- Recognizing spoiled foods (J, S)

Preparation
- Kitchen cleanliness: washing hands, cleaning utensils (A)
- Utensil usage: stirring, scooping, spreading, cutting (A)
- Careful use of sharp utensils: slicing, chopping, carving (J, S)

Measurement
- Following recipes: written or pictorial (J, S)
- Use of measurement utensils: pouring, leveling (A)

Appliance usage
- Can openers, blenders, electric mixers (A)
- Stove top, hot plates, electric skillets, oven, microwave, slow
  cooker, food processors (J, S)
- Coffee makers (S)

Serving foods
- Table setting (A)
- Decoration (J, S)
- Serving dishes: appropriate dish sizes, attractiveness of food (J, S)

Clean-up
- Leftovers (J, S)
- Clean dishes and appliances: including table and counter top (A)

E=elementary   J=junior high   S=senior high   A=all levels

Laundry and Clothing Care
Cleaning clothes
- Recognizing clean and dirty clothing (A)
- Sorting clothing (J, S)
- Using washing machine and dryer: measuring detergent, adding softener, selecting machine settings (J, S)
- Hand-washable items (J, S)
- Folding (A)
- Ironing (J, S)
- Using clothes hangers (A)
- Putting clothes away (A)

Basic repair needs
- Sewing buttons (J, S)
- Hems, straight seams: by hand and/or machine (J, S)
- Recognizing items beyond repair (J, S)

Personal Care and Hygiene
Basic cleanliness: overall appearance (A)

Toilet skills: includes washing hands (A)

Dressing (A)

Basic skills: e.g., buttoning, zipping, using snaps (A)

Choosing clothes that match (J, S)

Grooming
- Hair, teeth, breath, bathing, nails (A)
- Deodorant, make-up, hair styling, care of menstrual needs (J, S)
- Shaving (S)

Safety
Recognizing poisons: Mr. Yuk symbol, poison control (A)

Emergency numbers: 911, fire, police (A)

Basic first aid: increase complexity with age and functioning levels (A)

Personal safety: danger from strangers, dangerous situations (A)

Home Care
Cleaning

E=elementary   J=junior high   S=senior high   A=all levels

*Trainable
and Severely/
Profoundly
Mentally
Retarded
Students*

- Basic skills: dusting, sweeping, vacuuming, mopping (A)
- Decorating (S)

Home repair (S)

Telephone skills
- Telephone manners (A)
- Operator assistance (A)
- Emergency numbers: 911, fire, police (A)
- Using telephone book (J, S)

Community

Travel and Transportation
Crossing the street: traffic safety, "Walk" / "Don't Walk signs" (A)

Bicycle safety (A)

Using public mass transit systems (J, S)

Using a cab (J, S)

Other means: e.g., transportation services for the disabled (A)

Survival words: stop, danger, crosswalk, bus stop, railroad crossing,
    detour (A)

Restaurants
Fast-food restaurant
- Locating and waiting in line (A)
- Ordering: menu choice, waiting, paying (A)
- Money skills: identifying cost and paying appropriately (A)
- Eating meal: locating condiments, napkins, table; proper
    behavior, clean-up (A)
- Playground (E)
    (see **Recreation and Leisure** activities)

Conventional restaurant
- Seating: seating oneself, waiting for the hostess (J, S)
- Ordering: menu choices, addressing waiter/waitress (A)
- Eating meal: condiments, napkin, proper behavior (A)
- Paying bill: taken by waiter/waitress, paying at cash register (J, S)

E=elementary   J=junior high   S=senior high   A=all levels

Library (A)
Proper behavior

Locating items of interest: browsing, card catalog, librarian assistance

Check-out items

Other activities: films, listening centers; story times usually for (E) levels only

Post Office
Mailing letters: in mail box, slots, or at counter (A)

Counter assistance: locating correct line, waiting, purchasing stamps, picking up or mailing packages (J, S)

Stores and Shopping
Grocery stores (A)
- Locating purchase item(s)
- Choosing size and brand
- Requesting assistance (if needed)
- Paying: locating cashier, waiting in line, putting item(s) on conveyer, figuring tax, giving proper amount, waiting for change and/or receipt

Department store (A)
- Browsing
- Locating and selecting items
- Using fitting rooms
- Paying

Specialty stores (A)
- Browsing
- Locating and selecting item(s)
- Paying

Shopping malls (A)
- Using escalators
- Using elevators
- Browsing
- Locating and selecting items
- Use of fitting rooms
- Paying

E=elementary   J=junior high   S=senior high   A=all levels

319

*Trainable
and Severely/
Profoundly
Mentally
Retarded
Students*

Public Rest Rooms (A)
Locating correct rest room

Using facilities

Public Vending Machines
Telephones (J, S)
- Using telephone book
- Getting operator assistance
- Using coins
- Dialing

Snack machines (A)
- Using coin or bill slots
- Making selection
- Removing selection
- Removing change, if any

Newspaper (J, S)
- Locating coin slot
- Retrieving paper

Other: any public environment in which a specific student is likely to
be found

Recreation and Leisure

Activities Performed Alone
Hobbies
- Toys (E)
- Jigsaw puzzles (A)
- Reading (A)
- Photography (J, S)

Arts and crafts
- Painting (A)
- Drawing (A)
- Needlework (J, S)
- Building models (A)

Video games (A)

E=elementary   J=junior high   S=senior high   A=all levels

Audio/visual activities (A)
- Television
- Radio
- Records, tapes, compact discs
- Talking books

Spectator activities (A)

Activities with Others
Indoor or table games: choosing, turn taking, following rules (A)

Physical activities
- Sports (A)
- Aerobic exercise: tape or video cassette (J, S)
- Bowling (J, S)
- Skating (A)
- Miniature golf (A)

Spectator activities (A)

Vocational

Elementary Level (E)
Work-related attitudes
- Increasing amount of time on task
- Completing a task
- Willingness to try new tasks

Work habits
- Time awareness, passing of time (yesterday, tomorrow, next week/month/year, time-telling skills)
- Knowing personal information (recognizing printed name, printing name, writing name, knowing address and telephone number)
- Following directions
- Handling unexpected changes in routine
- Showing initiative

Performing classroom duties
- Feeding pets
- Erasing chalkboard
- Stacking chairs

E=elementary   J=junior high   S=senior high   A=all levels

Performing chores at home
- Daily chores (e.g., making bed, clearing table)
- Weekly chores (e.g., removing trash, cleaning room)

Receiving instruction and exposure to various types of jobs/careers
- Classroom unit work with community helpers (e.g., firemen, policemen, nurses, doctors)
- Field trips

Junior High Level (J)
Work-related attitudes
- Demonstrating desire to complete task
- Willingness to improve

Work habits
- Identifying personal information (name, address, telephone, legal signature — not printed)
- Time management (telling time, planning activities within a time range)
- Demonstrating safety awareness
- Increased endurance in length of time on task
- Seeking assistance when needed
- Ability to handle unexpected changes
- Showing initiative

Participating in work/study program in school
- Assisting custodian
- Assisting cafeteria workers
- Assisting office workers
- Assisting librarian

Receiving more exposure to various career/job duties and choices
- Recognizing career opportunities available to him
- Identifying duties involved in various careers

Senior High Level (S)
Work-related attitudes
- Demonstrating promptness
- Coping with criticism

Work habits
- Continuing to develop habits begun in the junior high program
- Demonstrating increasing ability to evaluate his own work
- Time management (planning and using break time appropriately)

Work/study program
- On campus
- Community job site (e.g., fast food, restaurants, car wash, service stations)

Choosing a career/job
- One that fits the student's skills
- One that the student will enjoy

323

*Trainable
and Severely/
Profoundly
Mentally
Retarded
Students*

Christian school educator or parent will have in discerning appropriate goals for a specific child is that which is given by the Holy Spirit.

Just as academic levels vary, levels of spiritual awareness and understanding will be different. It is important to realize that not all retarded children will have the mental maturity to understand even the Biblical concept of salvation. We believe that God gives grace to these children, just as he does nondisabled children who have not yet reached the age of accountability in their lives. This is not to say a disabled child's spiritual development should be neglected. The goal, then, is to provide the child with the instruction he needs at a level which he can understand. This may be as simple as exposing him to good standards in music and to basic Bible truths (e.g., God loves me, God made everything, we praise God with song). Some severely or profoundly retarded children may simply need to learn how to sit still enough to listen to a lesson for a few minutes before any other type of objective can be reached. (Teachers may be interested in considering a Bible curriculum for mentally retarded students called *Happy Time Course* [Hooten, McDaniel, & Schubert,1977].)

As the functioning level increases, the complexity of material presented can also increase. Sunday school curricular guides can be adapted for use in a Bible class. However, it may be necessary to take extra time in teaching the lessons. Lessons that are normally covered in one day for nondisabled students may need to be presented for several days or weeks in order to be learned and understood. Care must also be taken that the materials and the methods of instruction are appropriate to the students' chronological ages as well as their mental ages. While this particular curricular area may seem to be one of the most difficult to plan and implement, the benefits of perseverance may never be known until we reach eternity.

Implementing a functional curriculum for students with varying needs

We have seen that trainable and severely/profoundly mentally retarded students are vastly different from one another. Even those with the same classification labels may show markedly different personalities and achievement levels. As a parent or educator, one may wonder if it is even possible to use the same curricular outline for students with such varying degrees of differences. Let us look at some examples of how we can adapt specific functional objectives to meet such diverse needs.

Anne is a thirteen-year-old girl who is classified as trainable mentally retarded. She wears glasses to help her see distant objects, but she has no other physical disabilities. In her classroom, she has been learning to operate a calculator for practical uses. Anne's long-term goal in the community area is to increase competence while interacting in a variety of community environments. The following would be a specific objective designed to meet that goal: "Given a trip to a fast-food restaurant and varying amounts of money to spend, Anne will use her calculator to determine what menu items to purchase without exceeding her total to spend." Obviously, Anne is practicing a functional objective at a fairly high functioning level. How then could a student having less academic ability benefit from instruction in the same type of environment?

Joe is severely mentally retarded. A casual glance at him would not reveal anything unusual. However, closer observation would disclose several clues to his disabling condition. Joe doesn't talk, but he has several consistent vocalizations including a sharp yelping sound. He walks stiffly, slightly favoring his right side. His parents and teachers report that he is often resistant and will sit down in the middle of the floor when he does not want to continue an activity. In the past, these interfering behaviors would have kept him completely out of many community environments. Joe's long-term goal is to decrease interfering behaviors in community settings. His objective for a fast food environment is this: "Upon reaching the cash register, Joe will show the cashier his order card and wait for the food to come, without shouting or sitting on the floor." The objective is functional and meets a specific educational need of severely retarded children without imposing unrealistic expectations.

Earlier in this chapter you were introduced to a profoundly retarded child named Sarah. As limiting as her physical and mental disabilities are, she too can benefit from a functional curriculum. A long-term goal for her may be to develop and use communication skills in various community environments. A short-term objective for that goal could be this: "When a soft drink and a fish sandwich are held in front of her, Sarah will indicate a choice of one by turning her face or eyes toward the desired food item, within 15-20 seconds of presentation." Even though complete independence in the community will never be possible for a profoundly retarded child such as Sarah, a functional curriculum will allow her to be a part of the world in which she lives.

Teaching Materials and Environments

Each year much time and effort is spent by various school systems to determine what will be taught in their classrooms. Understanding the students' disabling conditions and the resulting needs is an important factor in that decision. Since the goal of education is to prepare a student for life, we must seek out teaching materials designed for that purpose. To reach this goal effectively, parents and professionals need to know what types of teaching materials are available and in which environments they are most effective.

Commercially available materials Educators and administrators are constantly flooded with catalogs and brochures for commercially available educational products. There are thousands of **curricular guides** available for purchase. Of these thousands, there are some that are designed for mentally retarded students. Some even include specific lesson plans. A growing number of the special education products are beginning to reflect a functional and age-appropriate approach (e.g., Ford, Johnson, Pumpian, Stengert, & Wheeler, 1980; Tawney, Knapp, O'Reily, & Pratt, 1979; for specific examples, please refer to Appendix 7). These curriculum guides often provide a sequence of specific skills and practical suggestions for implementation in the classroom. Such commercially available guides can be a helpful resource for the teacher if used wisely. The danger does not necessarily lie in the curriculum itself, but in an educator's attempt to follow it to the letter with every student in the class. Even the most thorough curricular guide is unable to provide for every student's unique needs. The teacher may need to devise an alternate strategy for a nonambulatory student or a student who is deaf. While commercially prepared curricular guides and lesson plans may be helpful, adaptations will almost always be needed.

Most students learn more quickly when they are allowed to work with **manipulative teaching materials**, as opposed to merely listening or watching how a task is done. This statement applies especially to mentally retarded students. Concrete learning materials are necessary in the classroom. Again, educational catalogs are filled with examples of products available for purchase, such as puzzles, cardboard representations of coins, object photographs, and dressing boards. In selecting these materials, the teacher must consider the student's age level and his ability to generalize. Special education teachers must be careful that commercially purchased materials do not hinder the student's ability to transfer the skill from the practice materials to the real situation.

Nontraditional classrooms Traditionally, a classroom consists of a teacher's desk, a chalkboard, a few bookcases, and some

327

*Trainable
and Severely/
Profoundly
Mentally
Retarded
Students*

neatly lined rows of student desks. The materials include textbooks, workbooks, charts, paper, and pencils. This design has proven successful in teaching students an academically oriented curriculum. However, it is unlikely that teaching mentally retarded students to complete phonics or math worksheets with 90% accuracy will help them meet the challenges of their everyday life. Even the physical design of this classroom would be impractical for students who also have physical limitations. Given students with various physical and mental disabilities and the need for a functional curriculum, one can readily see why an alternative to the traditional classroom and its materials is needed.

Nontraditional materials In choosing teaching materials for mentally retarded students, one must consider the types of goals and objectives they need. If a student needs to learn to sort laundry, it is best to have some baskets and clothing items for him to use in practicing. Other alternatives to traditional classroom materials might include real money, household furniture, toys for younger students, games, and cleaning products. Use of nontraditional learning materials will drastically change the "look" of a classroom, but it will also provide several practical benefits for trainable and severely/profoundly retarded students.

Creating a functional learning environment takes a little imagination and has the added benefit of being relatively inexpensive. While the initial expense of purchasing items used in daily life may seem sizable, the cost will be less later. Many of these learning materials may be purchased just once (e.g., dish cloths and towels, laundry baskets, coat hangers, small kitchen appliances, and games). Other items that have to be replaced periodically are often inexpensive (detergent, paper napkins, and food supplies). Students' families can provide some of the funds needed for their child's specific materials. After all, families of nondisabled students do the same when they purchase paper, pencils, notebooks, and other traditional supplies. Money can also be raised by the class itself. For example, the class may provide a weekly or monthly salad bar luncheon for the school staff. This will allow the students to earn money for materials while practicing functional objectives such as meal planning, shopping skills, and food preparation.

Use of nontraditional materials also helps to avoid problems with generalizing skills. A student may appear to have mastered a certain concept in theory while still being unable to apply it in reality. A student may learn to accurately determine "play money" sums, but when given actual coins and bills he may be confused. Much time would be wasted teaching him to count "play money" when using the real thing would have helped him achieve mastery more quickly. Since mentally retarded students have difficulty applying a learned skill to a new situation, it is advisable to use actual items when teaching a specific skill. Concrete practice with inexpensive everyday materials will greatly assist the student in his attempt to master the skills needed to prepare him for life. Where, then, should this practice take place?

Instructional environments If at all possible, the best choice for instruction is the actual environment in which the skill will be used. This will prevent problems the student may have in generalizing skills. It also allows the instructor to teach specific skills for specific needs. Some needs may not be discovered until the student is in the actual situation (such as maneuvering a wheelchair up a ramp). One of the greatest advantages is that it provides the student with exposure to real-life situations, and this provides the best preparation for life.

At other times, functional practice can be provided in the classroom. Classroom practice allows the student to practice a skill without the pressure of failure and embarrassment. It also helps to keep initial expenses low; for example, the student can

329

*Trainable
and Severely/
Profoundly
Mentally
Retarded
Students*

use a poster-board copy of a restaurant menu for several days in the classroom before going to the restaurant to purchase the food. However, classroom practice which does not progress to actual performance just teaches the student to function within a classroom environment. When the student graduates from the school program, he will still be unequipped to deal with daily life challenges. Therefore, a combination program of appropriate classroom practice which naturally advances to performance in actual situations will provide sufficient practice for mastery.

References

Bigge, J. L. (1982). *Teaching individuals with physical and multiple disabilities* (2nd ed.). Columbus, OH: Charles E. Merrill Publishing Co.

Burek, D. M., Koek, K. E., & Novallo A. (1989). *Encyclopedia of associations: 1990* (24th ed.). Detroit, MI: Gale Research, Inc.

Davis, W. E. (1980). *Educator's resource guide to special education: Terms–laws–tests–organizations.* Boston, MA: Allyn & Bacon, Inc.

DeVinne, P., Boyer, M., Ellis, K., Harris, D., & Soukhanov, A. (1985). *American heritage dictionary.* New York, NY: Dell Publishing Co.

Ford, A., Johnson, F., Pumpian, I., Stengert, J., & Wheeler, J. (1980). *A longitudinal listing of chronological age-appropriate and functional activities for school-aged moderately and severely handicapped students.* Madison, WI: Madison Metropolitan School District.

Freagon, S., Wheeler, J., Brankin, G., McDannel, K., Costello, D., & Peters, W. (1983). *Curricular processes for the school and community integration of severely handicapped students ages 6-21.* Dekalb, IL: Northern Illinois University.

Grossman, H. J. (Ed.). (1983). *Classification in mental retardation.* Washington, D.C.: American Association on Mental Deficiency.

Hallahan, D. P., & Kauffman, J. M. (1988). *Exceptional children: Introduction to special education* (4th ed.). Englewood Cliffs, NJ: Prentice Hall.

Hewett, F. M., & Forness, S. R. (1977). *Education of exceptional learners* (2nd ed.). Boston, MA: Allyn & Bacon, Inc.

Hooten, J. C., McDaniel, E., & Schubert, C. (1977). *Happy time course.* Wheaton, IL: Scripture Press.

Kirk, S. A., & Gallagher, J. J. (1983). *Educating exceptional children* (4th ed.). Dallas, TX: Houghton Mifflin Company.

Luftig, R. L. (1978). *Teaching the mentally retarded student: Curriculum, methods, and strategies.* Boston, MA: Allyn & Bacon, Inc.

Mercer, C. D., & Mercer, A. R. (1989). *Teaching students with learning problems* (3rd ed.). Columbus, OH: Merrill Publishing Co.

Reynolds, C. R., & Mann, L. (1978). *Encyclopedia of special education—A reference for the education of the handicapped and other exceptional children and adults.* New York, NY: John Wiley & Sons, Inc.

Tawney, J. W., Knapp, D. S., O'Reilly, C. D., & Pratt, S. S. (1979). *Programmed environments curriculum.* Columbus, OH: Merril Publishing Company.

Appendix 1

John J. McCormick

Laws Related to Special Education

1954: PL 83-531
Provides funds for research in mental retardation.

1958: PL 85-926
Provides funds for training college instructors who will teach teachers for the mentally retarded.

1963: PL 88-164
Provides funding for research and demonstration projects.

1964: PL 89-10
Provides educational programs for the disadvantaged.

1965: PL 89-313
Provides funds to support children in hospitals and institutions.

1966: PL 89-750
Created the Bureau of Education for the Handicapped.

1968: PL 90-480
Prohibits barriers for physically disabled children.

1968: PL 90-538
Establishes special education demonstration sites.

1969: PL 91-230
Recognizes learning disabilities of gifted children.

1972: PL 92-424
Mandates Head Start programs to serve disabled children.

1973: PL 93-112 *Rehabilitation Act*
Prohibits exclusion of disabled individuals from the benefits of
any program receiving federal assistance.

1973: PL 93-380
Requires states to take steps to protect the rights of disabled
children and their parents in placement changes. It also assures
that as much education as possible takes place in the regular
classroom.

1974: Family Education Rights and Privacy Act
Guarantees parents the right to see all official school records
involving their children and limits outsiders' access to records
without parental permission.

1975: PL 94-142 *The Education for all Handicapped
Children Act*
Provides for the identification, location, evaluation, and educa-
tion of all disabled children. The child must have an individual

education plan developed to meet his or her educational needs, and provisions must to be established to make certain the IEP is being followed.

1978: PL 95-602
Extended the vocational program established in the 1973 Rehabilitation Act for four more years and created a new program for comprehensive independent living services for disabled persons and a new National Institute of Handicapped Research.

1983: PL 98-199
Provides funds for the establishment and operation of regional centers to develop and apply the best methods of appraising the special education needs of disabled children.

1986: PL 99-457
Provides for a free appropriate education to all eligible children from 3 years to 21 years of age by 1991. Beginning in 1991, states must also have in a place a statewide system of early intervention services for eligible children from birth through age 2.

1990: PL 101-336 *Americans with Disabilities Act*
Provides civil rights protection to individuals with disabilities in private sector employment, all public services, public accommodations, transportation, and telecommunications.

1990: PL 101-476 *Individuals with Disabilities Education Act*
Represents a renaming of PL 94-142 — The Education of All Handicapped Children Act. It replaces the term *handicapped* with *disabled* and mandates a variety of other changes such as clearly identifying in the individual education plan the transitional services which will take place when a child transfers from one school to another.

Appendix 2

James A. Berg

How to Meditate Using the MAP Method

*F*ind a portion of Scripture relevant to your problem or find one that deals with a Bible principle or truth you wish to master. Always meditate on Scripture that God's Spirit "highlights" as you are reading the Word.

Memorize the Passage

This often occurs automatically if the passage is studied intensely enough in the next step. It is important when facing difficult times or temptations to know exactly what God said word for word. Satan was able to gain a toehold in Eve's life because she did not know exactly what God said. She had a general idea, but that is not good enough when dealing with an enemy as deceptive as Satan. A man who cannot remember

God's exact words is in danger of "lean[ing to his] own understanding" (Proverbs 3:5-6).

Many people find using the first letters of every word in a verse a helpful way of prompting them as they memorize. For example, Psalm 119:105 says, "Thy word is a lamp unto my feet, and a light unto my path." Using the first letters, this passage becomes "T w i a l u m f, a a l u m p." The first letters of each word (with the punctuation just as it appears in the text) give enough of a hint so that you usually can recall what the word is; but since the whole word is not present, you do not find yourself just reading the words mindlessly.

Analyze the Passage

Study the passage asking the Holy Spirit to give you a thorough understanding of its message.

1. **Intensive focus:** study of the words in the passage

   List the major words in the passage, and use an English dictionary to find out the meaning of each word. If possible, look up each word in a Greek or Hebrew dictionary or check out the meaning for each in *Strong's Exhaustive Concordance.* Once you are sure of each word's meaning, put the passage in your own words (paraphrase it).

2. **Extensive focus:** study of the context and purpose of the passage

   Use a commentary on the passage or study the notes in a good study Bible. Try to understand who the passage was written to and why.

Personalize the Passage

Plan out concrete ways for change in your life that are consistent with your understanding of the passage you just studied. Plans include schedules, details, techniques, steps, and procedures. Ask yourself, "When have I failed to do this in the past? When am I likely to meet it again? What will be my response the next time I meet this?" Think through the "game plan" thoroughly and in advance of the next temptation. Use the passage in personal prayer to God. For example, a person meditating on James 4:1-11 may begin a prayer like this:

> "Lord, you tell me here in James 4:1 that the conflict I'm having with John is the result of my own lusts, my own desires to have something my way. I know that isn't pleasing to You. Instead of responding in anger to John, I need Your help and grace which You promised in James 4:6 when You said that You resist the proud and give grace to the humble. Help me to humble myself instead of proudly insisting on my own way and to allow You to lift me up in Your time . . . "

Appendix 3

Kenneth Shore, Psy.D.[1]

Warning Signs that Suggest a Possible Educational Disability[2]

The following is a detailed (but not exhaustive) list of behaviors and characteristics that may suggest a possible learning disability. It can best be used *not* to detect an educational disability, but rather to decide whether your child might need further evaluation by a professional evaluation team. As you go through this list, you should keep certain principles in mind.

    1. Many children who do not have educational disabilities show some of these characteristics. In most

---

[1] Reprinted by permission of Warner Books/New York from *The Special Education Handbook.* Copyright 1988.

[2] The term *specific learning disability* is the term adopted by the federal government and contained in PL 94-142 and is the more frequently used term.

cases, there is little need for concern unless your youngster exhibits many of these characteristics or several clustered in one category, or unless your child shows one or more of these forms of behavior continuously and intensely.

2. Many of these characteristics are typical of very young children and only suggest a possible disability if your son or daughter exhibits them after a certain age. For example, kindergarten and first-grade children often reverse letters when they write; there is more reason for concern, however, if your child still reverses letters in the third grade. Some of these characteristics in the list suggest an approximate age by which most children master a skill. Review these statements with caution: the fact that your child has not attained a skill by the expected age may mean a delay in the development of that skill rather than an educational disability.

3. These characteristics may be present in some situations and not in others. It is not uncommon for a teacher to observe behavior of which you may not be aware, since the school setting often imposes different demands and elicits different responses than does the home setting. You therefore might want to ask about your child's behavior in the classroom rather than assume that it mirrors what you see at home.

4. A particular form of behavior may be the direct expression of an educational disability (a primary problem) or it may be a "side effect" of another difficulty (a secondary problem). For example, your daughter's angry outbursts may stem from intense frustration at her reading difficulties. In other words, the behavior problem may be secondary to the learning problem. Differentiating between primary

and secondary problems is a key to understanding your child's needs and planning helpful programs.

Health

Your child may have a health-related problem if he

- is lethargic and sluggish
- tires easily, falls asleep during class
- appears wan and pale
- drools
- requests to go to the nurse often
- complains often of headaches, stomachaches, nausea, or dizziness
- appears malnourished

Hearing*

Your child may have a hearing problem if he

- consistently turns one side of his head toward the source of sound
- holds his hand behind his ear when listening
- turns television sound up loud
- appears inattentive to what people are saying
- often requests that questions or directions be repeated
- is reluctant to participate in class discussion
- provides irrelevant or inappropriate responses to questions
- has speech articulation difficulties
- speaks very loudly or very softly

* *Adapted from a list provided by the U.S. Public Health Service, 5600 Fishers Land, Rockville, MD 20857.*

Vision

Your child may have a visual problem if he

- rubs his eyes or squints frequently
- complains often of dizziness or headaches

- tilts his head in an unusual manner
- is hesitant to participate in visually demanding games or tasks
- holds books close to or far from his eyes
- has difficulty reading or copying from the chalk-board
- confuses letters while reading (for example, *c* and *e*, or *g* and *q*)
- has difficulty aligning written work
- chooses unusual color combinations

Visual Perception

Your child may have difficulty with visual perception if he

- has problems discriminating among different shapes and letters
- has a hard time retaining visual images
- reverses letters or numbers while reading or writing after age 8 (for example, confuses *b* and *d* or *p* and *q*, reads *12* for *21*, writes *gril* for *girl*)
- reads words backwards (for example, reads *was* for *saw* or *on* for *no*)
- is easily distracted by extraneous visual images (for example, has difficulty with math problems grouped on a page but can do them when each is on a separate page)
- has spatial orientation difficulties (for example, is often confused in getting around school)
- does not consistently know left from right by age 8

Receptive Language

Your child may have difficulty understanding language if he

- has difficulty discriminating between sounds (for example, between consonant blends or between similar-sounding words such as *put* and *pat*)

- often fails to understand oral or written information (for example, teacher directions)
- frequently confuses language concepts (for example, *on* and *in* or *before* and *after*)
- has difficulty retaining what is said in correct sequence (for example, cannot follow two-step directions correctly by age 5)
- is unable to understand when background noise is present
- repeats a request or question before responding
- responds with an irrelevant answer

Expressive Language

Your child may have difficulties with oral and written expression if he

- is delayed in reaching speech milestones (for example, does not say first word by age 18 months or does not speak in complete sentences by age 4)
- distorts sounds or mispronounces words (for example, says *aminal* for *animal* or *hopsital* for *hospital*)
- fails to pronounce medial (middle) or final sounds of words
- stutters or hesitates to a significant degree while speaking
- confuses verb tenses or uses pronouns inappropriately
- has difficulty recalling names of familiar objects or people
- is unable to transfer thoughts to paper coherently (for example, writing is characterized by run-on sentences, incomplete sentences, or poor sequencing)

Thinking

Your child may have difficulty with orderly, rational thinking if he

- seems to think in an unorganized and incoherent manner
- has difficulty understanding abstract concepts (for example, interprets proverbs in a concrete manner)
- is preoccupied with details and misses the "big picture"
- does not consistently relate actions to their consequences or understand cause-effect relationships
- draws inappropriate conclusions
- misperceives social situations or the reactions of other people
- has a problem in making decisions

Learning

Your child may have a learning problem if he

- cannot identify letters of the alphabet by age 6
- has poor retention of learned material such as math facts, spelling words, days of the week, telling time ("she seems to know it one day but not the next")
- completes work much more slowly than others do
- has difficulty working independently and needs frequent teacher supervision
- has a hard time organizing himself and his materials (for example, forgets to bring proper materials home or to class, misplaces homework or turns it in late consistently, has a cluttered desk)
- has considerable difficulty in sounding out words
- reads one year below grade level in early grades or two years below grade level in later grades
- makes unusual spelling errors

- achieves poorly in some academic areas and highly in others

Fine Motor Skills

Your child may be deficient in fine-motor skills if he

- has difficulty manipulating small items
- is unable to unbutton by age 4 or tie shoelaces by age 6
- has an awkward pencil grip
- cannot draw a circle by age 3 or 4
- is unable to stay on the line while writing
- has too little or too much space between words
- forms letters poorly

Gross Motor Skills

Your child may be deficient in gross-motor skills if he

- frequently stumbles or runs into things
- has difficulty catching or throwing
- has poor balance (for example, is unable to balance on one foot for 5 seconds by age 5)
- is unable to walk a straight line or on tiptoe
- runs or jumps awkwardly
- cannot skip by age 7
- has not established either right- or left-handedness by age 5

Activity Level

Your child may have a below-normal or above-normal activity level if he

- seems in almost constant motion
- is fidgety in his seat
- is a restless sleeper
- lacks patience in waiting for his turn (for example, calls out in class without raising his hand)

- frequently acts before thinking, without concern for consequences
- hurries through schoolwork, giving rise to careless errors
- is much *less* active physically than peers (for example, moves in a slow and listless manner)

Attention Level

Your child may have an inadequate attention span if he

- has difficulty concentrating for even brief periods
- is easily distracted by background noise
- often appears to daydream
- takes a long time to complete tasks

Social and Emotional Status

Your child may have social and emotional difficulties if he

- is readily frustrated and gives up easily
- is prone to unpredictable and marked emotional changes ("He is happy one minute and in tears the next")
- shows signs of anxiety (for example, is fidgety, displays nervous habits, or complains often of physical ailments)
- appears sad more often than happy
- displays low self-confidence (for example, is easily discouraged or makes self-disparaging comments)
- is overly dependent on adults
- has trouble relating to peers or sustaining friendships
- is withdrawn and shy
- is defiant and hostile toward authority figures
- is physically or verbally aggressive toward peers

Appendix 4

National Organizations[1]

ACLD (Association for Children with Learning Disabilities)
4156 Library Road
Pittsburgh, PA 15234
(412) 341-1515
Each state has its own association branch. The addresses for
these branches can be obtained through the national association listed above.

Alexander Graham Bell Association for the Deaf
2317 Volta Place, NW
Washington, DC 20007

---

[1] While these secular organizations may not uphold Christian values, we believe
that they may provide helpful information for parents and professionals.

American Academy of Child and Adolescent Psychiatry
3615 Wisconsin Avenue, NW
Washington, DC 20016
(202) 966-7300

American Academy of Pediatrics
PO Box 1034
Evanston, IL 60204

American Association for the Education of Severely and
Profoundly Handicapped
1600 West Armory Way, Garden View Suite
Seattle, WA 98119

American Association on Mental Deficiency
5201 Connecticut Avenue NW
Washington, DC 20015

American Coalition of Citizens with Disabilities
1012 14th Street, NW
Washington, DC 20005
(202) 628-3470

American Council of the Blind
1211 Connecticut Avenue, NW
Washington, DC 20006
(202) 833-1251; 1-800-424-8666

American Council of the Blind Parents
Route A, PO Box 78
Franklin, LA 70538

American Council on Rural Special Education
National Rural Development Institute
Western Washington University
359 Miller Hall
Bellingham, WA 98225
(206) 676-3576

American Eugenics Society
230 Park Avenue
New York, NY 10017

American Foundation for the Blind
15 West 16th Street
New York, NY 10011

American Medical Association
Bureau of Health Education
535 N. Dearborn St.
Chicago, IL 60610

American Occupational Therapy Association
1383 Piccard Drive
Rockville, MD 20850
(301) 948-9626

American Physical Therapy Association
1156 15th Street, NW
Washington, DC 20005

American Printing House for the Blind
1211 Connecticut Avenue, NW, #506
Washington, DC 20036

American Psychological Association
1200 Seventeenth Street, NW
Washington, DC 10036

American Society for Deaf Children
814 Thayer Avenue
Silver Spring, MD 20910
(301) 585-5400

American Speech-Language-Hearing Association
10801 Rockville Pike
Rockville, MD 20852
(301) 897-5700

Association for the Education of the Visually Handicapped
919 Walnut Street, 4th Floor
Philadelphia, PA 19107

Association on Handicapped Student Service Programs in
Post-Secondary Education
PO Box 21192
Columbus, OH 43221
(614) 488-4972

Association for Persons with Severe Handicaps
7010 Roosevelt Way, NE
Seattle, WA 98115
(206) 523-8446

Autism Society of America
1234 Massachusetts Ave. N.W.
Suite C-1017
Washington, DC 20005

Boy Scouts of America
Scouting for the Handicapped Division
1325 Walnut Hill Lane
Irving, TX 75062
(214) 659-2127

California Association for Neurologically
Handicapped Children
Literature Distribution Center
PO Box 1526
Vista, CA 92083

Center for Independent Living
2539 Telegraph Avenue
Berkeley, CA 94704
(415) 841-4776

Center for Special Education Technology
1920 Association Drive
Reston, VA 22091
1-800-873-8255

Citizen's Alliance to Uphold Special Education
313 South Washington Square
Lansing, MI 48933
(517) 485-4084

Closer Look / National Information Center
for the Handicapped
PO Box 1492
Washington, DC 20013

Closer Look / Parent's Campaign for Handicapped
Children and Youth
1201 Sixteenth Street, NW
Washington, DC 20036
(202) 822-7900

Coordinating Council for Handicapped Children
220 South State Street, Room 412
Chicago, IL 60604
(312) 939-3513

Council for American Private Education
1726 M Street, NW, Suite 1102
Washington, DC 20036

Council for Children with Behavioral Disorders
1920 Association Drive
Reston, VA 22091

Council on Education of the Deaf
5034 Wisconsin Avenue NW
Washington, DC 20016

Council for Exceptional Children
1920 Association Drive
Reston, VA 22091

Department for the Blind and Physically Handicapped
Consult your local library for the services that are available for
the blind and physically handicapped.

Developmental Disabilities Administration
US Department of Health and Human Services
200 Independence Avenue, SW
Washington, DC 20201
(202) 245-2890

Disability Rights Center
1346 Connecticut Avenue, NW
Washington, DC 20036
(202) 233-3304

Down Syndrome Congress
1640 W. Roosevelt Road, Room 156E
Chicago, IL 60608

Education of All Children
1920 Association Drive
Reston, VA 22091

Education Resources Information Center (ERIC)
1920 Association Drive
Reston, VA 22091

Effective Advocacy for Citizens with Handicaps, Inc.
1705 19th Avenue S
Nashville, TN 27212
1-800-342-1660

Exceptional Parent Magazine
PO Box 4944
Manchester, NH 03108

FCLD (Foundation for Children with Learning Disabilities)
99 Park Avenue
New York, NY 10016

Federation for Children with Special Needs
312 Stuart Street, 2nd Floor
Boston, MA 02116
(617) 482-2915

Girl Scouts of the USA
Scouting for Handicapped Girls Program
830 Third Avenue
New York, NY 10022
(212) 940-7500

Goodwill Industries of America
9200 Wisconsin Avenue
Washington, DC 20014

Higher Education and the Handicapped
1 Dupont Circle, NW
Washington, DC 20036
1-800-54-HEATH

March of Dimes National Birth Defects Foundation
1275 Mamoroneck Avenue
White Plains, NY 10605

Mental Health Association National Headquarters
1300 North Kent Street
Arlington, VA 22209

Multiple Sclerosis Society
257 Park Avenue, South
New York, NY 10010

Muscular Dystrophy Association of America, Inc.
810 Seventh Avenue
New York, NY 10019

National Association of the Deaf-Blind
2703 Forest Oak Circle
Norman, OK 73071

National Association for Down's Syndrome
P.O. Box 4542
Oak Brook, IL 60522

National Association for Gifted Students (NAGS)
217 Gregory Drive
Hot Springs, AR 71901

National Association of the Physically Handicapped, Inc.
76 Elm Street
London, OH 43140

National Association for Protection and Advocacy for the
Handicapped Systems, Inc.
900 Second Street NE, Suite 211
Washington, D.C. 20002
1-(202)-408-9514
Each state is required by law to have a Protection and Advocacy System. Contact your local school district or your state
department of education for the office in your area.

National Association for Retarded Children
2709 Avenue East
Arlington, TX 76010
Ask for General Bibliography and Religion Bibliography.

National Association for Retarded Citizens
P.O. Box 6109
2709 Avenue E East
Arlington, TX 76005

National Association for Parents of the Visually
Impaired, Inc.
2011 Hardy Circle
Austin, TX 78757

National Association for the Visually Handicapped
305 East 24th Street
New York, NY 10010

National Association of Vocational Education
Special Needs Personnel
c/o Dr. Sheila Feichtner
Reschini House
Indiana University of Pennsylvania
Indiana, PA 15705
(412) 357-4434

National Autism Hotline
Douglass Education Building.
(304) 525-8014
Tenth Ave. and Bruce St.
Huntington, WV 25701

National Center for Law and the Deaf
Kendal Green Station
7th Street and Florida Ave, NE
Washington, DC 20002

National Committee for Citizens in Education
410 Wilde Lake Village Green
Columbia, MD 21044
(301) 997-9300; 1-800-638-9675

National Deaf-Blind Program
BEH
Room 4046, Donohoe Building
400 6th Street, SW
Washington, DC 20202

National Easter Seal Society
70 E. Lake St.
Chicago, IL 60601

National Federation of the Blind
1800 Johnson Street
Baltimore, MD 21230
(301) 659-9314

National Genetics Foundation
250 West 57th Street
New York, NY 10019

National Handicapped Sports and Recreation Association
10085 West 18th Avenue
Lakewood, CO 80215
(303) 232-4575

National Information Center for Children and Youth with
Handicaps (NICHCY)
PO Box 1492
Washington, DC 20013

National Instructional Materials Information System
National Center for Educational Media/Materials for the
Handicapped
Columbus, OH

National Library Service for the Blind and Physically Handi-
capped
Library of Congress
Washington, DC 20542

National Media Materials Center for Severely Handicapped
Peabody College
PO Box 318
Nashville, TN 37203

National Multiple Sclerosis Society
205 East 42nd Street
New York, NY 10017

National Network of Learning Disabled Adults
PO Box Z
East Texas State University
Commerce, TX 75428

National Neurofibromatosis Foundation
340 East 80th Street
New York, NY 10017

National Society for Autistic Children
Information and Referral Service
1234 Massachusetts Avenue, Suite 1017
Washington, DC 20005

National Society for the Prevention of Blindness, Inc.
79 Madison Avenue
New York, NY 10016

National Spina Bifida Association of America
P.O. Box 5568
Madison, WI 53705

National Spinal Cord Injury Foundation
369 Elliot Street
Newton Upper Falls, MA 02164

National Tay-Sachs Foundation and
Allied Diseases Association
122 East 42nd Street
New York, NY 10017

National Tuberous Sclerosis Association, Inc.
PO Box 159
Laguana Beach, CA 92652

The Orton Dyslexia Society
724 York Road, Dept. M
Baltimore, MD 21204
William H. Baker, Jr., Director, Research and Development
(301) 825-7837 (work); (301) 472-4728 (home)
The Orton Dyslexia Society has state branches. Contact the
national association for addresses.

Parent Advocacy Coalition for Educational Rights
4826 Chicago Avenue
Minneapolis, MN 55417
(612) 827-2966

Parent Educational Advocacy Training Center
228 South Pitt Street, Room 300
Alexandria, VA 22314
(703) 836-2953

Partners In Publishing (PIP)
Box 50347
Tulsa, OK 74510
Ask for *National Directory of Four-Year Colleges, Two-Year
Colleges, and Post-High School Training Programs for Young
People with Learning Disabilities.*

President's Committee on Employment of the Handicapped
1111 20th Street NW, 6th Floor
Washington, DC 20036
(202) 653-5044

President's Committee on Mental Retardation
Room 4063 HHS North Building
Washington, DC 20201
(202) 245-7634

Recording for the Blind
20 Rozel Road
Princeton, NJ 08540
(609) 45200606

Special Education Programs
US Department of Education
Switzer Building
330 C Street, SW
Washington, DC 20202
(202) 732-1007

Special Olympics
1701 K Street, NW, Suite 203
Washington, DC 20006
(202) 331-1346

Spina Bifida Association of America
343 South Dearborn Street, Room 319
Chicago, IL 60604

TASH: The Association for Persons with Severe Handicaps
7010 Roosevelt Way, N.E.
Seattle, WA 98115

United Cerebral Palsy Association
66 East 34th Street
New York, NY 10016

United Way Agencies

Western Law Center for the Handicapped
1420 West 9th Street
Los Angeles, CA 90015
(213) 736-1031

Appendix 5

Tests

*T*he number and types of tests on the market today are as diverse as the students to whom the tests are administered. Companies offer intelligence tests, achievement tests, screening tests, and readiness tests, as well as tests that determine overall ability, tests that determine ability in one particular subject area, and tests that suggest the most effective means (visual, auditory, or kinesthetic) through which a student learns. There are tests that assess a student's emotional state, his social aptitude, and even his career orientation.

Due to the number of available tests and the continued development and revision of additional tests, it would be extremely confusing to list every test on the market today. The information presented here is a listing of producers and tests that are frequently used. These tests provide the most reliable information necessary to help the classroom teacher understand the strengths and weaknesses of his students with learning difficulties. This list is by no means exhaustive. All of the companies listed will be able to provide additional information regarding other tests available from their catalogs.

Academic Therapy Publications
20 Commercial Boulevard
Novato, CA 94949-6191
(415) 883-3314
(outside CA 1-800-422-7249)

American Guidance Service
Publisher's Building
Circle Pines, MN 55014

- Woodcock Reading Mastery Tests
- Peabody Individual Achievement Test Revised (PIAT–R)
- Key Math–Revised

Consulting Psychologists Press
577 College Avenue
Palo Alto, CA 94302

Curriculum Associates
5 Esquire Road
North Billerica, MA 01862-2589
- The Brigance System
  - Early Preschool Screen (EPS)
  - Preschool Screen (PS)
  - K and 1 Screen–Revised (K&1–R)

- Inventory of Early Development–Revised (IED–R)
- The Brigance Comprehensive Inventory of Basic Skills (grades Pre–K to 9)
- The Brigance Inventory of Basic Skills (grades K to 6)
- The Brigance Inventory of Essential Skills (grades 6 to adult education)

Developmental Learning Materials
DLM Teaching Resources
One DLM Park
Allen, TX 75002
(214) 248-6300

- Woodcock-Johnson Psycho-Educational Battery– Revised
    (Includes the WJ–R Tests of Cognitive Ability and the WJ–R Tests of Achievement)
- Scales of Independent Behavior (SIB)
- Test of Language Development (TOLD)
    - Primary
    - Intermediate
- Test of Written Language–2 (TOWL–2)

Educators Publishing Service, Inc. (EPS)
1129 Garden Gate Circle
Garland, TX 75043
(214) 272-4862

- Slingerland Screening Tests for Identifying Children with Specific Language Disability

Jastak Associations, Inc.
1526 Gilpin Avenue
Wilmington, DE 19806
1-800-221-WRAT
- Wide Range Achievement Test–Revised (WRAT–R)
- Adaptive Behavior Scale–School Edition (ABS)

Learning Research Associates, Inc.
P.O. Box 39, Dept. 8
Roslyn Heights, NY 11577
1-800-331-3117

Pro-Ed
(Services for Professional Educators)
5341 Industrial Oaks Blvd.
Austin, TX 78758-9965
(512) 451-3246
- Detroit Tests of Learning Aptitude, Third Edition (DTLA–3)
- Detroit Test of Learning Aptitude–Primary, Second Edition (DTLA–P:2)
- Detroit Test of Learning Aptitude–Adult (DTLA–A)
- Test of Nonverbal Intelligence, Second Edition (TONI–2)
- Test of Early Mathematics Ability, Second Edition (TEMA–2)
- Occupational Aptitude Survey and Interest Schedule, Second Edition (OASIS–2)

Psychological Assessment Resources, Inc.
P.O. Box 998
Odessa, FL 33556
1-800-331-TEST

Psychological Corporation
Order Service Center
P.O. Box 839954
San Antonio, TX 78283-3954
1-800-228-0752

- Goodenough-Harris Drawing Test (1963)
- Stanford Achievement Test, Eighth Edition
- Otis-Lennon School Ability Test, Sixth Edition (OLSAT)
- Career Interest Inventory (1990)
- Stanford Diagnostic Reading Test, Third Edition (SDRT, 1984)
- Stanford Diagnostic Mathematics Test, Third Edition (SDMT, 1984)

Publisher's Test Service
Del Monte Research Park
Monterey, CA 93940

Slosson Educational Publications, Inc.
P.O. Box 280
East Aurora, NY 14052

- Slosson Intellegence Test–Revised (SIT–R)
- Slosson Oral Reading Test–Revised (SORT–R)
- Illinois Test of Psycholinguistic Abilities (ITPA)

Special Learning Corporation
42 Boston Post Road
P.O. Box 306
Guilford, CT 06437
(203) 453-6525

Stoelting
Oakwood Centre
620 Wheat Lane
Wood Dale, IL 60191
(708) 860-9700
Fax: (708)860-9775

- Kaufman Developmental Scale (KDS)
- Bender Visual Motor Gestault

York Press, Inc.
2712 Mt. Carmel Road
Parkton, MD 21120

Appendix 6

Educational Equipment and Resources[1]

A Beka Book
Pensacola, FL 32523-9160
1-800-874-BEKA

*[2]Academic Therapy Publications
20 Commercial Boulevard
Novato, CA 94949-6191
1-800-422-7249

---

[1] This list provides information regarding producers/distributors of educational equipment, including suppliers of products directed towards the physically and educationally disabled. Any items mentioned in the text that are available through a specific company are noted in the listing. The listing of a particular firm does not necessarily indicate endorsement of that company's products.

[2] *Indicates a supplier of special eduction materials

Alpha Omega Publications
2316 West Huntington Drive
Tempe, AZ 85282

*A.D.D. Warehouse
300 NW 70th Avenue, Suite 102
Plantation, FL 33317

*American Guidance Service
Publisher's Building
Circle Pines, MN 55014

ATD
135 Greenwood Avenue
Wyncote, PA 19095

*Attainment Company, Inc.
504 Commerce Parkway
Verona, WI 53593

Audiotronics
7428 Bellaire Avenue
North Hollywood, CA 91615
1-800-447-0381
        *Language Master

Barnell Loft Ltd.
958 Church Street
Baldwin, NY 11510

Basic Education
PO Box 610589
Dallas/Fort Worth Airport, TX 75261-0589

Beacon Enterprises, Inc.
PO Box 4745
Sonora, CA 95370
1-800-262-1776

Beckley Cardy
PO Box 2358
Lufkin, TX 75902

Bell
2096 South Church Street
PO Box 135
East Troy, WI 53120

Bob Jones University Press
Greenville, SC 29614
1-800-845-5731

Britannica Filmstrips
310 South Michigan Avenue
Chicago, IL 60604-9839

*Linda J. Burkhart
8503 Rhode Island Avenue
College Park, MD 20740
(301) 345-9152
        *Switches controlled by the physically disabled

*Cambridge Development Laboratory, Inc.
 214 Third Avenue
 Waltham, MA 02154
 1-800-637-0047

Childcraft Education Corporation
20 Kilmer Road
Edison, NJ 08817
1-800-631-5652

*Childswork/Childsplay
Center for Applied Psychology
441 North 5th Street, Third Floor
Philadelphia, PA 19123

Christian Mental Health
Counseling and Educational Services
Route 2, Popular Creek Road
Oliver Springs, TN 37840

Christian Schools International
3350 East Paris Ave., SE
PO Box 8709
Grand Rapids, MI 49518-8709
1-800-635-8288

Coronet/MTI Film and Video
108 Wilmont Road
Deerfield, IL 60015
1-800-621-2131

*The Council for Exceptional Children
Dept. K 1 0 9 2 1
1920 Association Drive
Reston, VA 22091-1589

Creation Science Evangelism
Dr. Kent Hovind
29 Cummings Road
Pensacola, FL 32503
(904) 479-8987

Creation's Ambassadors
PO Box 122
Fair Haven, NY 13064

Creative Edge Inc.
80 Pineview Drive
Amherst, NY 14228-2120
1-800-626-5052

*Creative Publications
5040 West 111th Street
Oak Lawn, IL 60453

Creative Teaching Associates
PO Box 7714
Fresno, CA 93727

Crestwood Company
6625 North Sidney Place
Milwaukee, WI 53209-3259

Critical Thinking Press and Software
PO Box 448, Dept. 17
Pacific Grove, CA 93950
1-800-458-4849

*Cuisenaire Company of America
12 Church Street
New Rochelle, NY 10805
    *Cuisenaire rods

*Curriculum Associates
5 Esquire Road
North Billerica, MA 01862-2589
1-800-225-0248

T. S. Dennison and Company, Inc.
9601 Newton Avenue South
Minneapolis, MN 55431

DLM (Developmental Learning Materials)
PO Box 400
1 DLM Park
Allen, TX 75002

EBSCO Curriculum Materials
PO Box 486
Birmingham, AL 35201

*Edmark
PO Box 3218
Redmond, WA 98073-3218
1-800-426-0856

Educational Design, Inc.
47 West 13 Street
New York, NY 10011

Educators Publishing Services, Inc.
1129 Garden Gate Circle
Garland, TX 75043
(214) 272-4862

ESP, Inc.
1201 East Johnson Avenue
PO Box Drawer 5037
Jonesboro, AR 72403-5037
1-800-643-0280

*Fearon/Janus
500 Harbor Boulevard
Belmont, CA 94002

Flaghouse
150 North MacQuesten Parkway
Mt. Vernon, NY 10550
1-800-221-5185

Follett Publishing Company
1010 West Washington Boulevard
Chicago, IL 60607

Goldencraft
5440 North Cumberland Avenue
Chicago, IL 60656-1469

Harcourt Brace Jovanovich, Inc.
School Department
6277 Sea Harbor Drive
Orlando, FL 32821

Hubbard Publishing Company
PO Box 104
North Brook, IL 60062
1-800-323-8368

Incentives For Learning, Inc.
111 Center Avenue, Suite I
Pacheco, CA 94553
(415) 682-2428
*Tok-Bac

Jesana, Ltd.
PO Box 17
Irvington, NY 10533

*Lakeshore Learning Materials
2695 East Dominguez Street
Carson, CA 90749
1-800-421-5354

The Learning Center
South Windermere Shopping Center
Charleston, SC 29407
1-800-397-1200
        *Alphamaster
        *Drillmaster
        *Skillmaster

Learning Labs, Inc.
PO Box 1419
Calhoun, GA 30703-1419

Learning Well
PO Box 3759, Dept. 7
New Hyde Park, NY 11040-1042

*The Library of Special Education
3000 Cindel Drive
Delran, NJ 08370-0001

*Lingui Systems
3100 4th Avenue
PO Box 747
East Moline, IL 61244
1-800-PRO-IDEA

Longman, Inc.
95 Church Street
White Plains, NY 10601

*Love Publishing Company
1777 South Bellaire Street
Denver, CO 80222

McDonald Publishing Company
10667 Midwest Industrial Boulevard
St. Louis, MO 63132
1-800-722-8080

McGraw-Hill Book Company
1221 Avenue of the Americas
New York, NY 10020

Modern Curriculum Press, Inc.
13900 Prospect Road
Cleveland, OH 44136

*Mosier Materials
61328 Yakwahtin Court
Bend, OR 97702

Nasco West
1524 Princeton Avenue
Medisto, CA 95352-3837

National Geographic Society
Educational Services
Washington, DC 20036

National LEKOTEC Center
2100 Ridge Avenue
Evanston, IL 60201
(708) 328-0001

*New Readers Press
PO Box 888
Syracuse, NY 13210
1-800-448-8878

*Opportunities for Learning, Inc.
941 Hickory Lane
PO Box 8103
Mansfield, OH 44901-8103
(419) 589-1700

Postive Action for Christ
PO Box 1948
Rocky Mount, NC 27802-1948

Prentice-Hall
Allyn and Bacon Educational Books Division
Englewood Cliffs, NJ 07632

Prentice-Hall
Book Distribution Center
Route 59 at Brookhill Drive
West Nyack, NY 10995-9900

Raintree Steck-Vaughn
310 W. Wisconsin Avenue
Milwaukee, WI 53203

Rehab Plus
745 State Circle
PO Box 1941
Ann Arbor, MI 48106

*Remedia Publications
PO Box 1788
Scottsdale, AZ 85252

Research Press
Dept. E
Box 3177
Champaign, IL 61826

Rifton
PO Box 901
Rifton, NY 12471-0901

*The Right Combination
Cornerstone Division
6025 Sandy Springs Circle, Suite 164
Atlanta, GA 30328

Rourke Publishing Group
PO Box 3328
Vero Beach,FL 32964

Fred Sammons, Inc.
145 Tower Drive
Burr Ridge, IL 60521

Saxon Publishers, Inc.
1320 West Lindsey, Suite 100
Norman, OK 73069

Scholastic, Inc.
PO Box 7501
2931 East McCarty Street
Jefferson City, MO 65102

Science Research Associates, Inc.
259 East Erie Street
Chicago, IL 60611

Scott, Foresman and Company
200 East Lake Avenue
Glenview, IL 60025

*Shepherds, Inc.
Union Grove, WI 53182

*Special Education
J. Weston Walsh, Publisher
321 Valley Street
PO Box 658
Portland, ME 04104-0658

*Special Learning Corporation
42 Boston Post Road
PO Box 306
Guilford, CT 06437

*Steck-Vaughn Company
PO Box 26015
Austin, TX 78755

Sullivan Educational Products
PO Box 1200
Palo Alto, CA 94302

Sundance
Room #122
PO Box 1326, Newton Road
Littleton, MA 01460

Super-Duper School Company
PO Box 17641
Greenville, SC 29606

Teaching Resources Corporation
100 Boylston Street
 Boston, MA 02116

*Thinking Publications
1731 Westgate Road
PO Box 163
Eau Claire, WI 54702-0163

TOPS Learning Systems
10970 South Mulino Road
Canby, OR 97013

*The University of Washington Press
PO Box 50096
Seattle, WA 98145-5096

*Zephyr Press
3316 N. Chapel Avenue
PO Box 13448-E
Tucson, AZ 85732-3448

Appendix 7

Educational Resources for Trainable and Severely/Profoundly Mentally Retarded Students[1]

Curriculum Guides

Ford, A., Johnson, F., Pumpian, I., Stengert, J., & Wheeler, J. (1980). *A longitudinal listing of chronological age-appropriate and functional activities for school-aged moderately and severely handicapped students.* Madison, WI: Madison Metropolitan School District.

This curricular guide provides a list of functional activities for various age levels (elementary, middle, and high school) and can be adapted for any functioning level.

---

[1] Except for *Happy Time Course,* the listings here are secular resources. While they may not uphold Christian values, we believe that they may provide helpful information for parents and professionals.

Freagon, S., Wheeler, J., Brankin, G., McDannel, K., Costello, D., & Peters, W. (1983). *Curricular processes for the school and community integration of severely handicapped students ages 6-21.* Dekalb, IL: Northern Illinois University.

This guide also provides a listing of functional activities for various age levels and can be adapted for any functioning level.

Hooten, J. C., McDaniel, E., & Schubert, C. (1977). *Happy time course.* Wheaton, IL: Scripture Press.

This program, designed for Sunday school classes of mentally retarded persons, can be used as a Bible class curriculum. While most of the lessons are geared for an elementary age level, the lessons can also be adapted for use with older mentally disabled students. Care should be taken to keep activities appropriate to the students' age level and functioning level.

Tawney, J. (1979). *Programmed environments: A curriculum guide.* Columbus, OH: Charles E. Merrill Publishing Co.

This guide presents teaching strategies and many task-analyzed programs which can be used for functional instruction of severely or profoundly mentally retarded students. It also gives excellent coverage to data collection and monitoring of student progress.

Teaching Mentally and Physically Disabled Students

Bigge, J. L. (1982). *Teaching individuals with physical and multiple disabilities* (2nd ed.). Columbus, OH: Charles E. Merrill Publishing Co.

This book provides practical information about the physical and educational needs of students with physical and multiple disabilities.

How to Find Help in a Local Area

1. Contact a local hospital system. Most hospitals will be able to refer inquirers to helpful organizations and programs for disabled persons in the area.

2. The education or special education department of a nearby major university is often very helpful in providing parents and families of disabled children with services and information. Some universities even provide a parent information center and support group services.

3. The telephone book or information assistance in your city may provide telephone numbers of various local organizations that may be helpful.

Contributors

Dr. Joe P. Sutton

Dr. Sutton is an associate professor and chairman of the Department of Special Education at Bob Jones University, Greenville, South Carolina, and serves on the Advisory Board of Hidden Treasure Christian School. He earned his bachelor's degree in mathematics education from Bob Jones University in 1978. His two master's degrees in educational administration and special education / learning disabilities were conferred by East Carolina University in 1985 and 1986, respectively. In the fall of 1986, he was awarded a three-year fellowship from the University of Virginia, where he completed his Ph.D. degree in special education in 1989. He has been a teacher for the last 14 years and has served in both public schools and private Christian schools in several states. His experience has ranged from elementary to secondary levels and across regular and special education settings. His last six years of teaching have been at the university level. Dr. Sutton holds professional memberships in the Council for Exceptional Children and Phi Delta Kappa. He has published articles in leading secular and Christian educational journals including *Learning Disabilities Research and Practice, Journal for Correctional Education, Journal for Christian Educators, Christian Educators Journal,* and *Balance.* In addition, he has recently co-authored two book chapters on specific mathematics disorders and effective teachers of mainstreamed students. He is a reviewer for *Exceptionality,* the official journal for the Division for Research of the Council for Exceptional Children, and has recently been invited to serve on the Advisory Board of the new *Journal of Research on Christian Education.* Dr. Sutton has also presented his research at a number of annual conventions of the Council for Exceptional Children, the Council for Learning Disabilities, and the Association for Teacher Educators. He is a registered special education consultant with the Home School Legal Defense Association, and he assists home educators in developing special education programs for their disabled children. As a certified educational diagnostician, Dr. Sutton serves a national clientele of parents and Christian schools in the area of special education testing and assessment. In 1992, he was included by *Who's Who Among America's Teachers,* which honors annually the top 5% of teachers nationwide. He is married to Connie Jett Sutton, who is also a special education professor. They are the parents of three school-age sons.

Dr. John C. Vaughn

Dr. Vaughn has pastored the Faith Baptist Church in Greenville, South Carolina, since 1977. He founded Hidden Treasure Christian School as a result of a tragic accident involving his wife and his daughter Becky. In May of 1978, the Vaughns' home was the scene of a fire in which these two were severely burned. By the grace of God, both survived and are doing well while undergoing regular treatment. This experience brought into existence the unique ministry of Hidden Treasure, which opened in 1981 with two students and has grown greatly every succeeding year. After receiving undergraduate preparation at Cumberland College in Kentucky, the University of Maryland, and the University of South Carolina, Dr. Vaughn completed a bachelor's degree in Bible from Bob Jones University in 1977. His master of ministries degree in 1991 and honorary doctor of divinity (D.D.) degree in 1989 were also conferred by Bob Jones University. Dr. Vaughn has enjoyed substitute teaching in regular classrooms in local public and private schools through the years. He is a frequent speaker at retreats, seminars, and school conventions, and his family's testimony has been featured on Dr. James C. Dobson's nationally syndicated radio broadcast entitled "Focus on the Family." Dr. Vaughn conducts a daily radio broadcast, "Foundations of Faith," and has authored various articles and studies in numerous publications including *Frontline*. He is a private pilot and serves as chaplain of the Greenville Police Department and the Greenville Squadron of the Civil Air Patrol. In 1989, he received the prestigious "Thomas C. Casady Chaplain of the Year Award." He serves as co-chairman of the Greenville County School District Sex-Education Advisory Committee, and he was appointed by the Greenville County Council to the Greenville County Human Relations Commission, serving as chairman for two years. He is also a member of the Crisis Response Team. He serves on the boards of several organizations, including the Executive Board of the Associated Gospel Churches and the Fundamental Baptist Fellowship, the American Association of Christian Schools, and serves as President of the South Carolina Association of Christian Schools. Dr. Vaughn was included in the 1989 edition of *Who's Who in American Christian Leadership* and the

1992 edition of *Who's Who in the South and Southeast.* He is married and the father of five children.

John J. McCormick

Mr. McCormick is the administrator of Hidden Treasure Christian School. He holds a bachelor's degree in business management, a master of science degree in educational administration and supervision from Bob Jones University, and a master of arts degree in special education from Furman University. Mr. McCormick has seven years of teaching experience in special education. In addition, he holds professional memberships in the Council for Exceptional Children and Orton Dyslexia Society. Mr. McCormick has conducted workshops on topics related to school administration and special education at state Christian school teacher conventions in Georgia and South Carolina. In 1988, he was nominated for inclusion in *Outstanding Young Men in America.* He is married and the father of three school-age children.

Mary Behymer

Mrs. Behymer completed a bachelor's degree in special education from the University of Cincinnati in 1986, and she is currently a graduate student at Bob Jones University pursuing a master of education degree in special education. She served four years as a special education teacher's aide at Clermont County Special Education Training Center in Owensville, Ohio, before taking her first severely/profoundly retarded students at Ft. Wright School in Ft. Wright, Kentucky.

After one year there, she moved to Greenville, South Carolina, where she was employed as a special education teacher at Hidden Treasure Christian School for two years. Mrs. Behymer is also on the Executive Board at Hidden Treasure Christian School. She is married and the mother of two children.

Ross Fichter

Mr. Fichter has been a special education teacher at Hidden Treasure Christian School for the last three years. He completed his bachelor's degree in elementary/special education at Bob Jones University in 1989. In addition to his teaching responsibilities, Mr. Fichter is responsible for coordinating the Special Olympics programs at Hidden Treasure Christian School. He is currently pursuing other writing interests in the area of books for children with the Institute of Children's Literature in Connecticut.

Katherine Young

Mrs. Young has a wealth of experience and an extensive teaching career in both public schools and private Christian schools. She has been employed as a special education teacher at Hidden Treasure Christian School for the last six years. She completed her bachelor's degree in elementary education at Bob Jones University in 1947. In addition, she has completed 21 credit hours of graduate work in special education at Furman University in Greenville, South Carolina. Mrs. Young is the mother of 14 children.

Author Index

Scripture Index

Subject Index